GOATWALKING

GOATWALKING

JIM CORBETT

VIKING

VIKING
Published by the Penguin Group
Viking Penguin, a division of Penguin Books USA Inc.,
375 Hudson Street, New York, New York 10014, U.S.A.
Penguin Books Ltd, 27 Wrights Lane,
London W8 5TZ, England
Penguin Books Australia Ltd, Ringwood,
Victoria, Australia
Penguin Books Canada Ltd, 2801 John Street,
Markham, Ontario, Canada L3R 1B4
Penguin Books (N.Z.) Ltd, 182–190 Wairau Road,
Auckland 10, New Zealand

Penguin Books Ltd, Registered Offices:
Harmondsworth, Middlesex, England

First published in 1991 by Viking Penguin,
a division of Penguin Books USA Inc.

1 3 5 7 9 10 8 6 4 2

Copyright © James Corbett, 1991
All rights reserved

LIBRARY OF CONGRESS CATALOGING-IN-PUBLICATION DATA
Corbett, Jim, 1934–
Goatwalking/Jim Corbett.
p. cm.
ISBN 0-670-82846-7
1. Corbett, Jim, 1934–   . 2. Goats—Sonoran Desert. 3. Herders—
United States—Biography. 4. Quakers—United States—Biography.
5. Sanctuary movement. 6. Sonoran Desert—Description and travel.
7. Simplicity—Religious aspects—Christianity. 8. Wilderness
(Theology) 9. Spiritual life—Quaker authors. I. Title.
II. Title: Goat walking.
BX7795.C755A3 1991
261.8'32—dc20   90-50557
[B]

Printed in the United States of America
Set in New Caledonia
Designed by Bernard Schleifer

Without limiting the rights under copyright
reserved above, no part of this publication
may be reproduced, stored in or introduced into
a retrieval system, or transmitted, in any form
or by any means (electronic, mechanical, photo-
copying, recording or otherwise), without the
prior written permission of both the copyright
owner and the above publisher of this book.

To Pat—
 Sancha to my Quixote,
 Quixote to my Sancho.

Calling myself "the herdsman Quixotiz" and you "the herdsman Pancino," we will wander among the peaks, the forests, and the meadows, singing here, lamenting there, drinking of the springs' crystal waters or from the unpolluted creeks or from the rushing rivers. We will be provided with sweet fruit in abundance by the oaks, chairs by the trunks of the hardy corktrees, shade by the willows, perfume by the roses, carpets of a thousand interwoven colors by the spacious meadows, breath by the clear and pure air, light in the night's darkness by the moon and stars . . .
—Don Quixote's last dream

Preface

TWO MILK GOATS can provide all the nutrients a human being needs, with the exception of vitamin C and a few common trace elements. Learn the relevant details about range-goat husbandry and something about edible plants, and with a couple of milk goats you can feed yourself in most wildlands, even in deserts.

Civilized human beings don't fit into untamed communities of plants and animals, as members of the community. Instead of adapting to wildlands, we tame them. The goat-human partnership can fit in, which opens a way for errantry. Goatwalking is errantry that takes the goat-human partnership's adaptation to wildlands as its point of departure.

Errantry is primarily concerned with communion, which in our age focuses on the harmonious adaptation of human civilization to life on earth. The first, decisive step into errantry is to become untamed, at home in wildlands. To be at home in wildlands, one must accept and share life as a gift that is unearned and unowned. When we cease to work at taming the Creation and learn to accept life as a gift, a way opens for us to become active participants in an ancient exodus out of idolatry and bondage—a pilgrimage that continues to be conceived and born in wilderness.

Leisure, solitude, dependence on uncontrolled natural rhythms, alert concentration on present events, long nights devoted

PREFACE

to quiet watching—little wonder that so many religions originated among herders and so many religious metaphors are pastoral. This dimension of the pastoral experience is as accessible to the goatwalker as it was to a preindustrial shepherd watching the night pass over.

Wildlands can wake us to forgotten harmonies if we return as participants who belong there rather than as appreciative aliens or as subjugating conquerors. As a survival technique independent of the market economy and land ownership, goatwalking works very well but is as self-defeating as any other self-centered activity. No one survives for long. As a way to cultivate a dimension of life that is lost to industrial man, goatwalking may put us in touch with a mystery more real than we are.

Goatwalking is a book for saddlebag or backpack—to live with a while, casually. It is compact and multifaceted, but for unhurried reflection rather than study. It is woven from star-gazing and campfire talk, to open conversations rather than to lead the reader on a one-way track of entailment to necessary conclusions. I prove no points. This is no teaching.

In common with other goat- and sheepherders, I talk to myself, or with my daemon, as this inner dialogue is sometimes understood. If, as you read, you pause in stillness now and then, you can continue the conversation on your own.

Contents

1. Going Out — 1
2. On Errantry — 12
3. Free and Easy Wandering — 27
4. Survival Tips — 49
5. The Cimarron Alternative — 71
6. The Civil Imperative — 87
7. Discovering the Church — 115
8. Pilgrims' Progress — 131
9. Weaving Sanctuary into the Social Fabric — 158
10. Going Up to Zion: The Extension of the Sanctuary Covenant — 183
11. Betrothal — 198

Appendix A: The Saguaro-Juniper Covenant — 211
Appendix B: Covenant Wisdom — 221

GOATWALKING

1

Going Out

> You think you do right to hide little things in big ones, and yet they get away from you. But suppose you were to hide the world in the world . . .
>
> —Chuang Tzu

TURNING AROUND

Maps made from personal itineraries are mostly guesswork; they suggest departure points for explorers. If used instead as territorial surveys, to stake claims, they cause boundary disputes. Here's how I propose to make a map for explorers that's both faithful and corrigible: I'll tell enough about my personal coordinates so each reader can correct for perspective.

To take possession and build fences, settlers need maps that show how to contain little holdings in bigger ones. To turn around toward exploring the Creation in its unbounded wholeness, one must learn to hide the world in the world, which is sometimes called "free and easy wandering."

I first learned about hiding the world in the world almost thirty years ago, when I was in my late twenties. My first marriage ended after five years, and I lost my three children. The possibility of a family breakup had never occurred to me. Without warning or a good-bye, they were gone.

I withdrew. When I didn't need to tend cattle, I stayed out on the Black Bear slope of Miller Peak, high in the Huachucas, in the

GOATWALKING

Arizona-Sonoran borderlands. I began learning Malay, a language I'd never heard, spoken on the other side of the world by a people I'd never met. I went to the state of Sinaloa, Mexico, where people wouldn't expect me to understand them. Then I went to the San Francisco Bay Area, where there was a good supply of library books written in Malay.

Sitting in the cheapest room I could find in Berkeley, I often concentrated on my heartbeat. When I concentrated on it, the stillness expanded and each beat became a sudden clutching, to keep from slipping away into final stillness. Each beat let me know that my heart still cared enough to clutch for life. As caring withered, the stillness grew and the clutching weakened.

About a month passed. Then, late one night as I sat waiting with indifference for each next beat of my heart, I realized it was slowing much more than ever before, to a stop. The last strands of caring gave way. I let go.

Out of the stillness that I thought was death, love enlivened me—or something like love that doesn't split, the way love does, into loving and being loved.

I gave away everything I didn't need, acquired a copy of the New Testament, and left Berkeley, hitchhiking. For a week or two I wandered. Everywhere, I saw I'd been living in conjured make-believe, yet I had no new beliefs. It was more like having always seen an optical illusion one way that seems meaningless and then seeing exactly the same relations another way that's completely meaningful. On the basis of quite limited information and no familiarity, I guessed I must have turned Quaker. Finding myself in Los Angeles, I located a Quaker meeting, attended, and decided I had.

I hadn't become a Christian. I'd become a Christian, briefly, when I was nine, because a preacher said that was how to live forever. I'd eagerly tried to bend my mind to accept everything he said I had to believe. I also read the Bible, doggedly and with limited comprehension, from cover to cover. After almost a year of saying I believed, I decided anyone who actually did believe would follow Jesus. But I had no more intention than anyone else I knew of following the way revealed by Jesus of Nazareth.

Even a child has the prudence to see that believers lose nothing if wrong, but unbelievers lose everything. (Later, I would learn that Blaise Pascal had given this common-sense calculation its classic formulation: "If you win, you win all; if you lose, you lose nothing" [*Pensées*, Sec. III, No. 233].) But even a child can tell the difference between prudent pretense and genuine belief. Faith built on cost-benefit analysis is a conjurer's trick.

The Christian beliefs I'd learned about when I was nine were of practical relevance only to rewards and punishments, but reward has nothing to do with the faith that had opened for me in Berkeley. This faithfulness is active dedication to fulfilling the covenant to become a people that hallows the earth, regardless of cost or failure; it has nothing to do with maintaining an unshakeable belief, regardless of improbability or absurdity.

Maybe Christians are right that the gospel calls for the profession of specific beliefs rather than the practice of a specific covenant. Yet, just as believers think it's incredible that an unbeliever would choose the way revealed by the gospel, I think it's questionable that believers actually choose the way rather than purported rewards—particularly if they just profess belief in the gospel without trying to follow it. If a faithful way of living is its own reward, afterlife would be a bonus that is irrelevant to the decision to be faithful; the only losers would be those who are conjured into professing beliefs rather than living faithfully.

Even after I turned Quaker, Christianity remained poisoned for me by the New Testament's emphasis on rewards. It would be many years before I began learning to read the Book of Job as the capstone of the Greek as well as the Hebrew books of the Bible.

Goatwalking is a way to learn about hiding the world in the world in desert solitudes that I know as home. It's no sham; I do tell of what I know from personal discovery. Yet, I can't include the vital first lesson that starts it all. The first lesson is where everyone starts: despair that clears the way. The Buddhists call it "the First Truth," universal suffering. Everyone tries to take possession, hiding little things in big ones, and we all fail.

Until I was almost fifty, I used Taoist and Buddhist traditions to provide a cultural context for goatwalking. I never sought guidance from the Bible. (Joshua's genocides and Abraham's near sacrifice of his son Isaac were the parts of the Hebrew Bible that I remembered most vividly from my childhood reading.) Yet, I couldn't avoid seeing that the way had already been blazed. Goatwalking reenacts the history of the prophetic faith. Contrary to my preconceptions and aversions, goatwalking is biblical—even liturgically biblical.

Goatwalking opened the way for me to read the Bible in the present, as covenanting in which I, as much as Joshua and Paul, am a participant. Learning to read the Bible in the present is the key to participation in the prophetic faith. All of us gathered here today stand at Sinai.

Much the way Abraham had gone *cimarron*[1] out of his father's land, Moses rejected the Egyptian court where he was raised, choosing the slaves as his people. His choice was no passive professing; he acted on it and then had to flee from Pharaoh into the desert. A stranger in a strange land, he learned to live as a herder. Then, meeting I AM PRESENT, he returned to open an exodus. Fleeing into the desert from Pharaoh, at the mountain of the burning bush, the escaped slaves covenanted to become a free people by living in a way that establishes justice as a communion

---

1. A *cimarron*—sometimes anglicized to "maroon"—is a domesticated animal or slave that goes free. The antonym of *cimarron* is *reducido* ("reduced"), used by the Spanish conquistadors as both adjective and noun to characterize and classify tamed Native Americans. The word in biblical Hebrew that is most often translated "stray" or "wander"—'*oved* אבד—has the same origin. ("God made me 'stray' from my father's house," Abraham tells Abimelech.) Nomadic pastoralists everywhere identify with the *cimarrón*, *kazakh*, or maverick.

In the Hebrew of later Israelite settlements, אבד came to mean "to stray away," "to be lost," "to perish," or "to be ruined."

אבד ('*oved*) should not be confused with עבד ('*oved*), the pronunciation of which is now usually the same but the meaning of which is "slave" or "servant."

that the moralities of slaves and pharaohs can neither know nor suspect.

The covenant—to become a holy people—requires that a hallowing way of life be established somewhere, in a specific land; the people covenants to hallow the earth through its way of life. As faithful errantry unwilling to settle for make-believe, Zionism is inseparable from the covenant; the cimarron generation raised in the desert therefore crossed the Jordan to take and settle Canaan. Joshua was faithful to the only way he knew; he led the children of escaped slaves to take possession of the promised land, as its masters. Many centuries would pass before another Joshua, Yeshua of Nazareth, would come up from the Jordan to renew and re-vision the Zionist task.

DOING NOTHING

To learn why you feel compelled to remake and consume the world, live alone in wilderness for at least a week. Take no books or other distractions. Take simple, adequate food that requires little or no preparation. Don't plan things to do when the week is over. Don't do yoga or meditation that you think will result in self-improvement. Simply do nothing.

Isolation distresses all social animals. To distinguish the human craving for company from the cultural compulsion to remake and consume your surroundings, go out afterward with congenial companions. When you want to be alone, seek solitude; when you want companionship, seek company. Just cease to intervene and plan. Do nothing but celebrate the goodness of the Creation—if you can.

Here's what you may learn: The most attractive surroundings removed from consumption and busyness will be a hell for you. To discover the uses of uselessness you must be reborn into the present.

In 1970, I taught at an "ecology summer session" near Nevada City, California, in the Sierra Nevada foothills, which was offered by John Woolman School for students in their late teens. Almost all the students were flower children, mostly from the San Francisco Bay Area. Other instructors taught biology, natural history, and environmental politics. I taught from Chuang Tzu's inner books—the uses of uselessness.

After several weeks of study and discussion, the students were to go out on a week-long fieldtrip. Some would backpack into the high sierra. Some would float down a river. Some would learn about agribusiness from migrant workers. My trip involved doing nothing on an idyllic bend of the Yuba River.

Most of the students that chose my trip already practiced one or another form of meditation. Their first two days on the Yuba could have passed as a reenactment of Arcadian scenes from *The Faerie Queene*. All were of a mellow, companionable disposition. They pursued their adolescent fancies, as free from jealousy as from constancy or inhibition. None suffered any physical discomfort. (The beachlike bend was relatively free from poison oak and mosquitoes, and skinny-dipping in the school's lake had already given them all-over tans sufficient to disprove my admonitions about sunburn.) None quarreled; the weather was good; time cycled uneventfully from night to day. But on the third day they began to be desperate for distraction. By the fifth day, most had returned to the school, explaining that they had to tend to things that they'd left hanging.

Awakening into the fullness of the present yields unrestrained intimacy; awakening into the present is communion; but one awakens from despair, not from self-gratification. Despair shouldn't be cultivated, just allowed to surface. Being useless uncovers despair, and the same empowerment occurs when the optimist ceases to grasp at the future, when the mourner ceases to grasp at the past, or when the bereft ceases to grasp at what might have been.

GETTING NOWHERE

Backpacking skills are helpful for goatwalking, but backpacking attitudes are not. The goatwalker wanders but rarely hikes. Goatwalkers are not trying to conquer intervening space in order to arrive at a destination. Their packs usually weigh less than twenty pounds. They sit more than they walk. They use available food daily without concern for the next day's supply.

Modern man is able to go into the wilderness or up to the moon and be comfortable as long as he takes enough of his world with him, but he remains an outsider. For the goatwalker, wildlands themselves are the life-support system. Goatwalkers are comfortable and secure to the degree that they understand and adjust to their immediate environment. Their economy is self-sustaining and runs on sun, rain, and soil, with no need for machines, machine products, or fossil fuels. Products of modern technology such as metal pots, sleeping bags, tarps, ropes, matches, toilet paper, and knives are convenient but inessential.

The goatwalker reaps but does not sow. Cultivators must continually intervene in the natural order, clearing and preparing a plot free from existing vegetation, then warding off invading plants and animals. Free-range pastoralists simply take what nature provides. Good farmers must be hard workers; good herders must be alert observers. The farmer alters the land to suit his needs. The herder moves about to take advantage of conditions as he finds them. The farmer gains security from food preservation and storage; the herder, from relatively unencumbered mobility. For the farmer, food is necessarily the product of labor. For the herder, food is a gift, eternally regenerating itself.

Pastoral nomadism is similar to most hunter-gatherer cultures in its concentration on the present, in its reliance on and adaptation to the given aspects of nature, and in its emphasis on unrelenting observation and awareness. Peasant and commercial economies, on the other hand, place their emphasis on the work needed to transform and develop unimproved conditions and raw materials into wealth. For the nomadic hunter-gatherer or pastoralist, wealth is created by sun, rain, and soil. To think of one's life as time to be invested or to sacrifice the present to an uncertain future is foolishness for man-in-nature; it is as obvious that life is a gift rather than a reward as it is obvious to man-in-time, who labors for future fulfillment in an ever-dying present, that life can be supported only by work, investment, the accumulation of wealth—above all, that the past is dead and the present moment in which one's life is trapped is just the point where the future dies. Man-in-time labors in an empty present that is death; he grasps for a future that must die when he touches it.

For civilized man laboring under Adam's curse, the Sermon on the Mount is worse than foolish. That we should give our wealth to the poor, fail to protect our property from plunderers, and cease to take thought for the morrow—this teaching that we should no longer lay up treasures on earth is immoral. If we are to meet our social and familial responsibilities—if, in fact, we are to live at all—we must serve Mammon rather than the God proclaimed by Jesus of Nazareth. Subjugation to Money—the owner-master that an ancient agricultural age called Baal—is so obviously the price of civilization that these passages from the sermon don't even merit the lip service professing Christians pay those other embarrassing commandments concerning strict nonviolence and loving one's enemies. The only civilized people who can afford the pretense of totally rejecting Mammon are those who are supported by the rest of us. (Maybe tithing and responsible stewardship are what He really had in mind and He just didn't express himself clearly.)

Archaeologists generally maintain that, with a few possible exceptions such as Lapp nomadism, pastoralism emerged as a spin-off from cultivation. For those who try to devise models of human cultural evolution that demonstrate an inevitable, linear, cumulative development from primitive ways of living to our own, pastoral nomadism is an untidy dead-end—as though some human beings, after learning how to earn their bread by the sweat of their brows, realized that a symbiotic relationship with ruminants opens an unguarded back gate to Eden; they simply took their animals and went feral.

Man compulsively weaves conceptual nets in which to catch the world, and then traps himself. When we make a classification scheme to sort the kaleidoscopic variety of human cultures into a related, understandable pattern, we may end up earnestly talking about the classification scheme when we think we are still talking about human cultures. If we find ourselves at the culmination of cultural evolution, bound by history not to evolve backwards and bound by the exhaustion of alternatives to make our civilization ever bigger, more powerful, more complex, and more inclusive, with no further chance of qualitative cultural change of the kind that occurred when we stepped out of nature into history, then we have trapped ourselves in our own words. We may yet turn out to be the missing link—or we may be just another abortive experiment, soon to be scrapped.

LOSING HOLD

As a form of wildland pastoralism that can be adopted by individuals and small groups, goatwalking provides the economic foundation for a practice that would otherwise be virtually impossible for members of industrial civilization: withdrawal from society in order to cultivate detachment or selflessness. Because such detachment is essential to the unfolding of the primal insight that permits us to participate in life rather than living by possession, anyone who intends to try goatwalking should learn about this practice in some depth.

Students of mysticism often assume the mystic is a romantic who seeks seclusion in nature for its peace and quiet, that intense meditation is possible only in such surroundings free from the noise and physical distractions of civilized life. Actually, most of us can be much more isolated from physical distractions in our own homes—eliminating noise by using earplugs or other devices if necessary—than we can be in a natural setting subject to the vagaries of weather, insects, and the enormous variety of life and activity always present in wildlands. Mystics seek seclusion outside society because a person addicted to social busyness cannot become adequately detached, and the most direct way to break the addiction is to withdraw from society. Having arrived at some measure of detachment, a person might return to society without suffering a relapse, but the person who has never experienced solitude can't even understand his addiction or the nature of detachment.

Attachment—as used here, synonymous with greed or self-centered craving—is the emotional analogue of delusion. Intellectually, our alienated condition is the result of delusion; emotionally, it is the result of greed.

Greed feeds on the continual busyness of the man-made world. Withdrawal from this busyness is necessary if one is to begin developing the detachment that comes from an elimination of selfish craving. To be detached, in this sense, does not mean the elimination of involvement. The mystic seeks total involvement, unlimited relationship, complete intimacy, inclusive empowerment. Detachment is freedom from the self-centering that destroys our ability to relate.

At one time or another most of us want to get away from it all and live a simple, natural life in seclusion, but this escapist urge and the romantic images associated with it have little to do with the true nature of solitude. Wandering purposeless and without human companionship, one sometimes experiences emotional crises that are in some respects similar to culture shock and in other respects similar to cabin fever—culture shock from social vacuum rather than social displacement, cabin fever in the sense that one finds unrelieved association with one's self intolerable. Sigmund Freud's claim that repression is the price of civilization seems to work in reverse. In the absence of socially supported identities we may discover ourselves possessed by naked demons who have the good manners to appear only in acceptable disguises when we are in polite society. During extended periods of isolation working as a sheepherder and cowboy, I discovered little of this kind of emotional conflict. After all, I was doing a job and earning a living. Each day had its work and objectives, and if I was separated from human society I was still of it. But in full solitude—free and easy wandering without purpose or schedule—the demons appear.

Society provides most of the make-believe that prevents one's hells from surfacing into full consciousness. No matter how dissatisfied, one can always find distractions within society. But whoever leaves the world to wander alone in wildlands should be prepared to meet a devil or two, when busyness ceases to drown out the dream side.

During a goatwalk of more than two weeks, the boundary of

the dream side becomes less certain, but devils don't actually walk into waking life. Rather, the dream side asserts its own reality. Old wounds become fresh injuries. Unresolved terrors become immediate threats. I've come awake in the close darkness of a cloudy new-moon night, sobbing from an early-childhood rejection, so overcome with its lasting presence that I could only gradually remember my way back into middle age. I've come awake old and senile, awaiting death with dumb, motionless panic. There are good dreams, too, but they come during times of brightly intense wakefulness.

Existentialists have sometimes searched for angst the way nineteenth-century romantics cultivated melancholy, as a literary device. One can look at hell in all its horror and enjoy a delicious shudder. But why search out one's inner anguish in actuality? To take the step beyond life in time, one must overcome the delusion of possession—on the dream side, of being possessed; on the waking side, of possessive busyness.

The Buddha advised that speculative theorizing is a waste of time, that what he could teach about the way to selflessness is strictly empirical, embodied in practices leading to direct insight. Mysticism usually rejects speculation and clears away preconceptions because nothing meaningful can be said about the ultimate source of meaning; definition is meaning's heir, not its parent. Can life be meaningful? Only if we are active participants in the Creation. Can the possessing self be the source of meaning? Whatever I try to possess is gone the moment I grasp at it. Can the elimination of self-centering open the way for meaningful living? This is a matter of personal discovery, not propositional proof, of cocreativity rather than entailment, of life rather than doctrine.

2

On Errantry

> A marsh pheasant has to take ten steps to pick up a mouthful of food and thirty steps to get a drink, but it does not seek to be nourished in a coop.
>
> —CHUANG TZU

QUIXOTE AND THE CONJURERS

BEFORE GOING TO the San Francisco Bay Area and turning Quaker, when I withdrew to the Black Bear slope of Miller Peak, I considered fitting in—finding something to do that would pay better and be more respectable than cowboying or sheepherding. (In college, I'd planned to become a philosophy teacher, but the main thing I learned from studying philosophy was that I knew nothing to teach.) Mulling it over, I saw that I was really concerned with doing something notable with my life. When I sorted it out, I made a memo to myself:

> Life is just a moment, they say. One's name must be carved deep into history's bedrock, to last a moment longer through time's endless erosion, they say.

> On the prairie, when the wind wails a dirge and snow sifts in rivulets through the sagebrush, I've hugged the sticky-pink, death-chilled body of a newborn lamb under my coat, and its heart fluttered in reply.

> And on a desert mountain, amidst the hush of soaring

ON ERRANTRY

granite, I've opened a forgotten spring. The few who remembered thought it had long ago gone dry, but I found the hidden place and dug down until a stream ran clear and cold in the summer sun.

So what are epitaphs to me? I've shared life's warmth with a lamb. I've opened a desert spring.

Still in my twenties, I could already write as good a remembrance as any I could imagine for myself at ninety: "He kept a lamb or two from freezing; he found and opened a forgotten spring."

That settled, I came down from the Black Bear and went to Sinaloa, Mexico, taking a copy of Cervantes's *Don Quixote* to read. I can't recall how I'd come to think Quixote might be my daemon. I hadn't yet grown into looking like him. (In recent years, to meet strangers in crowded airports or plazas, I tell them to look for Quixote wearing glasses, and they spot me immediately.) He was my constant and only companion in Sinaloa and has accompanied me on subsequent wanderings.

Goatwalking is a way to be at home in wildlands, living on milk and wild foods. It is a means of subsistence. It is also a form of errantry.

Errantry means sallying out beyond a society's established ways, to live according to one's inner leadings. This looks like, and in a sense is, madness—Quixote's Madness. Both the lunatic and the visionary create a life outside the ready-made roles prescribed by their society, adjustment to these roles constituting a society's understanding of sanity. As social animals, ants are invariably sane, but human beings are typically alienated.

Our anxiety, restlessness, make-believe, compulsive intervention, freedom, and creativity are all rooted in the reflective awareness that distinguishes humankind. We aren't called to cure alienation by destroying reflective awareness with surgery, drugs, discipline, or meditation. The world has enough ants. Mere survival would constitute adaptation if we were simply living creatures. As life become reflective, we must choose either to adapt demonically, by trying to possess the world, or prophetically, by actively participating in creation.

In its quest of full communion, errantry neither waits for recruits nor compromises to gain allies. It shrugs off the arguments of all theological or political parties, each of which claims to have discovered the right way to fracture time and the world into good ends and effective means. It is therefore an insecure, impolitic, minority way of life. Errantry disdains adaptive pretense, majoritarian morality, and all politic forms of solidarity because it is based on the Quixote Principle: *To open the way, a cultural breakthrough need not involve masses of people but must be done decisively by someone.*

Errantry's archenemy, "the Conjurer," substitutes symbolic appearances for the lived actuality, contriving a name to replace the quest. Conjuring often takes the form of organized religion. For example, in a society at war with man and nature, a religion of peace and love might be fantasized into creeds, rituals, and otherworlds while its professed adherents continued to live by conquest. The Conjurer also deludes both the religious and the irreligious into assuming that errantry, rather than conjured make-believe, is the fantasy. This contrast has to do with two radically different meanings of faith: For errantry, faith is fulfilled here and now as cocreativity; for conjuring, one's faith is professed rather than lived, as a belief in good goals to which the living present is a sacrifice.

QUIXOTE, FRANCIS, AND THE PILGRIM CHURCH

Francis of Assisi began where Quixote quit, when the pursuit of knightly glories foundered in a reversal that required a farewell to arms. Young Francis had dreamed of a great hall in a magnificent castle. The walls were hung with weapons and shields from history-making victories. An incomparably magnificent lady presided. And a voice that rang with unquestionable authority proclaimed that this was the high court of Francis Bernardone and his knights.

ON ERRANTRY

No need for Francis to make do with a barber's basin as his helmet or with a stumble-footed nag as his charger. His father, the town's rich cloth merchant, bought him the best available armor and war horse. After all, it was his father, Pietro, who had dubbed little Giovanni "Francis" to identify his son and his family's future with the chivalric culture of France—that is, with the ideals disseminated by the troubadours. Pietro Bernardone had made the family rich; he raised Francis to make it noble. Everyone else in Assisi took the tales of Roland and of the Round Table as entertaining diversions from real life. Francis knew the troubadours' songs of chivalry as the lineaments of his identity.

He sallied out to fight for Pope Innocent III, got as far as Spoleto, and the same voice from the dream side ordered him back.

> Why are you leaving the master for the sake of a servant, a rich man for the sake of a poor man? Turn around!

What man could be richer and more powerful than the pope? What forces were then winning more triumphant victories than the papal armies of the Norman knight he was to join? What glory could be greater than crushing the enemies of the Church? And what could be more ignoble, after sallying out with pomp and fanfare, than to return a few days later, defeated and in retreat before even having reached a battle?

Francis turned around, to face Assisi's scorn. Two years before, when the Assisi townsfolk had been defeated by the Perugia townsfolk at the Battle of San Giovanni Bridge, rumormongers spread the tale that Francis had surrendered prematurely, from cowardice. Now everyone believed it. And as a prisoner he had, of course, been held with the aristocrats, since his father could pay ransom. There was much for commoners to resent and aristocrats to deride about the phony nobility of the rich merchant's fanciful son. Pietro Bernardone could buy Francis fine armor and a place with the knights of the papal armies, but the Bernardone riches could only buy a counterfeit, posturing, tradesman's nobility.

Francis made a cave his daytime home and tried to understand his turnaround. Who was the lady in the castle? To recognize her would be to sort out the reversal of master and servant, rich and poor, that had been proclaimed by the voice at Spoleto. Her knights would surely know true nobility and genuine errantry, for which the troubadours' chivalry was apparently just a metaphor.

Sometime in the course of the year after his turnaround, while he was in the cave, Francis recognized her. Only Poverty empowers her followers to make errantry a way of life.

Quixote convinced himself that Dulcinea was really an incomparably elegant lady whom the conjurers had changed into a peasant girl; Francis saw that Poverty is the preeminently majestic Lady behind the troubadours' enchantments. Quixote's problem was not that he went to extremes in trying to live chivalry into the world but that he failed to go far enough. His problem was that he failed to go as far as Francis. He was plagued by conjurers who made armies look like sheep and giants look like windmills, turning all his adventures into absurdities, but he never suspected that conjuring is much more pervasive than even a Quixote could imagine—that conjurers blind all whose Lady is less than Poverty to the ever-present adventure in meeting sheep, windmills, lepers, beggars, birds, flowers . . . fire, water, sun, moon—everything—as a brother or sister, to be loved rather than possessed.

Only a few years after Francis sallied out in the name of his incomparable Lady Poverty, Pope Innocent III had a dream that the Lateran Basilica, the mother church of Christendom, was leaning and had begun to topple when a skinny beggar in the brown frock of a common laborer jumped forward to hold it up. It was Francis, who at first sight had seemed no different from the countless madmen and heretics who then roamed Europe and threatened the stability of the Church with topsy-turvy visions of renewal. Pope Innocent was far too shrewd to be guided by every disruptive intimation from the dream side, but this vision broke into his deliberations with self-validating certitude. He granted Francis's petition, that Lady Poverty's brotherhood be authorized to wander throughout Christendom, to proclaim the gospel "as the Lord reveals it to you. And when the Almighty has multiplied your number, then come back to me and I will charge you with a greater inheritance."

Shortly after recognizing that Poverty was his Lady, Francis found himself drawn into the tumbledown church of San Damiano, where he prayed intently that his mission be revealed. A soft voice from the cross answered, saying, "Francis, don't you see how my house is in ruins? Go and restore it!" He began by rebuilding the walls of San Damiano. But by the time he petitioned the pope to recognize Lady Poverty's brotherhood, he knew the quest was not the reconstruction of a San Damiano—nor even the Lateran Basilica. In later years he would persist in the mission by struggling to tear down the walls built to settle and assimilate Lady Poverty's church-errant.

All talk about church invites misunderstandings. "Church" may mean a building where worship takes place, such as San Damiano—or, at least, the building symbolizes the congregation that meets there, the church being wholly present in each such gathering. "Church" may mean a denominational management, the corporate structure of a religion such as Roman Catholicism. And "church" may mean the religious society formed by communities that covenant to become a holy people. As a building, a church is built with such things as quarried stones and mortar; as a corporation, by hierarchical organization, obligatory creeds, and prescribed rites; as a society, by practices established through covenanting.

Francis set about restoring the church with practices that constituted a society-forming religious rule. Practices that he gleaned from the Gospels, rather than mortar or dogmas, were his building materials. Yet, he always insisted that nothing about the unsettled church of the Way conflicts with making houses for congregational worship or with managing ecclesiastical organization. He just tried to rule out any dedication of Lady Poverty's lesser brotherhood to buildings and ordination.

Insofar as human beings can respond to a call to build or restore the church, the visible church is at issue. The visible church has three faces: the ecclesiastical organization, the housed congrega-

GOATWALKING

tion, and the covenant-formed society. Before his turnaround, Francis had set out to win victories for the organization; afterward, to rebuild San Damiano; and then to found a rule that observed all the essentials of gospel errantry. Building the church with armed struggle could never have occurred to the Francis who restored San Damiano; constructing congregational housing could never have occurred to the founder of the Franciscan Rule. By the time he founded the rule, Francis had seen that the church is built through errantry—that, whatever else it may be, it must be a pilgrim community formed by those who walk the Way.

As set out in the gospels, the Rule of Lady Poverty's church-errant is unambiguously simple:

1. Go, sell what you possess, and give to the poor (Mt 19:21).
2. Take nothing for your journey, no staff, nor bag, nor bread, nor money (Lk 9:3).
3. If any man will come after me, let him renounce self, take up his cross, and follow me (Mt 16:24).

The Vinaya of the Buddhist Sangha was remarkably similar to the Rule of the Franciscan order. Initially, for both communities, begging was also an important element of the discipline; they complied with the precepts of nonpossession by living in symbiotic relation with those who *did* store up (and share) earthly treasures.

"Be Unprepared" could be the motto for all errantry—that is, adapt directly rather than trying to tame your surroundings to fit you. Rather than seeing a flawed Creation that needs fixing, errantry sees adventures. It is therefore at home in wildlands rather than cityscapes. But how could one follow the precepts of nonpossession in wildlands, where no one is storing necessities that could be begged?

In the desert, sister goat would be a particularly helpful companion, when she's in milk. This step into legendary Arcadia completes the metamorphosis of chivalry, from the ideal of the *caballero andante*, the knight-errant, to that of the *cabrero andante*, the goatwalker.

ON ERRANTRY

THE PASTORAL TROUBADOUR

From the time man-and-woman tasted the fruit of knowledge and, becoming self-conscious, stepped out of nature into history, we have dreamed of the age when we were—or will be—at peace with all that lives. That place before and beyond exile has many names. In the poetries of the Western world, it is Arcadia.

Poetic traditions reveal much that religious traditions conceal. Religion's versions of the myth channel longings for lost Eden into guilt, taming us (by denaturing communion) into flocks under pastoral care. In Arcadia, where life is shared rather than owned, poets rather than priests shape communion. Song formulates faith. All spirit is carnal.

To enter Arcadia, one must learn to commune with objects. Beneficial use must be subordinated to active worship.

Objects are assessed for their usefulness and beauty. They are just there as the self's external environment, but persons are recognized and are looked to for reciprocal recognition. How can communing with objects make sense?

The reason we need maps to avoid getting lost in unfamiliar country is that the landscape is a nonperson to be passed without recognition, catalogued according to its characteristics, maybe photographed as scenery. The recognition of another as an active presence capable of reciprocal recognition determines whom we consider a person. Savages, small children, lunatics, and poets meet, recognize, and address mountains, springs, trees, clouds, birds, and many other "things." When primitives do it we say that they are animists who think there are selves called "spirits" inside all objects. Poets use personification as a literary device. Lunatics are irrational; small children are prerational.

Animism is a technocratic theory attributed to pretechnocratic societies; the savage's awareness that presence is unfragmented and is met in all others is interpreted as a belief that every object has a self in it. Is there more reason for believing that each human body you meet has a self inside it than there is for believing that mountains, trees, and springs do? Are you sure there's a self in

19

your own body? Why do savages refer to spirit as the air we breathe, people living in spirit instead of spirits living in people?

Gods as well as animals once spoke to us. Now each self talks to itself. But have you ever tried to find the self who speaks? Elusive, isn't it? Maybe the subject self is unobservable because it really isn't there at all. But if I'm not the one talking to myself, who is? Daemons—that is, angels—are said to be messengers who shape primal presence into specific, personal points of view, so, unlike the self-addressing self, they account for the primacy of shared meaning and for the rhythm of aspiration and inspiration manifest in poetry, prophecy, and the other ways of expressing communion.

The assumption that meaning must be centered in the self-conscious self dies harder than its geocentric analogue. Technocratic man has extracted all explanatory content from mythopoeic insights concerning the daemonic in order to distill a residue of pure superstition—the self-addressing self—that functions as the referential center around which his worldview revolves. (Since daemons appear only in disguise and are also fond of irony, they probably invented the masquerade.)

Zen Buddhism uses the *koan*—a special kind of riddle—to overcome the constrictive fabrications of the egocentric hypothesis. The "answer" to a *koan* must be found rather than made. But koans must also be personally prescribed and may be culturally specific. There is one analogue of the *koan* that is generally suitable for clearing away the egocentric fabrications that keep us from recognizing the active presence of "objects": the kind of versification that humankind is said to have learned from Pan.

Legend has it that King Midas was asked to judge a poetry competition between Pan and Apollo. Pan is identified with poetry's rustic preliterate origins; Apollo, with its refinement into the quintessence of belles lettres. Poor Midas preferred Pan's unembellished folk ballads, so Apollo transformed his ears into those of a burro.

Because Pan is so closely associated with Dionysus, this legend might seem to contrast Dionysian and Apollonian art—roughly, the romantic-classical polarity—but the rustic folk mode clings unromantically to repetitiously fixed forms, and Pan, the herder, teaches attentive stillness directed outward rather than inward. In Pan's Arcadia, ballads are the preeminent form of verse, and the Arcadian goatherd-errant is a finder (*troubadour*) rather than a maker (*poietes*) of verses.

Poetry often takes the form of verse—of repetitiously rhythmic language that may also be rhymed and alliterated. (By "poetic" I mean the characteristic of inspired forms that opens human consciousness to communion.) Versification is a way to play with words. It is also mnemonic. It resists alteration when passed from person to person, generation to generation. It allows a large gathering to pray in unison. It can make an orator's words ring, a jester's jokes jingle, and a hawker's cries echo insistently in one's memory. It intensifies insults. It tests and tempers competitive displays of wit. It makes conjuring credible and gives unintelligible incantations the patina of immemorial antiquity. It merges with melody, percussion, and dance. The use that ties verse most closely to poetic insight is its function as a purely formal koan that fixes concentration while resisting what one wants to say.

Verse can also make false "inspiration" obvious, even when a line almost fits. Why record one's failures, when Shakespeare and Milton are at hand? Because verse is an antidote. To what? To the same malady for which koans are prescribed, the attempt to contrive inspiration. A line that fails to fit is obvious to metaconscious awareness, which recognizes contrived inspiration the same way it recognizes an idol. A line that fails to fit holds attention in the present, while the composer stops to listen for the line that has metaconscious approval.

THE BODHISATTVA VOW AS A PILGRIM COMMUNITY'S COVENANT

Some religious traditions tell of Bodhisattvas who take a vow of open, unqualified errantry: to be the last of all beings to enter nirvana; to wander through time and serve in every hell until all have been freed from the sufferings of life-in-time. As a precondition for insight and a preparation for service, the Bodhisattva goes out into wilderness to cultivate detachment from civilization's struggle to bend the world to human will. The wanderer goes out away from purpose-driven entanglements to seek eternal presence and renew the vow to hallow all life. When a community goes out into Sinai stillness, could it, too, take the Bodhisattva's vow of perfect errantry? Can detachment from busyness be socialized somehow by a community that covenants to become a people that hallows the whole Creation?

For "savages" survival means learning how to fit into an untamed habitat, but for the civilized it means learning how to use natural resources to make a tamed habitat. I therefore refer to primitive societies to illustrate differences between technocratic civilization and communion, but I recommend no regression to a precivilized condition. Life on this planet urgently needs to evolve beyond human possession, but regression would just lead to repetition, because pretechnocratic societies disintegrate when brought into contact with technocracy.

They disintegrate because technocratic civilization vastly extends the human ability to experience and do many things. Living *is* the striving to preserve and extend one's existence as agent. All that empowers, insofar as it does empower, affirms life. If communion displaces domination as the foundation for cultural evolution, it will do so because it expands civilized humanity's activity and awareness. Neither regression nor repression will preserve human life and the world; those who preach an ecological conscience that requires altruistic sacrifice are therefore of Moloch's party, unwittingly.

At the dawn of history, two adaptive systems emerged that permitted human beings to establish dominance over their surroundings: farming and nomadic pastoralism. As a way to assert ecological dominance, nomadic pastoralism was a cultural dead end that often led to damaged land with reduced productivity. Nomadic pastoralism's mode of production is the wildland ecosystem itself. The system won't work for one of its members who rises up as a conqueror and claims it all for himself. Farming replaces wildland biotic communities with other habitats designed

ON ERRANTRY

to be ruled by man. This is the technological foundation for civilization and the beginning of material progress, of man's growing power to bend the biosphere to his will. Cain, the Bible tells us, also built the first city. The ecological concerns of our day reflect an emerging awareness that, for all our ingenuity, this other form of ecological dominance is also a dead end. The ecosystem won't work for an animal that rises up as conqueror and tries to take possession—unless dominion itself continues to evolve, beyond dominion.

Goatwalking interweaves a warp of practicalities with a variegated reflective weft. The shuttle that weaves the practical warp and the reflective weft into a single fabric works on the principle that right livelihood and communion are inseparable. Right livelihood actually *is* practice that reflection knows as communion. Wrong livelihood is known as the complementary master and slave moralities that take the glories of command and the rewards of obedience as the ultimate sources of virtue. Only through right livelihood can reflection see the virtue—the life-enhancing power—of the cocreative community's masterless morality.

No way of living can be right that is part of a livelihood system that destroys rather than supports life. All others are primarily subjects rather than objects. And genuine communion is inseparable from right livelihood. How, then, can members of technocratic civilization enter into communion?

When communion is conceived technocratically, as an end state to be superimposed or achieved, they can't. Communion is always here and now rather than an end state. Technocratic civilization is itself irreplaceably good, in its time, because it is the womb of contractual property relations among strangers, which grow into the societal forms that must precede any realization of the covenant to extend civility to humankind and all that lives. In their time, social philosophers were right in claiming that human civilization had to be founded on slavery. In their time, they have been right in claiming that war is the natural relation of one state to another and that national security must override human rights. And industrial civilization's free markets and private property are also essential for the realization of human rights and for the emergence of a land ethic that establishes rights for the biotic community—that is, for extending civil association beyond (and in spite of) national borders and for accepting everything that lives as a member of our consociation.

THE MASTERLESS MORALITY OF THE SABBATICAL CIMARRON

Why should goatwalking as an unlikely way of living be packaged with way-of-life issues that confront everyone in a technocratic society? Goatwalking happens to be the easiest way I know to feed myself by fitting into an ecological niche rather than a social hierarchy. It also happens to be the only way I've discovered to share and bequeath the outlook and practice of symbiotic covenanting within a technocratic society. To those for whom wildlands are truly home, they reveal what is to be learned by living in harmony with an untamed community of plants and animals. As one's adversary, raw material, preserve, or scenic retreat, untamed life hides its inner teachings because one is there as an alien.

Goatwalking is errantry that happens to work as an emergency survival system. But errantry is the opposite of the survivalist preparations for Armageddon that have become popular since we realized that the greenhouse effect, the destruction of the ozone layer, a lethal contagion, or some other impending disaster may soon destroy our civilization. Survivalism assumes that life is in one's self rather than among us. Goatwalking works as an emergency survival system, but only because it goes the other way from survivalism, toward communion. All forms of errantry do take survival seriously—much more seriously than does survivalism. Taking survival seriously means serving and celebrating life rather than the separated self.

Cutting one's tie to the industrial life-support system is just a beginning. No matter how much is known about living within a wildland habitat, we can be at home in wildlands only when certain cultural disabilities are overcome. To live peacefully as members of wildland communities, human beings who have been domesti-

ON ERRANTRY

cated to live by possession must become untamed. This is the heart of errantry.

Goatwalking is errantry that is primarily concerned with opening a way through the adversities faced by any people that covenants to treat no one as an inferior, enemy, or alien. To choose freedom is to cease collaborating with organized violence. But ceasing to collaborate means errantry of one kind or another; in the eyes of pharaohs and slaves, it means straying out into the desert.

Learning to go cimarron opens an exodus. Learning to live by fitting into an ecological niche rather than by fitting into a dominance-submission hierarchy opens human awareness to another kind of society based on equal rights of creative agency for all. This awareness develops even when untamed living is a practice apart from one's ordinary livelihood. Living cocreatively rather than possessively seems impossibly demanding because it *is* virtually impossible in our kind of society, for individuals and families. Errantry's special virtue as a community practice is that the covenant community can open the way where its members are individually powerless, while at the same time it greatly enhances its members' personal and familial abilities to undertake covenanted tasks. Covenanting, rather than the individual's adaptation to wildlands, is the fundamental practical concern of any posttechnocratic human being who seeks to go free. The radical individuality of the cimarron is realized only in the kind of consociation in which everyone is a fully empowered partner.

Covenanting is the fundamental adaptive concern of anyone who seeks to become fully human, because the basic covenant community empowers its members to be cocreators of a social order in which humankind lives in harmony with one another and all that lives. There are, of course, many less inclusive meanings of the verb "covenant"—as many meanings as there are ways that human beings can choose to bond into partnership with one another—but I will ordinarily use "covenant" to refer to the enactment by consensual agreement of societal and other symbiotic harmonies that would reach completion in communion. I will sometimes call the pilgrim people constituted by all such covenant peoples "the church," but I can only speak of this gathering of the covenant peoples from my own specific place within the church.

As the gathering of covenant peoples, the church is cultivated rather than built, discovered rather than described. It is a multicultural, interfaith people of pilgrim peoples whose errantry is an open-willed quest to fulfill shalom—in each day, through their lives, and in the life of the entire people, on earth as it is in the high heavens (as the *Kaddish* puts it). It covenants to transform civilized humanity away from living violatively, as the possessors of the earth. The personal side of this pilgrimage—errantry—scouts a way into uncharted time.

Errantry seeks the cultural breakthrough that opens the way for civilized humanity to live by communion rather than possession, much as agriculture opened the way for human bands to take possession of the earth and in doing so to step from life-in-nature into history. Individuals sometimes take this next step in which history is overarched by eternal presence, but the search for a cultural breakthrough has to do with the emergence of cocreative communion as a people's chosen way of life, transmissible through succeeding generations.

3

Free and Easy Wandering

When man began his first farming operations in the dawn of history, the goat was the king-pin of the pastoral life, making possible the conquest of desert and mountain and the occupation of the fertile land that lay beyond. The first of man's domestic animals to colonize the wilderness, the goat is the last to abandon the deserts that man leaves behind him. For, ever the friend of the pioneer and the last survivor, the goat was never well-loved by farmers on fertile land. When agriculture produces crops that man, cow, and sheep can consume with more profit, the goat retreats to the mountain tops and the wilderness, rejected and despised—hated, too, as the emblem of anarchy.

—David Mackenzie, *Goat Husbandry*

TAKING CAPTIVES, TAMING SLAVES, MAKING FRIENDS

THE GOAT IS THE natural emblem of anarchy. It is the most adaptable pastoral animal, and pastoral nomadism remains the only form of livelihood that permits subjugated communities to walk away from the state. Quick-witted, social, and educable, with a capacious, high-speed digestive system, a thorn-chewing mouth, cliff-climbing hooves, and a relatively undiscriminating appetite for low-grade roughage, goats thrive on a wider range of plants and in more varied terrain than any other large herbivorous mammal. On range where other domesticated animals would starve, goats often provide both milk and meat for their human partners. Because goats will readily admit human beings into herd membership, they can be managed and moved without fences, corrals, hobbles, tethers, or any of the other mechanical devices used to control other livestock. From the Alps to the Empty Quarter, Java to Baja, with the goat as a partner, human beings can support themselves in most wildland environments.

In canyonlands or other rough country, goats are at home on cliff faces where human beings can follow only with difficulty. They instinctively seek the safety of heights and want to climb up into the highest castlerocks to bed down at night. The herder must therefore cultivate and maintain a bond with the herd that is so strong they will come down, against instinct, when he calls.

Other herd animals respond to the approach one must use with goats, but since other kinds of livestock are so easy to handle with mechanical restraints such as wire fences and ropes, and because they can be driven so easily with threats, sedentary pastoralists herding other animals have little reason to spend the time necessary to develop personal trust and mutual understandings. (Because nomadic herders have no fences to substitute for social cohesion, much of what I say about making friends with goats applies as well to the herding of other livestock under nomadic conditions.)

Origin myths from all parts of the world refer to the time when people and animals talked with each other. This is neither fiction nor hyperbole. Social animals of different species do learn to talk with each other. To learn how to talk with other animals, a human being just needs to live with them on their own terms.

Here's an exercise: Go with a small group of friends to meet some range cattle, sheep, horses, burros, or goats. One at a time, walk up to the animals and, if possible, mingle with them. Watch what is said by each person's way of moving and looking and the way the animals respond. If you were a personnel manager trying to fill a position requiring responsibility and efficiency, would you hire anyone as unassertive and easygoing as the people animals greet? Next, sit quietly for an hour or two, but don't freeze in place. What kind of person do animals want to meet? Is he wired to become so distressed by stillness that he will be highly productive

FREE AND EASY WANDERING

in even the most meaningless jobs? Why is it usually easier for women to become friends with animals?

Domesticated animals learn enough human for basic communication with people by means of conventional signals. Sheep, cattle, and horses can be herded with ritual threats. Goats are quick to learn vocal commands or other signals, but they don't really herd in this sense. They must be led. And to lead them one must be accepted into the herd as a leader. Unlike pets, goats never seem to think they're human, but they tolerate physical differences and allow properly behaved human beings to become fully accepted members of the herd. If range goats should decide that the herder has become a genuine threat, they will escape.[1]

John Woolman School once arranged to send groups of high school juniors and seniors to Arizona for semester-long courses of study with my wife, Pat, and me. In addition to the study of ways human beings have lived, the program included brief experiences with basic economic systems: subsistence gardening, Mexican village agriculture, gathering, and pastoral nomadism. The experiences with pastoral nomadism consisted of goatwalking. When the program began, Pat and I only kept a couple of goats for goatwalking and family milk supply, so I began looking for a small herd.

About ten days prior to the first group's goatwalk, I found

---

1. The only English-language book I know about that deals with range-herd ethology as an important part of goat management is David Mackenzie, *Goat Husbandry*, 4th ed. (London: Faber & Faber, 1980), 67–68.

"The psychological relationship between man and his domesticated animals, horses, cows, sheep, dogs, and poultry, is . . . different from the behaviour towards man of their wild counterparts in captivity. The relationship is the product of centuries of selective breeding and may be said to constitute their domestication. In this sense goats are not domesticated. At times they treat man as they treat members of their own species, at other times they treat man as their wild ancestors do in a natural state. There is no qualitative difference between the behaviour towards man of wild goats captured young and that of so-called domesticated goats.

"Anyone who has the care of goats soon realizes that the relationship between the goatherd and his flock is a great deal more personal, more intimate and more delicate than is usual in the farmyard. It is in fact similar to the relationship with a gregarious animal that has been tamed wild."

suitable range goats. They came from a herd of grade Saanens a woman had been running on a desert mountain for about forty years. They were small, inbred, and wild. Their only water was in the woman's corral, so if her customers needed more milk or if she wanted to sell or eat one, she trapped them when they came into the corral for a drink. Normally, they ranged out and cared for themselves.

I selected and we managed to catch five freshened does that were from two to six years old. During the next three days, my classes suffered while I spent most of my time with the goats, even sleeping in their corral. The goats soon accepted me as a milker, but on the third day, when I decided to risk taking them out for a walk, something startled them and I spent the next two days getting them back. On the tenth day we left for a two-week goatwalk through a seventy-mile stretch of roadless rough country. Day and night, the goats ranged free. They followed when we walked, foraged when we stopped, and bedded down wherever we made camp at night. When we needed milk, I simply milked them as they foraged. As far as they were concerned, we were a single herd, and I shared leadership with "the White Queen," their herd queen. For foraging, she led; for trailing out, I led.

About two years later, when the school program ended and Pat and I were moving, I arranged to leave most of the herd, which by that time had increased to about a dozen, with a group of tepee hippies who were to caretake the small farm where we had been living. A few weeks after we moved, I heard that most of the goats had gone feral.

The herd had never been penned after the first week I'd had them, and a number of them had been born on the place. They never ranged out more than a mile or two from the area where they bedded. Some had gone on many goatwalks with several different student groups, and all were accustomed to the presence of strangers. When the hippies moved in, the goats were a nuisance around the tepees, so most of the interaction was negative. On about the third day, a wether was caught and slaughtered while the herd watched. The next day the goats left. During the following months a few reports came in from cowboys about goat tracks found around waters in the nearby mountains along the Mexican border, but I couldn't return to look. I like to imagine them playing among the castlerocks in that part of the Sonoran desert, but in the Arizona-Sonoran borderlands feral goats rarely survive predation by mountain lions for long.

Because goats are herd animals, they need company and will do whatever is necessary to get it. If only the herder is available, a single goat will stay with him or her, no matter how poor or threatening his herd manners happen to be. The problem in this case is leaving her. Goats must have companions. In some cases animals other than goats may provide companionship, but generally no less than two goats should be kept.

The herder must gain the herd's confidence that he or she will protect them from danger and lead them to pasture and water. Then they will leave good feed to come to the herder's call and will follow him against instinct across shallow streams or in the face of other dangers. But milking requires still more intimate relations of trust and affection. A doe will give her milk down completely only if she regards the milker as a suitable surrogate for her kid. This is particularly true for milking on range, when does are neither restrained by stanchions nor bribed with feed.

Milking is very simple in theory, but most beginners take about a week to do a passable job. First, learn the theory. (See Mackenzie's *Goat Husbandry* for an explanation of goat milking technique and related considerations.) Next, persuade a goatkeeper to let you try your skill with one of his goats and under his supervision, and only then commit yourself to milking a goat on your own. Many experienced milkers have bad habits, so don't skip the theory. People who know how to milk cows should learn the important differences between milking techniques for cows and goats. Goats' teats should never be stripped or tugged as forcefully as is common with cows. Generally, goats' teat sphincters are much weaker than cows', which makes them easier to milk, but their teats and udders are also easier to injure.

Beginning milkers often think they aren't squeezing hard enough to get a good stream of milk, but this is rarely a problem with goats. My hands are so weakened and deformed by arthritis that I'm unable to hold most water glasses one-handed and often have trouble turning doorknobs, yet I can still milk two-handed and fairly fast. I can only make contact between my thumb and my index and middle fingers, the joints of which are fused (which is the way one must milk short-teated goats, in any case). If the neck of a teat is pressed closed so milk will not flow back into the udder, pressure below will squirt milk from the sphincter. A lamb nipple or rubber glove attached to a bottle full of water can be used for practice; it should have a sphincter that is no more than a pin hole.

Goats that are determined not to be milked will work out ingenious deterrents, so the herder may need to invent countermeasures. Training methods should never be painful, and the trainer should never lose his temper. Domination must finally be superseded by the kid-doe relation; training is completed by bonding.

Range goats should not be bribed to stand still to be milked. When a goat has accepted a milker, she will placidly chew her cud while being milked. Goats accept more than one milker, just as they accept more than one kid, but the relationship should be regular and predictable. A milker who has the wrong approach can make a doe a serious problem for everyone else who milks her.

During the first hour or two after kidding, the doe will repeatedly turn to smell her kids as they begin to suck, making it difficult for them to get much at a time. This interaction is associated with bonding. If the kid is removed during these first few hours, the mother may refuse to claim it later. If the herder unobtrusively joins in the bonding process, allowing the doe to associate him with her kids' sucking, she will often accept him along with the kids, standing to be milked by him without being restrained. If the herder misses the opportunity to bond the goat to him when she kids, gentle handling along with firm restraint should soon persuade her to accept him. If, prior to their first kidding, goats are handled gently and their udders are occasionally massaged, training them to stand to be milked is usually no problem.

If a goat runs away when approached to be milked, a nonchafing tether that is free of any knots that might hang up can be left on her so she can be stopped from a distance by stepping on the tether. One-inch nylon webbing works well for this, always tied with a bowline or in some other manner that will prevent it from tightening on the goat's neck. Have a tasty handout to offer each time, such as a mesquite bean or a prickly pear fruit, and approaching her will soon be no problem. At first, tie her to a post or tree for milking. When she settles into this procedure, she should next be restrained only by the milker's keeping his weight on the tether while he milks. Soon she will be ready for the tether to be removed. It should be removed as soon as possible or whenever the goats are untended, since any tether will sometimes weave its way into bushes or under boulders and hang up.

Kicking is often a response to painful milking, particularly when the milker's hand works above the teat and pinches the milk glands in the udder—an error that can cause permanent damage as well as pain. If a goat stands patiently while her udder is full and then kicks when she's almost milked out, either the milker is pinching her milk glands or else she's fearful that he will.

If a doe is bonded to the milker when she kids, she will stand to be milked—unless a subordinate goat is within about ten feet, in which case she will insist on running the subordinate away beforehand. The same territoriality can be seen when a doe's kid starts to suck while subordinate goats are standing nearby. The doe should be led a little way from the herd, then held by the hock of the near hind leg and milked one-handed until she begins to cud. (One usually milks on the right side, in which case the right hock is held by the left hand while milking right-handed.)

Goats should usually be milked in their order of dominance. Otherwise, a dominant doe eager to be milked is likely to butt a subordinate the herder is milking. When approaching a doe, call her name in a tone of voice and with a tune that is different for each goat. Give her a handout of some kind. Soon, each doe will come when called. Just as goats distinguish their kids' calls from any others, they quickly learn to respond to a distinctive human call.

Goats maintain an order of dominance and submission that

governs virtually all their interactions with one another and the herder. The herder must learn a given herd's dominance patterns, affinity groups, aberrant personalities, and unresolved feuds and power plays. Older, horned, male goats tend to be dominant. The younger, hornless, female, and newly arrived goats tend to be submissive, although sheer determination to dominate sometimes overcomes these disabilities. Dominant goats are most insistent on the formalities of submission from subordinates of the same sex, although protocol is often ignored among close friends.

During the breeding season, the herder may be challenged by the buck. When this happens, avoid coming to blows and never mimic the challenge. Dipping your head in a way that could be interpreted as a challenge invites serious concussion with any goat. Crouch and advance, maintaining a predatory stare, then, the moment he stands on his hind legs to challenge, step to the side, grab his horns, and bulldog him. If he's hornless, bring one arm around the neck to grab the far front leg above the elbow, grab high above the stifle of the far hind leg, then lift with a knee on the near side while flipping and busting him (the way large calves are busted for hog-tying). Never grab legs in other ways that could pull them out of joint. When he's down, hold down on a horn or up from underneath the muzzle, put a knee on his neck, and hold the underneath front leg folded back at the fetlock. When he ceases to struggle, let him up.

BLACK MAGGOTS, PASTORAL HARMONIES, AND URBAN ANTIPATHIES

Pastoralism is one of the few ways human beings can be at home in arid lands. If the human population is limited to the numbers that can be sustained by the low-ebb livestock carrying capacity and if pastoral use is for direct life support rather than commerce, then pastoralism is also the way that human beings can have the least impact on a wildland community that supports them—compared, for example, to hunting and gathering. Yet, pastoralism is responsible worldwide for the destruction of arid lands.

FREE AND EASY WANDERING

Goats are the livestock species that is potentially most injurious to wildlands. Goats make deserts. They are "the black maggots of the Middle East," the herbivorous plague that swept across the slopes where Lebanon's cedars once flourished, leaving nothing but parched gullies. Chewing at the base of the food chain, plant eaters can become a plague destroying whole communities of plants and animals. And goats are in a class with locusts as notorious destroyers of plant life.

Wherever livestock have been used on arid lands, they have been destructive. Goats are more destructive than other livestock because, when protected from predators, they are better survivors; in most deserts, the elemental human-goat partnership is *the* way to adapt to adverse and unpredictable conditions. Goats survive long after sheep, cattle, horses, and even burros have died out. Yet, the very characteristics that have made goats the most destructive livestock species can also make them beneficial. Because they are such good survivors, they give their human partners many more choices, for harmony or disharmony. This flexibility is particularly important when annual rainfall is low, spotty, or fluctuates from one extreme to another. But before reviewing the ways goat pastoralism can contribute to the health of a wildland community, I must mention another source of the goat's notoriety, as the natural emblem of anarchy, which often colors settled people's point of view.

The comic-strip goat foraging in garbage, raiding clotheslines, and butting the unwary embodies deep antagonisms between sedentary peasants and nomadic pastoralists that reach back to the dawn of civilization when the first Cain came to blows with the first Abel. Satan inherited Pan's horns, goatee, and hooves for reasons that remain fundamental even if long forgotten. We are Cain's descendants.

Goat eradication can serve much the same purposes as nineteenth-century buffalo eradication—that is, the exclusion of nomads by pioneer landowners and the settling of nomadic tribes in order to bring them under government control. There is ample evidence, though, that nomadic patterns of livestock use are essential to avoid or minimize livestock damage to arid wildlands.

The settled pasturing of livestock on arid lands is always destructive, unless settlers imitate nomadism by rotating the use of available pastures. For example, in a painstaking examination of the Alanya-Antalya area of southwestern Turkey, John Kolars discovered that the forests and watersheds surviving in good condition are in remote areas that have the region's highest goat population and that have been the summer pastures for goatherding nomads for at least five hundred years, but near the region's settled areas forest destruction and soil erosion are extreme.[2]

Wherever plant life has evolved in the presence of large herbivores, pruning may be beneficial for a plant species or for the biotic community of which it is a member. For example, many browse plants may be prevented from overgrowing their root structure by the pruning activities of browsers, and during periods of drought, when such plants need to reduce the ratio of superstructure to roots, hungry herbivores may also prune back old growth that would not be touched during better years. Herbivores are especially important for ecosystem circulation because they act as decomposers; they harvest, package, and distribute plant life in a way that makes the fertility it contains available to new life. In cold or dry climates, many forms of plant life decompose readily only when eaten by herbivorous mammals.

When allowed to range free, goats seek out ridgetops for bedgrounds. They dislike canyon bottoms or low spots where predators could sneak up on them. As a result, their days are spent collecting plant materials along the slopes of mountains, canyons, or hills and then hauling much of it up to vantage points at night. This is one of the few cases in which fertility regularly migrates uphill.

Both in chaparral and in the transitional grasslands where fire prevention has resulted in woody-plant invasions, goats can promote the kind of stability once maintained by frequent cool burns and can also recycle more fertility and maintain better watershed conditions than was the case with frequent burning. Introduction of balanced foraging by goats discourages fuel buildup and in areas

---

2. John Kolars, "Locational aspects of Cultural Ecology: The Case of the Goat in Non-Western Agriculture," *Geographical Review*. 56 (1966):577–584.

where summer rains are adequate opens the way for colonization by perennial grasses. Particularly where solid stands of manzanita have established themselves after a hot burn, temporarily using such areas as bedgrounds for goats will open the way for colonization by other plants. (Manzanita is one of the many plants browsed by goats that are rarely touched by other herbivores.)

Range-improvement studies traditionally ignore browse plants or else classify all woody plants as undesirables to be eradicated by chaining or herbiciding. This is understandable, since browsers (goats and many wildlife species) make the best use of browse plants and grazers make the best use of grass, and most range-improvement schemes are for the benefit of grazers rather than browsers.

Browse plants offer the herder important advantages. First, they usually remain green and palatable during dry seasons. Second, the deeper roots of browse plants reach moisture and minerals unavailable to grasses, normally bringing three or four times as much soil into biotic circulation and in some cases multiplying the depth of soil use a hundredfold; this same process can also build fertile soil to much greater depths. Third, many browse species retain a high nutritional value during cold seasons when most grasses are of low value. Fourth, only the new annual growth on browse plants is usually harvested by foraging animals, so the plants maintain an efficient use of available sunlight and moisture even when total annual growth is cropped, but a grass plant that is cropped close to the ground must grow new leaves before it can make much use of sun or water. (Using all or most of annual growth is generally destructive, though, for browse as well as grass.)

The very characteristics that make goats the most destructive livestock when they are mismanaged or overstocked make them the least likely to damage the range plant community when they are properly managed and stocked. More plants are palatable for goats than for other livestock. Goats sometimes relish spiny, thorny, bitter, and woody plants that other livestock ignore. They are at home in rough, steep areas inaccessible to other livestock. The goat's greater rumen capacity and superior ability to digest fiber free it from dependence on the most nutritious plants; its high mineral requirements lead it to eat a little of almost everything when it forages. Other livestock concentrate their foraging near water, along canyon bottoms and trails, and on relatively flat areas, but unherded goats tend to cover their range evenly and prefer not to take much from any one area before moving on—in part because range goats fastidiously refuse to nip a twig that smells of another goat's bite.

Goats can also contribute to the proper grazing distribution of other livestock. In the United States during the last thirty years, many woolgrowers have replaced herders with net fencing. Unfortunately, unherded bands of sheep chew out some pasture areas while ignoring others, the problem becoming worse as the untouched herbage grows coarser. A few goats mixed with a band of sheep will lead the band to distribute its grazing use better than would normally be the case even if the band were herded.

FITTING IN AND CULLING OUT

Human beings find goats either admirably clever or else intolerably mischievous because, in common with primates, goats have a three-dimensional spatial intelligence. Grazing animals such as horses, cattle, and sheep see the world as a two-dimensional surface; they go directly toward food and water or away from danger. Goats evolved as cliff dwellers and are convinced that there must be a way, no matter how devious, to reach every apparently inaccessible ledge. Kids delight in solving three-dimensional problems of this kind. Their quick wit and athletic prowess make them delightful companions in rough country and a frustrating nuisance when one must try against their will to keep them in or out or off. If pen-raised kids must be selected and trained for goatwalking, the worst rogues are also often the best because they are usually the most intelligent.

Adaptation is a matter of education as well as inheritance. Although all goats enjoy browsing and will show elation at the sight and feel of a craggy cliff, the culturally deprived adult goat never develops its full potential as a forager. The beginning herder must also learn how to become a herd member and will do this best if the herd is free from the retardation and neuroses common among bottle-raised pen goats. A knowledgeable herd queen who works well with the herder is particularly important for educating any newcomers brought into the herd.

Next to the intelligence and education necessary for survival, milking persistence and resilience are the most important traits in a free-range milk goat. Persistence is the tendency to continue producing large amounts of milk as long as the feed is good. (Natural selection generally favors animals that go dry and start putting on weight shortly after their young reach weaning age.) Some milk-goat strains are exceptionally persistent, and most good milk goats can be milked for two years without kidding. When run through (without kidding) for two or more years, the milk production of goats in the Northern Hemisphere will dip in the fall and rise in late winter but will rarely rise again to the highest level, which is normally reached a week or two after kidding, following a dry period of two or more months.

At times arid rangeland may support the production of only one pint daily, and at other times the same range may support production of a gallon daily. In hot desert areas, annuals often respond rapidly to a good rain but also wither quickly under the blast of a dry wind. Resilience is the ability to recover high levels of milk production on good feed after periods of depressed production resulting from poor feed. Resilient milkers are persistent, but many does that are persistent when kept on a consistently high level of nutrition are not resilient.

Desirable traits often conflict with each other. For example, a high metabolism that promotes milk production also reduces an animal's tolerance of heat stress or periods of low nutrition. In general, exceptional productivity reduces survivability; more intensive care by the herder must always accompany selection for increased production.

The rumen is a "fermentation vat" in which microflora predigest nitrogen compounds such as urea and ammonia into true proteins essential for a mammal's body maintenance and milk production.

Ruminants therefore thrive on plants that other mammals can't eat. "Roughages" contrast with "concentrates" such as grain that do have a concentration of nutrients that most mammals can digest. Breeders who push production with concentrates and fail to select for optimum production on a ration restricted to roughages are therefore breeding out the characteristic of ruminants that is basic to adaptation to untamed lands.

Traits that are undesirable or of no importance in pen goats may be desirable in range goats. Optimum size for range goats is lower. Traits that make a pen goat a restless, mischievous, disruptive rogue may make a range goat an industrious, versatile forager whose leadership contributes to the herd's well-being. Soft, white hooves may be of some advantage for a pen goat or one that runs out on improved pasture, since white hooves wear and trim more easily, but hard, black hooves may be important for goats that must cover extensive areas on rocky range. Extra-long hind legs give a show goat a slightly sway-backed appearance but are advantageous for goats dependent on browse and will also reduce the risk of udder injuries. A strong herd instinct is important for herding range goats but may cause high stress and undesirable behavior in show goats.

As a species, goats adapt well to hot climates. All of the major dairy breeds do well in hot, dry climates of the kind found on the Sonoran desert, but some breeds, strains, and individuals adapt better than others, and heat tolerance is always a limiting factor when breeds from temperate climates are introduced into areas where heat is accompanied by high humidity.

The ability to conserve water is a particularly valuable trait wherever animals must roam out some distance from limited stock-watering facilities or when stock water must be hauled. With the exception of camels, goats are superior to all other livestock in the efficient use of water.

A good rangeland milk goat is generally small or medium-sized, has extra-long hind legs and a long feminine neck, shows the typical "dairy wedge" that goes with a well-developed rumen, has a well-attached udder carried high off the ground, and has hooves that have not become deformed from the goat's being penned without regular trimming. (When looking at adult pen goats, try to find one with hooves that have not become deformed; such goats are rare.) A good range goat lifts and places her feet the way a deer walks; a poor forager—sometimes one that has been nearly crippled by being penned without trimming—drags her feet forward in a slovenly fashion. The way goats walk is particularly important in cholla country, where those that walk like a cow will kick cactus joints up onto their udders.

ON KILLING AND EATING ONE'S FRIENDS

Living primarily on milk rather than meat reduces the need for slaughter. Persistently resilient milk goats need to be bred only every two or three years, so they reduce the need for slaughter. Breeding and herding to develop high-producers, so that one or two goats will be plenty for supporting a human being, reduces the need for slaughter. But slaughter can't be avoided. Attempts to avoid culling and slaughtering just magnify the need to do so. Culls suffer least when slaughtered on their home range by a familiar herder who follows the most humane procedures.

Anyone concerned enough to search will find a wealth of biblical, koranic, and talmudic support for the position that anything less than the most humane form of slaughter is also less than kosher. Most people have erroneous ideas about what will knock out or kill an animal and sometimes become involved in ugly attempts to kill a struggling, screaming animal by stunning it with a hammer or by letting it bleed to death while fully conscious. An animal shot from above at the base of the skull, just above the point where the neck attaches to the skull, with the bullet angling through the center of the brain, loses consciousness instantly. If a goat who knows and trusts the killer is shot while it is eating one of its favorite foods from a small container, there is little risk that it will move its head at the decisive moment. If its throat is then cut immediately, the heart will continue pumping long enough to bleed the carcass.

Meat that has not been bled won't keep or cure as well, but it loses nothing in flavor or nutritional value.

Adequate exploration of the ethical issues associated with slaughter would involve an open-ended study of agricultural ecology, agribusiness economics, human nutritional requirements, cultural factors determining human diet, and subsistence alternatives to the commercial life-support system. No preconceived formulas or creeds can tell us, with respect to each community of plants and animals, what choices would preserve its integrity, stability, and beauty. Just as medical practice can sometimes turn the preservation of life into a prolongation of dying that is akin to torture, the avoidance of killing (as though life were encapsulated within individual creatures) can sometimes serve death in relation to the life among us.

Most meat eaters see nothing wrong with humane slaughter but now consider animal sacrifice a barbaric religious practice because the killing of meat animals has been desacralized along with the rest of nature. The rejection of animal sacrifice by the civilized religions follows from their denaturing of communion.

Among the various reasons that can be given for the kosher slaughter and meat handling requirements that are common among Semitic peoples, the functional explanation that fits ecologically is that relying on a diet of blood and milk, which is an everyday practice among some pastoralists south of the Sahara, would lead to a disastrous increase in herd mortality among desert nomads. Unlike blood, milk is usually produced from nutrients that are surplus to an animal's needs.

This is ecologically reasonable, but the explanation found in the Bible touches a deeper concern that is common to all primitive hunters and pastoralists:

> If any man of the House of Israel slaughters an ox or goat . . . and does not bring it to the Tent of the Meeting to present it as an offering to the LORD, before the LORD's Tabernacle, bloodguilt shall be imputed to that man: he has shed blood; that man shall be cut off from the people (Lv 17:3–4). For the life of the flesh is in the blood, and I have assigned it to you

for making expiation for your lives upon the altar; it is the blood, as life, that affects expiation. . . . You shall not partake of the blood of any flesh, for the life of all flesh is its blood. Anyone who partakes of it shall be cut off (Lv 17: 11,14).

The primitive hunter feels the need to sacralize the killing and eating of the game he hunts; through myth and ritual, the taking of the animal's life may be seen as its voluntary gift to the human band it feeds—a self-sacrifice on the animal's part. The primitive farmer feels a similar need concerning his enslavement and possession of the land, which entails that he kill untamed life by exclusion as well as direct action. He hacks and digs out a piece of God's land as his personal possession. But the pastoralist brings this primal religion-forming tension to its highest pitch, killing and eating animals who are members of his own personally known community.

The pastoral metaphors of the nomad religions—metaphors about good shepherds who lead their flocks through desert dangers to cool water and green pastures, who protect their herds from wolves and make a special effort to recover every stray lamb—express the religious inspirations of peoples who regularly slaughter and eat the innocent lambs in their care. The mythic meaning of Abraham's willingness to sacrifice his son Isaac to God and of God's sacrificing his son to us is lost if the integral role of animal sacrifice in these religions is screened out of consciousness. The civilized religions that screen out primal communion are screening out primal *religio*, which is concerned with rebonding the full communion that our living on life otherwise breaks. Where primal *religio* is concerned with the "re-ligation" of human livelihood into full community, the civilized religions that desacralize Nature are concerned with little more than the personal anticipation and fear of one's own death.

In primordial religion, communion is sacrificial killing and eating. Civilized religions often transform the killing and eating of hallowed life into a ritual meal that bonds cocommunicants to one another through a purely spiritual divinity, which means desacralizing the communicants' primal communion with the life that is actually eaten. Suppose the bread and wine at a Christian mass actually were to become the flesh and blood of Jesus, in all sensed and digestible respects. As a miracle, it would just prove that God has a sense of humor.

We don't eat family and close friends or even members of our own species. When members of other species that we do eat are adopted into our family, we become averse to eating them. For example, Pat and I eat goats, but we couldn't eat the White Queen. This has more to do with mammalian ethology than with human ethics. Ethically, meateaters probably shouldn't waste good food.

I slaughter animals, eat meat, and seek to live nonviolently. I needn't eat meat, but I can't live nonviolently on the Sonoran desert if I fail to cull animals from the small herd that enables me to adapt without injuring the land. The converse is also true. Much of the time I now live in the Sonoran desert, in the city of Tucson, by means of modern industrialism, which is the most violent way of life yet devised—violent to the point of terminal ecocide. If I were to become vegetarian, it wouldn't make this way of living less violent—at least, no more so than reducing my gasoline consumption by a tank or two each year. An earth without wilderness, populated by billions of mechanized vegetarians and their grain fields, would be an earth reduced, enslaved, and deadened—an earth systematically violated.

This ecological understanding of nonviolence conflicts with the traditional understanding of Buddhists, Hindus, Jains, and many Quakers, for whom "nonviolence" translates the Sanscrit term *ahimsa*. The *Yogashastra* explains *ahimsa* as follows:

> In happiness and suffering, in joy and grief, we should regard all creatures as we regard our own self, and should therefore refrain from inflicting upon others such injury as would appear undesirable to us if inflicted upon ourselves.

Ahimsa is the Silver Rule of Hillel, Confucius, Hobbes, and all other proponents of a morality based on commensurate justice: Don't do to others what you don't want others to do to you. If life on earth is an undivided communion, no other is a violable alien, and every sentient creature is my neighbor, a cocommunicant. From the inception of life, every sentient being strives to survive and tries to evade death and suffering. In this we are all alike and have an equal right to life, so don't kill or injure other sentient beings.

The fundamental choice between *ahimsa* and symbiotic nonviolence is easier to see by considering abortion rather than vegetarianism, euthanasia rather than the slaughter of meat animals—areas where the distinction is within humanity and usually within one's own family. In the case of euthanasia, it's also becoming a choice that modern medicine forces many of us to make for family members—that is, the decision to unhook life-support systems.

My mother and I had to decide when my father should no longer be kept alive. I've never felt any conscious anguish about deciding the time had come to disconnect his life-support system, except from the dream side. The dream side's metaphors mock at all euphemisms that call our killings by other names. In dreams, authorizing the disconnection of my father's life-support system is mixed together with the occasions when I've killed one of our dogs or cats. These are the test cases to which I look for guidance, to see how killing can be communion rather than violence.

Puck was a sheep- and cowdog who was my companion and coworker during much of his fifteen-year life. As a puppy, he'd accompanied me on my rounds when I did range analysis for the U.S. Forest Service, snuggling to me under the flap of my sleeping bag at night and running to me for protection when he tangled with bees or skunks. When barely a year old, he helped me herd a band of more than eight hundred ewes with their early lambs through spring blizzards and over the Bureau of Land Management trail from south of Shoshone, Wyoming, up into the Bighorn mountains, with virtually no losses. In his middle age, when he decided he could no longer keep up for cow work, Pat and I were living on the Sonoran desert near the Gila River, in an old adobe that had a rattlesnake den under its concrete slab. Through our first year there, as more than a dozen large coontails came out, he kept watch to warn us when they crawled onto the porch or tried to come through the cooler. He was a friend and guardian through the years that I, too, ceased to be young.

In 1973, when he was fifteen, Pat and I spent the summer at the AY Ranch line cabin in Blind Indian Creek, on the Hasayampa slope of the Bradshaw Mountains south of Prescott, Arizona. Puck had become so arthritic that he could walk only on level ground. I had to carry him over the difficult parts of the trail as we packed in. I strengthened his medication for the trip, but my picking him up still caused him severe pain. At one dangerously difficult place, where the trail dropped down along the face of a natural rock dike, I simply had to ignore his howls of pain and hold him as I concentrated on keeping my balance. Pat and I saw that he wouldn't be going back.

My children and niece stayed with us through the summer, and I think Puck found considerable goodness in his rapidly waning life, even though by the end of the summer he could scarcely walk and lived almost entirely on the dream side. When the mornings turned nippy and it was time to pack back across the mountains to the ranch headquarters near Cleator, while Pat was away for several days, I got out the pistol and shot him.

From late spring, when I knew the time was coming, I'd mulled over my doubts that killing him could be genuine communion. I wanted no solacing make-believe. If it was just a matter of doing the dirty work when life goes bad, I wanted to know it. I had no doubt that for him it was the best of the bad options that remained and that I should and would kill him. Any hallowing of Puck's death would have to germinate and grow in my life, out of the killing.

After killing him, I wrote the following memo to share with Pat:

> Immediately after killing Puck, I pressed my hand against his body and waited for the spasms and muscular twitching to pass. There was little movement apart from the wagging of his tail. I wasn't conscious of grief, loss, guilt, horror, regret—although all of these had been a major part of my anticipation. A strong sense of warmth and affection welled up in me with the sudden release of tension. It stayed with me as I loaded

the body on the improvised travois, dragged it to the grave, and buried it. Some of the rocks I used to fill the grave were taken from the slope rather than the streambed, and I thought that on this occasion it was proper, to celebrate change rather than mourning impermanence. The strands of Puck's being were now released, for Nature to weave into new harmonies.

After doing what needed to be done, I grieved. I will grieve the loss of those I love. I will not try to deny that part of being human.

Grief, when it comes with an awareness and affirmation of eternal transformation, is the beginning of compassion. All individuated being is *dukkha* [suffering]. But the impermanence of individuals is also the harmony of eternal transformation. Compassion is the ear of those who hear.

May all beings come at last to full tranquillity.

May all share, according to their nature, in the love that defines us.

May the love that bound me to Puck relate me to all that lives.

The concluding lines paraphrase a Buddhist prayer, and my conceptual framework here is distinctly Buddhist. Yet, virtually all Buddhists consider any killing, for whatever reason, to be injury rather than *ahimsa*. Buddhist insights remain instructive, nonetheless, because the Buddha, like Job, refuses to be consoled by theological fictions.

In primordial religion, the altruistic ideal of noninjury is undifferentiated from Nature's communion, in which life lives on life. When, for civilized religion, the altruistic ideal challenges Nature's communion, the old ways of sacralizing slaughter won't work; following our expulsion from Eden, the human side of communion among fellow creatures who eat one another must henceforth incorporate reflectively deliberative cocreativity. In some circumstances, shooting a friend like Puck may be loving-kindness that leads toward creational communion, but this doesn't go very far toward addressing the anguish of the herder who lives in symbiotic friendship with animals he intends to kill for food. Maybe the herder who is truly a member of the herd must now give those he kills to be eaten by others, much as the hunted animal was once thought to give itself as a sacrifice, that the cycle of life living on life may remain unbroken. Seen in its symbiotic unity, the herbivore-human herd makes its sacrificial offering.

Whatever the anguish of slaughtering animals that are members of one's immediate community, this remains the unavoidable reality: For human beings who live in wildlands as herders, the violence that can't be hallowed is the refusal to cull and kill.

The Hopi tell of ancient times when they wandered throughout the North American continent in search of the right place—the place to practice a sacramental way of life that preserves the universe. From jungles lapped by both oceans, they walked north to the Arctic icefields, east to the shores where leafy forests meet the sea, and west to the shores where giant redwoods overlook crashing surfs. No place anywhere on the continent equaled the high desert mesas where they finally settled. When explaining to outsiders, they sometimes observe that the home of a peaceful people must be in places that others consider wastelands.

Part of the reason the Hopi could be at home on their mesas was that they bred a corn that could grow and produce where other corns would wither. To be at home in desert solitudes, peaceful peoples must enter into partnership with other highly adapted life that permits them to walk gently over a land that is ruthless to misfits. To be at home in deserts, a gentle, peaceful people must also be ruthless. Sentimentalism is a luxury of the rich and violent.

4

Survival Tips

> One goes wherever the water commands.
> —Don Isidro Gutierrez Aguilar
> (a South Baja herder)

SOME BASICS FOR PERSONAL ADAPTATION TO ARID WILDLANDS

I HAVE A CONFESSION to make. I want my grandchildren to learn how to goatwalk, even if they have no interest in errantry. I'm a survivalist where they're concerned. Industrial civilization has destabilized the earth's climate beyond the point of no-return. The fair-weather agriculture on which our civilization depends is doomed. In the course of the next century, much of North America will probably become desert. Even if it doesn't, annual rainfalls and temperatures will fluctuate too wildly to sustain the agricultural systems on which we now depend. If humankind doesn't self-destruct, my grandchildren will have to get along without industrial agriculture as it now exists. Maybe a more sustainable industrial adaptation will emerge, but I want them to know enough to survive the old-fashioned, nomad way, in case that's the viable choice.

Although we undoubtedly have a good deal to share with one another, preindustrial peoples that are at home on the land generally have more to teach us than we have to teach them. Our fossil-fueled adaptation to life on earth, which we push as the universal answer to humanity's material needs, has become so narrowly specialized and generally destructive that we've lost our ability to go on living either with it or without it. Communities that live by adapting to untamed land are therefore the best teachers of realistic survivalism to people who don't know how. My tips about basics are just a starter, like the sentences in foreign-language phrase books for travelers.

(i) *water*

On the Sonoran desert in the unusually wet winter of 1972–73, I took a meandering walk with two little range does and their four kids, from Tucson through the Tortolitas and the Ninety-six Hills to the South Butte area of the Gila. One of the does was the White Queen; the other, a range-raised Nubian-Alpine crossbred from purebred parents. Each was giving about a gallon of milk daily during the third month of lactation, on an unsupplemented diet of desert plants—predominantly wild mustard, filaree, patata, catclaw, ironwood, and staghorn cholla fruit. With the milk and greens, the four kids and I had all the nourishment we needed.

During the first ten days, the Nubian-Alpine refused all water and the White Queen drank less than a quart. Even while producing large amounts of milk, they really needed no water to supplement what they were getting from plants, and I needed no water to supplement what I was getting from their milk. Free from the need to find water, we wandered at ease and without schedule through desert where a human being must ordinarily follow a rigid itinerary of dirt tanks and windmills.

Goats' need for water varies according to circumstances. A doe in milk and eating dry feed may need four or five gallons on hot days. During summer on the desert a human being needs as much. Goats do not like brackish water, but when there's nothing else they can serve to filter and purify some water that is unfit for human consumption, converting it to milk. They tolerate saltier water than human beings do and will sometimes sip sea water, possibly because they dilute it with plant moisture. Goats have occasionally thrived on islands where plants were the sole permanent source of fresh water.

Cows need water at least every other day, so one of the easiest ways to locate water in many arid areas is to find a cow or cow tracks, then cut for a water trail. When cattle trail in for water, they often walk single file. They usually graze back out from water, so a trail on which most of the tracks go in one direction and that is joined by similar trails should lead to water. Game trails often make similar convergence patterns toward water. Even on level ground, European breeds of cattle rarely go farther than three miles from water; Brahman crossbreds will usually be within six miles of water. Water trails are normally unmistakable within a half-mile of water, but trails along fences and in the bottoms of canyons may not be water trails. If you can tell the difference between a thirsty cow and one that has just had a drink, you may also find one that will lead you to water. (If you can't recognize a thirsty cow, go to a waterhole during hot, dry weather and look at cattle before and after they drink.)

Before going into unfamiliar arid country, study maps that show the location of water. Grazing-permit maps for areas administered by the U.S. Forest Service or the Bureau of Land Management will indicate most waters, including temporary springs and seeps that are not on U.S. Geological Survey maps, but inaccuracies of one-quarter mile or more are common on the Forest Service and BLM maps, so don't put all your faith in them—or in anything else. Life on the desert is always for real; little mistakes can be fatal.

Boiling to sterilize water reduces its potability when evaporation has already raised its salt and other solutions to the critical point; there are no universal answers to drinking-water problems on deserts. To remain fully functional day after day during the hot months on the Sonoran desert, a person must drink about four gallons daily. With exertion, more is needed, and strenuous exertion during the middle of the day can dehydrate and kill a human being in a matter of minutes. The risk of drinking too little or too late must often be weighed against the risk of drinking water that's dangerously contaminated.

For example, while I was tending a herd of young bucks in the South Baja sierras near Mulegé during the summer of 1980, which was a time of severe drought when all the cows were dying, the bucks decided to climb toward some castle rocks where several cimarron does hung out. If they reached the does, they'd decide to follow them rather than me, climbing up cliffs where I couldn't follow, so when other diversions failed I decided to panic them after me. Goat herders take control by panicking an unruly herd in much the same way a rabble-rousing politician takes over a mob, by getting out in front and then diverting it to his purpose. The herder moves out to take the point, signals alarm, and runs, trying to stay in front as the herd panics after him. By the time I had the herd under control and settled, it was midafternoon and simmering hot; I was dangerously overheated and dehydrated; and the only water nearby was a small tank in bedrock, fed by a seep that ran slower than the daytime evaporation rate—a natural tank that happened to be a favorite hangout for the area's feasting vultures, which had white-washed all the surrounding rock with their droppings.

The greenish water smelled of carrion and seethed with putrefactive bacteria. I drank more than a gallon, which got me and the herd back to a clean spring before diarrhea started cleaning me out. I spent the night drinking water that took just a few seconds to go through me, but nightlong diarrhea was much better than being dead.

I should have had containers and water purification tablets to treat the water before drinking it. That was the only time I ever became sick from drinking water in the sierras. (I sometimes theorized that maybe the high temperatures and aridity kill pathogenic bacteria on the drainages that feed the *tajos*—the hand-dug dirt tanks that are the only source of water for herders and their animals in many areas of the South Baja sierras. When staying with the seminomadic herders who live there, I always drank it freely and never became sick, but I may have developed some immunities from drinking out of dirt tanks when I was tending cattle in Arizona.) Strangers to the desert generally take the opposite risk of drinking too little when all the water is contaminated; and they often think, mistakenly, that survival tips about getting water from a barrel cactus or a clear plastic solar still can do something more than slow their rapid rate of depletion on a hot day. A good compromise is to carry a couple of gallons of treated water and some purification tablets at all times, but when living on the desert it's often impossible to adhere to the safest discipline.

Water is a special problem for goats when it comes as streams to be crossed or as rain. They avoid walking in water or mud. Few can be driven or coaxed across streams that are more than six inches deep, and they may panic rather than swim if they get in over their heads. Goats are good at balancing across on tree trunks and at using strategically located cliffs and boulders to jump from one bank to another, but most goats must be tugged, carried, or ferried across when water must be forded.

When the only available water is in a pond surrounded by mudbanks, the goatwalker may need to carry water to the herd in a container. Because goats are extremely fastidious and cautious about water, they always drink better at a new camp if watered individually from a familiar container. This is particularly important before crossing dry country, when the herder wants them to tank up. They will often refuse certain kinds of contaminated water, sometimes refusing just because the herder has put his mouth in the waterhole to drink. (When seriously dehydrated they will, of course, drink almost anything liquid.) When the color of their urine indicates inadequate water consumption, their milk production will drop.

(ii) *shelter*

Goats run for shelter at the lightest sprinkle. Unlike acclimated cattle, sheep, and horses, they often chill and become sick if they get wet. As a result, the goatwalker must carry adequate shelter for them and must be able to erect it quickly when a shower starts. When there is steady rain for more than a day, the goatwalker may need to bring brush and other forage to the goats at the shelter. To keep warm in wet, cold weather, goats need feed that is high in fiber, low in moisture, and low enough in energy to make them stuff themselves full in order to satisfy their appetite. (For ruminants, high-energy foods cool, high-fiber foods warm. High-energy foods such as mesquite beans, prickly pear, and saguaro fruit, by satisfying the goats' appetite and thus reducing the volume of fiber fermenting in the rumen, help cool them in summer, but sugary foods may also imbalance the rumen's microflora and result in the production of lethal toxins. Feeding concentrates such as grain or sugary fruit in amounts to which a ruminant is unaccustomed cultures toxin-producing microflora that will kill it, which is the leading cause of death for pen goats tended by uninformed or careless goatkeepers.)

If the shelter is crowded, the goatwalker must referee territorial disputes to prevent dominant does from driving others out. Goats' dislike for water can be used as a quick, painless way to impose discipline; the herder wets his fingers and flicks a few drops at the offender, who will then immediately back away. Goats soon learn that a flick of the hand means "back off and behave yourself" and will respond without being sprinkled. This is also an effective way to teach them what to leave alone in camp.

Once, for about a week in high, cold, rainy country, my son and I shared a two-man tent with a goat, and she always stepped outside to urinate, but I would have been more relaxed about having her in the tent if the floor had been sandy soil rather than plastic-coated nylon. On wet feed a goat can wait only about four hours between urinations. Immediately before defecation, her tail lifts, and before urinating she will squat. She will defecate immediately after urinating. When a goat squats or lifts its tail, holding the tail down will usually stop her long enough so she can be led to a more suitable place. This is how goats are housebroken. They learn quickly when young and will make every effort to comply, bursting out of a shelter or car with unmistakable urgency when confined too long, but their high-speed, large-volume digestive system can't be inhibited for long at a time. The punitive methods commonly used to housebreak dogs should not be used on goats.

After considerable trial and many errors, I concluded some years ago that the best portable dwelling for warm arid climates is a tarp strung up in the apparently haphazard fashion sometimes seen in photographs of Bedouin encampments. The basic principles are as follows: (1) Start with a sturdy tarp no less than ten by eight feet and preferably larger. (2) On the upwind or uphill side, weigh the length down with heavy rocks or else peg it, adding dirt or sand if it will be used more than a day or two. (3) Tie lines from the other side and the ends to rocks, pegs, or trees, and use forked sticks to prop the line taut where it ties to the tarp. (4) Use a pole or stick that is longer than the props for the lines (the latter usually being between two and three feet in length) to prop up and add tension to the center of the tarp, wrapping the upper end of the pole in extra clothes, plant fiber, hides, or anything else that will prevent it from wearing through the tarp.

The props need not be very strong or heavy. To tie a line where a grommet is lacking, put a smooth, round stone on the underside of the tarp and tie around it from above. As long as the props keep rope and tarp taut, the shelter will not whip in the wind the way it will if it's anchored like a tent, without props. When lines are tied to large rocks rather than pegs or trees, tension can be quickly adjusted and flaps raised or lowered to suit circumstances. In a hard storm with high winds, most of the outer props are pulled and the tarp's edge weighed down with rocks. The whole shelter becomes a free-form structure continually changing to adjust to weather or the occupant's whims.

(iii) *salt and supplemental minerals*

Milk goats must have salt, especially when lactating or on sappy feed. In arid country, salt can usually be found in a number of different plants and adjacent to damp ground. In South Baja, where the need for salt is high, goat herders never give their goats salt, but I've seen no indication that the goats suffer from a salt deficiency. They apparently get all the salt they need from available sources. Nonetheless, I prefer to carry my own supply of iodized salt.

Because of their unusually active thyroids, good milk goats need more iodine than other livestock. High milk production also requires more of other minerals. Range goats do a good job of balancing their mineral requirements, as long as the minerals are on their range, but most arid rangeland will be high in calcium in relation to phosphorous. If dry bones are collected and then crushed on flat rocks adjacent to their bedground, goats will usually maintain an adequate calcium-phosphorous balance. If the goats don't eat the crushed bones, they don't need them. If they do need them, they will search for and chew them, so the observant herder will easily collect a supply.

(iv) *packing*

Packing of one kind or another is an integral part of any form of nomadic living. Very little in the way of equipment or supplies is needed for goatwalking, and goatwalking is most enjoyable when one's backpack weighs no more than fifteen pounds, but in some circumstances pack animals are needed. Unless they must carry water to cross dry areas, milk goats should not be used for packing, since their energy is more profitably spent foraging and producing milk. In relation to their weight, people are better pack animals than four-legged animals, so where body weight is about the same people should do the packing. Generally, no more than eighteen percent of an animal's body weight should be packed. No animal should carry this much until it has all its adult teeth.

Before trying to pack, learn how to tie and use two knots: the bowline and slip knot; two slings: the basket and barrel slings; and the one essential hitch: the diamond hitch. If you know no one who can teach you, consult Joe Back's *Horses, Hitches, and Rocky Trails* (Chicago: The Swallow Press, 1959), which inexperienced packers ought to read first, anyway.

For the goatwalker, pack animals generally create more problems than they solve. First, the foraging needs and habits of another species will be different. Second, methods of control will be different. Third, no other domesticated stock can go everywhere goats go, so range will be more restricted. To accompany walking human beings, burros are generally better pack animals than horses and mules. They are smarter than horses—more adaptable and less accident-prone. Unlike many mules, they usually have a sunny disposition. They bond more readily to the packer and sometimes develop a doglike affection for human beings. They can go into rougher country. They get along on coarser and sparser feed, often thriving on brush diets. Even in mountains, their hooves are dense enough for daily packing unshod—at least, if their hooves are black rather than white. Although they can pack only about half the load carried by a horse or mule (because they weigh about half as much), good burros can usually be bought for about one-eighth the price of a suitable horse or mule. Burros are particularly well-adapted to goatwalking because most of them learn to like milk and can therefore be fed for hard work and attracted to the halter each morning without the use of grain.

Burros often chase, strike, and bite small animals. When raised with a herd of goats, they become part of the herd and must be watched only when kids are young—except for jack burros. Jacks are always dangerous, to people as well as smaller animals, so only jennies and geldings should be run with the herd. New burros must be watched carefully and kept hobbled or on a rope until they integrate into the herd.

The easiest way to prevent burros that are not bonded to the herd or herder from straying is to use two of them, keeping one tied while the other grazes. But if a burro is bonded to goats or herder, a second one may alienate its affections. If a burro is bonded to the goats but does not like the herder, it will try to drive the herd away. Burros that are bonded to the herd and herder will follow on their own when packed; if they aren't bonded, they're usually easier to drive than to lead.

(v) *tethering, belling, protecting from predators*

When only a few goats are involved, tethers can help the goatwalker compensate for a dull subconscious. If goats are to be tethered at night, they should be tied close enough to each other to feel secure, yet far enough to prevent tethers from tangling together. Tie them in their order of dominance; don't tie a subordinate herd member while dominant goats are loose. Young subordinates will stay with the older goats, so they rarely need to be tethered.

When tying to a tree or bush, use a bowline to make a loop that will tend to pull around as the goat circles. Most goats soon learn how to unwind their tether after wrapping it around a tree, but they need help at first. Problems of this kind can also be avoided by tying to a line that has been stretched at ground level between trees or bushes. A variant is the running tether, a short tether tied to a ring through which the ground line is run, the ring being blocked by obstacles near the end of the ground line so the goat won't wind its tether around the objects to which the ground line is tied. A stake with tie-ring is another way to tether that eliminates the need to teach a goat to unwind the tether when it wraps around a tree or bush. Don't tie goats next to a log or rock or ledge where they might jump over and hang themselves. Always tie at ground level. Use a tether (not manila) that will not burn or chafe the doe's udder when she runs out and pulls it up taut between her legs. Don't leave while goats are tethered.

If a few of the goats are belled, the herder has an easier time keeping track of them in brush. The herd itself is less likely to separate if one or two are belled. Goat bells are rarely audible for more than about one hundred yards, so the herder still must move with the goats when in new country. From time to time during the night, satisfied goats turn to lick their sides, which makes their bells sound like a burglar alarm. I sleep better when all bells are removed each evening, but bells do reduce risks from predators such as mountain lions. Bells are unnecessary when goatwalking with only one goat because a single doe won't go far from the goatwalker anyway. If bonded to the goatwalker, a group of four or five goats will usually behave much the same way, running to him or her when startled, going hungry if he is farther than forty or fifty yards from feed.

When bedding down among goats in bear or lion country, I've sometimes wondered whether a bear or big lion or jaguar that happened by would consider me a goat among goats or would feel that the goats should be left alone because of my presence. Deer, for example, have a different attitude toward me when I'm sitting among the goats, often coming up close to puzzle over us. I don't like to have a fire burning near goats because they lack the fear of fire characteristic of most animals and may injure themselves by walking in coals. So sometimes after seeing impressive lion tracks, and always in bear country, I hang clothing and urinate around the circumference of the camp at night in order to emphasize my presence. I've never had a problem with predators during a goatwalk, although I've occasionally found lion tracks that showed we were scrutinized during the night.

(vi) *tracking*

Goats sometimes panic and may run far enough to get lost. When they do panic, the flightiest one takes the lead, her fear confirmed by the goats that are running wildly behind her, their fears confirmed by her panicky flight. When they are accustomed to their bedground and know their range for a radius of two or three miles, they rarely panic or get lost. When they leave their bedground to forage at night in a strange place, they easily become startled, break, run, and get lost. The risk of panic increases on windy nights; the rare occasions when they panic away from familiar range are usually on windy days.

Full goats are less likely to panic than hungry goats. The smell of bear or lion may also set them off if they are in flatlands or can't easily climb to a vantage point. A spooky doe will set off the whole herd, and if the herd queen also happens to be spooky the nomadic herder will lose a lot of sleep. Herders usually snap awake whenever the herd moves, acts nervous, or begins to stray. Those who fail to develop this unsleeping awareness of the herd's activities and moods must become good trackers.

Goats prefer rocks to soft ground, often choose to travel along rocky, windswept ridges, are as likely to go up and over a bluff as around it, go right under barbed wire fences, and zigzag or double back on themselves as readily as they travel in a straight line. When goats stray where the ground is hard and rocky, only an exceptional tracker can catch up until they settle. If, after a herder has tracked strays all day, their sign is colder than it was in the morning, the best procedure is to try to cut their trail several miles ahead by checking surrounding washes, trails, and roads where their tracks would easily be seen, coming around full circle if no tracks are found, and then narrowing the circumference of the search until the strays or their tracks are located. If more than one person is searching, one can carefully trail while others cut for tracks, always agreeing on rendezvous and message locations before separating. When several people are involved, one person should move camp and carry messages so that the others can travel light and also so they can keep in touch with each other well enough to regroup and reorganize quickly when fresh tracks are cut. Heliographic communication is often convenient on such occasions, so a small mirror should be a part of everyone's pack. The procedure is laborious and requires painstaking and unrelenting observation of the ground, but it will systematically narrow down the strays' location until they are recovered.

Casting about at random in an effort to sight strays is a hit-or-miss approach that never gets anywhere or narrows any possibilities until the searcher is lucky enough to happen across them. Goats on unfamiliar range may travel ten or fifteen miles each day and could be almost anywhere in a very large area after two or three days. After rain, snow, or high wind, a random search may be necessary, but the searcher should still look more for tracks than for the animals themselves. As night approaches, though, check the high spots. A sentinel will usually stand on a vantage point next to a bedded herd. Tracking involves no secrets or special knowledge—just careful observation and a buildup of experience concerning the way observations correlate with events. Tracking is learned by tracking.

(vii) *wild foods*

Theoretically, anything organic is edible if properly processed and detoxified. Practically, many wild "edibles" should be left alone. Some of the best regional guides to wild foods are anthropological studies of Native American material cultures that were made before reliable informants died out. No matter what your source of information, though, when sitting down to a meal of recommended but unfamiliar wild plants (or insects), go slow and eat only a little at a time. If you have not positively identified the plant, don't eat it. Just a little of some plants can be fatal. Also, your digestive

SURVIVAL TIPS

system has not been trained and may not have evolved to handle foods that were everyday staples for local hunter-gatherers. Learn about individual wild foods in depth before trying for much breadth; work out a menu of a few common plants on which you can rely for both quantity and digestibility, then gradually expand your repertoire.

The local Indians will usually have relied on a common, easily-stored or else nonseasonal high-energy food, rounding out their diet with assorted greens, animals (including edible reptiles and insects), and seasonal fruits. With a daily supply of three or more quarts of milk, you won't need to worry about protein and calories, but sources of vitamin C, iron, copper, manganese, and fiber must be added. Nonetheless, it's still best to start by learning about one or two common high-energy foods because these are essential if you lose your milk supply. That a plant can be eaten is not enough. You must find enough calories to keep going.

In southern Arizona's desert at elevations between two thousand and six thousand feet, the common energy foods are saguaro fruit, the fruit of the prickly pear cactus, mesquite pods, mescal, acorns, and honey. With the exception of mescal and honey, they are only seasonally available, but mesquite pods and acorns store indefinitely if protected from moisture, rodents, and insects. In the Southwest, mesquite pods are generally the high-energy food to learn about first. In much of California and some of the Arizona chaparral, acorns would come first.

Mescal is a common invader on some overgrazed range but is a protected plant in Arizona and elsewhere in the United States, so it should be used only in emergencies. Mescal and other "century plants" are like giant artichokes. They store carbohydrates in the heart and at the base of the leaves. The heart of a mature mountain mescal is likely to weigh about thirty pounds. (Southwestern Indians formerly traded roasted mescal heart; the Mescalero Apaches, who specialized in the mescal trade, were named after it.) It is also a good source of fiber for thread, cloth, and rope, and is the source of the sacred Aztec drink, pulque, from which mescal (the hard liquor customarily bottled with a white worm in it) is distilled. (Redistilled, mescal becomes tequila.)

GOATWALKING

The raw juice from the mescal is poisonous. It causes photosensitivity if eaten and a painful rash if it touches the skin. The leaf tips are dagger-sharp spikes that easily make deep punctures, which the plant's poisons cause to ache intensely. (Emiliano Zapata is said to have relied on mescal's special properties to torture captured enemies and suspects.) But if the heart is pit-roasted for about thirty hours, it becomes a highly nutritious food similar to sweet potatoes.

Honeybees can be followed to their hive by catching a number of them at a water or a honey plant and then releasing one at a time. However, inexperienced honey thieves run a high risk of falling if they try to rob a colony located in a cliff (which is one of the most common locations of wild colonies in the Southwest), and many colonies are in saguaros or other living plants that should never be injured. I recommend that only knowledgeable beekeepers integrate honey collection into goatwalking.

In most cases, edible seeds should be slightly roasted, ground, and then soaked or boiled before being eaten. The most useful greens are common in many parts of the United States; many are garden pests. My favorites are lamb's-quarter (*Chenopodium album*), and pigweed (*Amaranthus palmeri*, also known as careless weed, redroot, and amaranth—a leading invader of gardens). Filaree (*Erodium cicutarium*), watercress (*Nasturtium officinale*), purslane (*Portulaca oleracea*), and assorted wild mustards are also seasonally abundant in many areas. Cholla buds and the new growth of prickly pear are sometimes abundant. Rosehips are often found on wild rose bushes that sometimes grow in damp areas in mountains; they can be collected to assure a regular source of vitamin C.

If I had to choose between a metal pot and a metal knife as a survival tool, I would choose the pot. I would also prefer both pot and knife to a rifle. Containers are easy to find or make, but for the processing of foods the metal pot provides us with an enormous advantage over Native Americans who could boil water only by dropping hot rocks into the water held in containers that could not withstand direct flames. Ground acorn meal is leached by boiling and then straining it. (In the absence of a straining cloth, the water

SURVIVAL TIPS

can be carefully poured off while blocking the meal in the pot.) Small spines that cannot be singed off cactus fruit and are laborious to trim off are quickly softened and made harmless by boiling water. Boiling makes many foods, such as staghorn cactus fruit, ground manzanita berries, ground seeds, and greens, more palatable and digestible. Sweet juices are preserved by boiling them down to a syrup. A whole range of important foods formerly available to human beings only after tedious processing are quickly and easily prepared when one has a metal pot.

Some vitamins are destroyed by cooking, and many health food enthusiasts have concluded that all cooking and processing of food is therefore bad. Few greens can be eaten in quantity when raw. Other nutritious foods are poisonous when raw. Little research has been done to determine the nutritional value or the dangers of wild foods, so pay attention to what your own senses tell you. Don't force yourself to eat any wild food just because you think it's good for you, and don't assume plants that make good cooked greens can be eaten raw.

(viii) *poisons and medicines*

Many plants contain poisons. Many poisons are medicinal in the right dose for specific ailments. Some medicines may be good for many ailments and have no overdose, but they would then be more of a food than a medicine—or maybe a persuasive placebo. Some plants, such as Mormon tea (which is an "upper" that gives symptomatic relief for allergies), seem to work well in catch-as-catch-can dosages, but the medicinal use of many plants is problematic because there's no way to be sure of dosages or long-term effects. So little research has been done on most medicinal plants that, as a rule of thumb, I recommend ingesting only food plants, and then with caution. Without arguing the point, I'll just illustrate my reasons with some anecdotes.

In La Purísima, on the other side of the Baja sierras from Mulegé, I once met a *curandera* (a folk doctor who relies primarily on medicinal plants) who insisted that jimson weed in any amounts is good for all ailments—contrary to the Merck medical manual that just says eating it results in hallucinations, convulsions, coma, and then death. (Castaneda's Don Juan was a *brujo* or wizard who used this "Devil Weed" spiritually rather than medicinally, but in folk medicine one man's *curandera* is another's *bruja*.) Maybe, since jimson weed is such a strong poison, it's good for some things in some amounts. Maybe this *curandera* gives it in a way that causes patients to vomit an overdose; it certainly smells so rank that it must be difficult to chew, swallow, and keep down. Her patients will surely discover her medicine is persuasively potent, if they survive.

Throughout South Baja's sierras, I found that almost every plant that is reported to have medicinal properties is said to be good for kidney infections. People think a lot about their kidneys, if they must move whenever they can no longer drink the rapidly evaporating solution in a *tajo*, but none of the plant cures they take for kidney infections is likely to be as good as clean water. My prescription would be filters and solar stills.

The plague that kills most goats in the sierras of Baja California Sur is called *la huilera*. During severe droughts it more than halves many of the herds. When I first saw it, I thought of the way loco weed affects cattle; a goat first loses locomotion in the hind quarters and tries to drag herself forward, but she eventually goes down and seems to give up. Unable to move, she soon dies of thirst or starvation. There are loco weeds in Baja, but only at the highest elevations where the herds never suffer from *la huilera*. Asking in La Paz about poisonous plants that would cause these symptoms, I learned that one of the Livestock Service veterinarians had been using goats to do extensive tests on a plant the sierra people call "cacachila" (*Karwinskia humboldtiana*), which has a poison that destroys the body's ability to produce an enzyme that is essential to nerves' signal transmission. His description of cacachila poisoning fit *la huilera*.

Back in the sierra, I learned that *la huilera* only occurs during dry times, that cacachila remains green and is often eaten by goats during dry times, and that cacachila bushes are particularly abundant around springs at the foot of the high cliffs that are the eastern boundary of the sierras, which is where the herds go during dry times. When eating cacachila, goats often use their prehensile lips to pick its dry berries, which the veterinarian had found to have a concentration of the poison. But none of the sierra people would believe that cacachila could be poisonous because, when the berries are boiled to make a tea, it's their preferred remedy for colds.

I checked with the doctor in Mulegé, to see whether he ever ran into a disorder among the sierra people in which their limbs went limp, and he said that, as a matter of fact, he'd run into a number of puzzling cases, which he had at first diagnosed as *myasthenia gravis*. As in *myasthenia gravis*, the patient would briefly regain strength when an injection temporarily substituted for the deficient enzyme, but in other respects the diagnosis had failed. I told him about cacachila, and when he then asked each of these patients about it, each had, indeed, been drinking cacachila tea prior to becoming disabled. I returned to the sierra, to indict cacachila, but no one believed me. Everyone knew that cacachila is a better cold medicine than anything available in town, and from time immemorial all the sierra people have used it whenever they catch cold.

I've sometimes disregarded warnings, as superstitions, that turned out to be well-founded. (Maybe one of the reasons my Ozark ancestors have a reputation for show-me skepticism is that they know much of what they share as folk wisdom is actually superstition but is now the foundation of too many good yarns to be recanted.) For example, the sierra people warned me never to stay in the shade of a bush called *"yerba de la flecha"* (*Sapium biloculare*), which has a milky sap that was used by the Indians to poison their arrows. If you should get a droplet of its sap on your finger and then rub your eyes, you will go blind, quite painfully.

Many years before, I'd cowboyed with a Sonoran who would warn me against sitting in the shadow of a number of different trees that he said cast a shade like the evil eye—for example, that it is as bad to sit in the shade of an ash tree as it is to let an owl stare at you. I thought the warning against *yerba de la flecha* was an extension of the same superstition, with some associational logic based on the great danger of being exposed to its sap. In many areas of South Baja's Sonoran desert, *yerba de la flecha* provides the only solid shade, and, when the temperature goes up around 120 degrees Fahrenheit, solid shade is important; anything that stays in the sun tends to bake. But when I disregarded the warning, I soon felt as though I were in a Mexico City smog; my eyes stung and my lungs became congested. Examining the twigs, I saw that they are quite flexible and exude little droplets of poison when bent. Dust devils or other strong gusts of wind (which are unpredictably sudden on hot days in the desert) act as atomizers to squeeze out, dry, and puff the poison around each *yerba de la flecha*.

I also disregarded the sierra people's warning about bat urine. They would take great risks, climbing down the face of cliffs and walking through rough country, to reach a shelter at night, even if it was just an abandoned jacal or ramada, and they often urged me to quit sleeping on the desert wherever nightfall found me. When they talked about danger from snakes, scorpions, spiders, and rabid animals, I countered by pointing out that, as they knew, the shade and palm fronds of their shelters are among the best habitats for the reptiles and arthropods they fear, and the risk of being bitten by a rabid animal is probably about the same in an open-air shelter as it is under the open sky. When they talked about lions, I said that if a lion should decide to try eating human beings, it would know where to find them. (Now and then, a lion that becomes too old or crippled to catch deer and goats takes to raiding the corrals at night, to grab a goat that can't escape.) Then they would warn me that the urine of flying bats might sprinkle me. Bat urine, they said, burns much worse than battery acid.

Once, when goatwalking in mid-August along Eagle Creek (above the Gila, just below the mouth of the San Juan, near the New Mexican border), I camped for about a week close to one of the largest bat caves in North America. All night, swarms of bats fluttered overhead, which turned out to be an ideal place for me and the goats to escape the mosquitoes that plague the high Sonoran desert at that time. Since a cloud of low-flying bats had been no problem, I saw no reason to be concerned about an occasional Baja bat flitting overhead. Then, one morning when Pat was out with me, she woke with a burning itch on her hand. In spite of repeated washing, a large red blotch appeared and began to blister. We were at Corral Blanco, where our friends Libui and Chueco (who often urged me not to sleep out at night) identified it immediately: bat piss. For several months after the blister drained, Pat had a purple-red blotch over much of her hand; we thought it might be permanent, but it eventually disappeared. I now try to remember to take some baking soda along, when I'll be sleeping under South Baja's bats.

Sometimes folk wisdom should be heeded; sometimes it shouldn't; and only after living in an area for years will an outsider have much basis for sorting it out. Practices that seem irrational may have some basis, even if they're just a way to do something about what can't be helped. For example, when a cow or goat becomes too weak to stand, the sierra people cut notches at the base of its horns down to the core, to draw blood. During dry times, cows must often be tailed up to keep them foraging, and maybe notching their horns helps them to keep struggling to survive, but I've never seen any reason to think so. Lactating cows are the first to go down in dry times, stretching their heads back along their body in the pose that's characteristic of milk fever (which dairymen know as a mineral imbalance often suffered by high-producing cows fed first-cutting alfalfa). An intravenous feeding of an inexpensive solution that reestablishes her mineral balance has a cow that's down with milk fever back up and foraging in a few minutes. Nothing else works. But the sierra people will always insist on notching her horns as well—and rarely consider using the milk-fever serum when outsiders aren't around to urge it.

Traditional societies survive by sticking to their ways. Some of their ways seem irrational and outworn to outsiders—and may be—but outsiders have only external, conscious criteria for judging. A fiesta that squanders all surplus wealth on one big blowout isn't the way to thrive in industrial society, but it may be exactly what's needed to maintain the balance and integrity of a seminomadic, preindustrial livelihood. If I could have persuaded the sierra people to treat milk fever with the serum rather than horn notching, some of their cows would have lived longer before starving, but most of the cows in South Baja will die every few years anyway—the sooner, the better, for them and the land. (A palo verde called *"dipugo"* [*Cercidium microphyllum*] that is the only forage that can be gathered and fed at these times has ceased to regenerate and its survivors are being pruned to death during the droughts, wherever there are cows on South Baja's Sonoran desert.)

And the deceptively deadly cacachila that I denounced so ineffectively may actually be the savior of the Cuesta's ecosystem, culling the goat herds down to carrying capacity during the dry times—and, over the longer run, thereby saving the goats and people, who are dependent members of the community of plants that cacachila preserves. Poison is often the best—and sometimes the only—medicine.

(ix) *milk, yogurt, and cheese*

Yogurt or clabbered milk, cheese, and kefir are staples for pastoralists from Mongolia to Morocco who often live on a diet consisting almost exclusively of milk and milk products. Yogurt is probably the most common milk product consumed, but it's rarely the carefully cultured product promoted by health-food stores. It is milk clabbered by whatever bacteria happen to drift in for free. The flavor of the yogurt depends largely on the bacteria one happens to catch and the strains that are favored by a given incubating temperature, although goat's milk normally makes a milder, less sour yogurt than cow's milk. The bacteria one catches in wildlands are less likely to produce obnoxious flavors than bacteria commonly found around barns and settled areas, but the risk of off-flavors from barn milking is minor as long as good sanitation is practiced. (My grandmothers made cottage cheese and buttermilk all their lives without even knowing that starter cultures could be purchased.)

SURVIVAL TIPS

During cool weather, milk may take a long time to clabber, so a way must be worked out to keep it warm. Milk must also be cultured at the same temperature to retain the same bacterial mix. For this, an old sheepherder's trick for saving firewood and cooking beans without tending a fire works well. Dig a pit or make an enclosure with rocks that will have a radius at least six inches greater than the radius of the container to be used for the milk to be clabbered. Pack it full of dry grass. Force the pot in and pack the grass tightly around it. When camping in the same place for several days, wet the grass and let it dry to the pot's shape. Slowly heat the milk to about 110 degrees Fahrenheit while constantly stirring. (Learn how 110 degrees Fahrenheit feels on the inside of your wrist sometime when you have a thermometer.) Don't overheat the milk. If it is pasteurized, nothing will happen; many bacteria fail to survive heat over 120 degrees Fahrenheit. If you do pasteurize the milk or accidentally raise the temperature too high, sprinkle bark scrapings into the milk from trees or bushes that are known to have sap that isn't poisonous. (Experiment to see which barks are associated with bacteria that produce the best flavors. I've found that pine bark usually produces a pleasant cheddary flavor.) Cover the pan; pack more dry grass over it; and in about twelve hours it should be ready. Fully clabbered milk will taste much better than milk that is just blinky (beginning to turn sour). When you have a batch of clabbered milk that is particularly tasty, it can be perpetuated by keeping some to put in the next milking. This will also speed the clabbering process. (In addition to making milk edible for people who have difficulty digesting lactose, clabbered milk is a good cure and preventative for many kinds of bacterial diarrhea.)

Milk can also be curdled with rennet or with acids such as lemon juice. Rennet comes from the lining of an unweaned calf or kid's milk stomach. When a calf or kid is slaughtered, the milk stomach is saved and dried, then strips of it are dipped in small amounts of warm water to add to milk. After the milk curdles, the whey is drained and the curd is salted and pressed. This is the way most Mexican cheese is made, with no bacterial culturing, although commercial rennet in liquid, powder, or tablet form is used to make Mexican white cheese in large quantities, as in South Baja's sierras.[1]

Reportedly, most people develop an allergy to lactose after they're weaned, except for Caucasians and some tribal people who live by pastoralism. Making yogurt, buttermilk, or cheese solves this problem by converting lactose to lactic acid. Some people are allergic instead to milk proteins. On occasion, switching from cow milk to goat milk takes care of this protein allergy, but goatwalking won't work for anyone who is truly allergic to milk proteins.

I've found that people who go goatwalking return with an increased appetite for milk and milk products and that a minor lactose intolerance soon disappears as the "yogurt-making" microflora in the digestive system flourish on the regular supply of milk. Nor do goatwalkers burn out on milk, yogurt, and cheese the way they do when forced to live on an exclusive diet of other less-balanced foods. Instead, any aversions they feel toward curdled milk soon disappears. On a goatwalk, milk also assumes a sacramental quality. It is life.

> You know, O my son, the first thing God created when he created the world was milk. And from this milk came all life, first mankind and then camels. Just as our own mothers gave us life with their milk when we were young and helpless, so the she-camels mother us all and keep us alive. The most precious of God's gifts to mankind and the world is milk. Those who follow the camels and live most exclusively off their sweet milk are the ones who live in greatest harmony with the universe.
>
> —Al Hudayb, a Bedouin of the Empty Quarter[2]

---

1. For a much more detailed explanation of the way to make Mexican goat cheese, see Jim Corbett, "The Goat Cheese Economy of the South Baja Sierras," part one, *The Dairy Goat Journal,* (July 1979), 15, 66–67. This two-part article (July and August 1979) also has information about other aspects of the material culture of the goat-herding seminomads of the South Baja sierras.

2. National Geographic Society (U.S.), *Nomads of the World* (Washington, D.C., 1971), 63.

5

The Cimarron Alternative

> Calves are easily bound and slaughtered
> Never knowing the reason why;
> But whoever treasures freedom
> Like the swallow must learn to fly.
>
> —*"Donna, Donna,"* a Yiddish song

ESCAPING PHARAOH

NOMADIC PASTORALISM MAY have originated among primitive serfs who saw that their herds combined agriculture's food-production security with the mobility needed to escape subjugation. When humankind learned how to produce surplus wealth by farming, the warriors among them discovered ways to take it away, cultivators' dependence on a plot of ground anchoring them so they could be subjugated, taxed, and conscripted. When warriors established a territorial system of organized violence, a primitive state was born. There are many theories about stateless societies and how they could be created, but only in symbiotic relationship with herbivores have subjugated human communities escaped. Maybe the Israelites' escape from Pharaoh is a paradigm for all pastoral nomadism, the one and only way entire peoples can go feral, but, in any case, an outlook that is rooted in the cimarron's experience of liberation is radically different from the outlook of a community that has never been subjugated or that has never gone free.

The state ideologies of ancient Egypt, Persia, and China described the Habiru (Hebrew), Turanian, or Hiung-Nu (Hun) as a type tied to no particular nationality, a wanderer or stray who neither conquers nor is conquered and who represents the Powers of Darkness against the Powers of Light (represented by the state). Babylonia built its Wall of the West, Egypt its Wall of the Ruler, and China its Great Wall to exclude the cimarron peoples who, on their side, disdained " 'the peasant tied to his clods, and the cowardly townsfolk, who seek to protect themselves behind walls and who serve a lord as slaves. . . .' In all these peoples, their way of life is more than a form of livelihood; it is a kind of faith."[1]

Going feral allows small groups to live through the cultural evolution that brought us here, which is an educational prerequisite for going free. According to a well-worn biological dictum, *ontogeny* (the developmental history of the individual) repeats *phylogeny* (the developmental history of the species). In education, cultural ontogeny *must* repeat cultural phylogeny. Educational growth requires cultural roots. The alternatives are brainwashing and conditioning—programming that may produce a marketable individual but that fails to prepare a person to participate creatively in cultural evolution. (I'm not suggesting we must read about phylogeny, although that may be helpful. Only a radically empirical education leads to the discoveries one must make for oneself.)

Here are two iconoclastic suggestions about our fundamental educational needs: First, everyone should learn how to feed himor herself. Second, everyone should live at least briefly as a member of a wildland band.

Ethologists have devoted considerable attention during recent years to the evolutionary conditions that have made us what we are. At times their methods are reminiscent of medieval scholastics' inquiries into the nature of gravitation. The surmised lifestyles of australopithecines or the social behavior of chimpanzees are in themselves interesting studies and also raise important questions

---

1. For elaboration and further citations, see Martin Buber, *Moses* (New York: Harper & Row, 1958), 23–32.

about human behavior. But they don't answer the questions about human behavior that they raise. Goatwalking is one way to discover firsthand what life is like in the kind of band that cradled human evolution.

Goatwalkers are members of industrial civilization who sustain themselves for a few weeks or months in a wildland environment. Learning how to cut our ties with the commercial life-support system will not change our cultural identity any more than learning Chinese will make us Chinese. Nonetheless, many of the characteristics of a tribal band do emerge in a group that lives on its own for a few weeks. The members of such a group act like tribesmen because they are living tribally.

Small groups living on their own tend to make decisions by consensus, become more concerned with one another, and readily contribute according to ability and share according to need. When they compete, it is for status as providers. Living in wildlands by mutual support and their wits, human beings get along much better than they do when they live by competing to retain and improve their niche in society.

Until this century, the cultural development of the individual did, at least among country people who were the preponderant majority everywhere, repeat important aspects of the cultural development of humankind. With respect to the economy, if cities collapsed, as they sometimes did during periods of famine, plague, and war, country life went on. If agricultural markets collapsed, country people could get along without money as long as their land was not mortgaged or subject to confiscatory taxation. If crops failed, farmers turned to hunting and gathering. All previous livelihood systems remained operative. And when times were good, country people continued to use many wild foods and to grow the food they ate because only a fool would gamble his family's fate on the market's stability.

Most inhabitants of the industrialized nations have burned their bridges to the life-support systems that were used prior to this century. Our agriculture is now as dependent on fossil-fuel technology as any other modern industry, and it also relies on an enormous capital investment and rapid cash flow that ties its fate to the fate of the market. Corporate agriculture is replacing the family farm, but where families survive in farming they usually buy their food; a diversified operation consumes extra time, and time is money. Not just individual farms, but entire regions have abandoned diversity in favor of a market specialty. The pace is frantic, and high indebtedness is so widespread that most of the remaining "family farms" are occupied by families who work seventy-hour weeks at less than the minimum wage for a lending agency that owns both their land and their time.

At the beginning of the century, a majority of Anglo-Americans were country people. Most country people rarely ate food they had not grown or collected. They felt insecure until they stored enough to last out a bad year. My grandmothers put up a three-year supply and would have been as mortified at being caught opening a tin can as my grandfathers would have been by having a mortgage on their land. They and all their neighbors knew there would be times of drought and hail and frost and flood. Sometimes depressions would drive relatives back from the cities. And they still remembered how it was when the bushwhackers burnt-out one family after another until just about everyone was living off the woods. For their generation of Ozarkers, the regular gathering of wild foods and the preparation for hard times were more than acts of prudence; religious duty required a person to share God's bounty with those in need and to avoid becoming a burden to others. Even during the hardest of times, no loaded guns were kept with the food supply. Rather, children were taught always to set an extra place at the table and never to eat the last helping, just in case someone happened by. (Pigs and chickens assured that nothing would be wasted.)

Prior to a cousin's reunion of my father's clan one year, one of the cousins volunteered to provide the banquet for the more than two hundred people who would gather. She insisted on providing it all herself, but, because she and her husband had a poor, forty-acre hill farm and no cash, and drought had caused a total failure of crops in the region that year, my father visited to be sure it

THE CIMARRON ALTERNATIVE

would not run them short. He found that there would be plenty for the banquet and more years of drought. That was only sixty-five years ago.

During the Nixon administration an operation was launched to close the Mexican border to drug smuggling. The borderlands were supposed to be under constant aerial surveillance, coordinated by radio with units on the ground. At the time, I happened to take a group of goatwalkers into the mountains west of Nogales. We wondered whether the federal units could track us down when they either saw us or else cut our tracks. After wandering around the area for about a week, during which the surveillance planes failed to notice us and we failed to find any ground units, we concluded that, for all the equipment and manpower being budgeted, the border remained unsealed—a view that was confirmed by itinerant *alambristas* (Mexicans who had come north over the border fence). Another time, I took a group goatwalking on land belonging to the San Carlos Apache. Unknown to us, someone became worried about the van we left parked on the desert, and Apache trackers were sent to find us. They didn't. The experience of the U.S. military forces in Vietnam also indicates that small groups that are at home in the land are very difficult to find and catch or to prevent from crossing borders, even with practically unlimited manpower, fleets of helicopters, advanced electronic and photometric technology, indiscriminate air attack, and an elaborate network of spies. (Anyone who knows how to track knows how to evade trackers. Beyond that, evasion becomes a game of wits and a test of one's ability to do the unexpected or unthinkable. In *Pasó por Aquí*, Eugene Rhodes writes of a man who shakes a posse by catching and then riding off on a steer. That's the way to lose trackers, if you're good at riding steers.)

Before the age of fossil fuels, pastoral nomads enjoyed the strategic advantages now associated with guerrillas. More mobile than any other human society and having no fixed bases to defend, they could choose the time and place for attack and, if necessary, retreat indefinitely without sacrifice. Militarily, all of their attention and resources could be devoted to attack, because escape substituted for defense. For centuries these inherent strategic advantages made pastoral nomads the scourge of large areas of Asia, Africa, and Europe, nomadic hordes sometimes forming under a Genghis Khan, Attila, or Tamerlane to sweep over the vast grasslands of Eurasia. In the Western Hemisphere, nomadic hunters who turned horse pastoralist were quick to understand these same advantages. If Native American tribes had been organized for sustained action, with the horse they might have held the arid West during the nineteenth century, even without full mastery of firearm technology. Yet, for the same reasons that cavalry has become obsolete, pastoral nomadism could no longer provide the base for armed resistance to an industrial power. Pastoral nomadic skills remain useful for escape—increasingly useful as modern man has become roadbound—but not for attack.

Only within a very special and limited political context could goatwalking be used for nonviolent resistance. For example, it could be used to assert the right to live free, without asking or earning anyone's permission for access to subsistence. In seventeenth-century England a movement of dispossessed peasants, "the Diggers," claimed the right to use the commons to produce food for themselves, maintaining that no economic system can rightfully deny a person the small plot of ground needed for survival. For a little more than a year the nonviolent Diggers planted and replanted crops that troops repeatedly trampled. They were often assaulted and many were jailed. And, for all practical purposes, the Digger movement died. If the Diggers could have claimed their rights the way nomadic pastoralists always have, by telling the authorities "Catch me if you can," the right of every human being to subsistence from the land might have come to be considered as inalienable as the right to worship as one chooses. At times, Thomas Jefferson apparently thought it was. Rights to life and liberty lack a firm foundation for the landless who are entirely dependent on someone's willingness to give wages or welfare. But the Founding Fathers forgot to put it in the Bill of Rights.

When a person or group is faced with extermination or enslavement, going free may be a more responsible choice than at-

THE CIMARRON ALTERNATIVE

tempting to resist. The black maroons who escaped to form their own societies created both an example and a refuge for those who were still enslaved. If we're lucky, few of us will ever face political conditions that would make escape necessary for survival, but knowing how to escape, should the need arise, can still strengthen one's sense of independence. A slave who only knows how to live by slavery is in no position to struggle for freedom.

Knowing how to go free is a nonviolent analogue to the right to bear arms. When every citizen is armed, the state's ability to rule by coercion is limited. At some point, oppression sparks rebellion. But rebellion is successful only when the state is overthrown or brought to terms—no easy task for an armed citizenry in an age of tanks, high explosives, napalm, and air power. Rebellion also requires a high degree of consensus. Those who go free simply declare their independence, as a community rather than as a territory. In this case the state's control is limited by its ability to find, keep, and manage the people it would subjugate.

While the state's power may come from the barrel of a gun, its ability to apply power comes from the tongues of its informers. Violence is power only when combined with information. Villagers living under the most tyrannical of ancient despots often had more control of their lives than do the citizens of a modern democracy; the despot had no way to know about and direct the details of everyday living. Because everyone in a commercial economy must get money in order to live, modern governments learn all they need to know to control their subjects by monitoring the details of personal cash flow. Refinements such as telephone and mail surveillance, the bugging of homes and offices, and the acquisition of school, medical, and other institutional records are of minor importance compared to tax, social security, credit, and banking records.

These days, despotism's basic strategy is to shroud important governmental decisions and operations in secrecy or misinformation while accumulating as much information as possible about the citizenry. When modern information technology is in the hands of a governmental body established to maintain secrecy and gather intelligence, the most explicit constitutional restraints fail to check the growth of despotism; any governmental body whose activities

77

are secret is operationally above the law. At the same time, modern information technology empowers such a governmental body to operate in every area of a subject's daily life.

Nonetheless, much of the technology involved is also impossible for the state to monopolize. Almost everyone can get in touch with almost everyone else. Information flows across borders uninspected and unapproved. International movements spring into being overnight. Concerted resistance by a handful of people may have a widespread political impact when it echoes through the communications system, magnified and duplicated into millions of concurrent electronic events. Groups can go into uninhabited areas, yet stay in touch and even regain social initiative.

A person or group might also choose to walk out on society for essentially the same reasons a conscientious objector refuses to go to war. Some conscientious objectors refuse to bear arms but will do military service as medics or in some noncombatant function. Many conscientious objectors refuse any form of military service because they believe all jobs within the military support the warmaking mission, that medics or cooks are as much a part of the war effort as foot soldiers. But when industrial nations go to war, civil society itself is the war machine. Any useful, productive role within a warmaking society therefore contributes to the war effort; there is no place for nonparticipants, only for collaborators and resisters.

Active and visible conscientious objection to war, to the destruction of the environment, to racism, to the exploitation of economic colonies—to any form of organized and socially accepted brutality or injustice—is often the most effective way to sensitize one's society and stimulate change, particularly when the objector maintains a relationship of goodwill that prevents the hardening of adversary positions. Attitudes change through example rather than arguments. The uncompromising attempt to live one's highest ideals openly and consistently is therefore the most effective social action one can take. To live in opposition to the principles one proclaims is also the surest way to destroy them as social options. If, to avoid betraying one's conscience, a person must walk out on society, then by all means let him walk out.

Yet, "betrayal of conscience" is a catchphrase that leads to confusion. It is not the health of something called "conscience" that is at issue but the victims of socially sanctioned violence. If conscience becomes an object of concern, the conscientious objector confuses cleaning up the mess with washing one's hands of it.

But how can a systemic mess be cleaned up when the key choice is between collaboration and resistance? Life turns sour when it is dedicated entirely to resistance and is cut off from constructive social activity. During the sixties, war resisters therefore tried to drop out of the established system and create a peacemaking counterculture. The result was little more than an assimilated subculture and new fashions. The counterculture was as self-absorbed as the kind of conscientious objection that is primarily concerned with conscience rather than objectionable violations.

One's complicity can be reduced by limiting acquisition and consumption to necessities; failing to limit consumption means that other living beings are injured to make the difference. Nonetheless, any productive member of a society at war with man or nature can also be sure that he is one of its soldiers, no matter how considerately he lives. To serve life, technocracy's conscripts must go beyond simplicity and do more than desert; they must gather into basic communities that open an exodus.

SHABBAT SHALOM

Goatwalking is one of the few ways that a group of people who have been tamed to serve technocratic civilization can cease (*shabat*) for a time to live by making war on life. As a sabbatical basecommunity livelihood, goatwalking's religious roots are more biblical than Buddhist, which poses a problem for many readers who are *too* familiar with the biblical account to see what it reveals about sabbath.

When young Moses learned he was a foundling—probably the abandoned child of a slave people—he ceased to speak freely. His mouth would labor to shape thought into speech, mutilating courtly Egyptian's self-assured accents into word fragments that stuck spastically on his tongue.

The obstruction vanished whenever he spoke rhythmically, in verse. Cut off from spontaneous conversation with others, searching in solitude for suitable meters, he discovered a companion who sometimes breathed words into his mouth. Instead of speaking to his hearing, the way one usually talks to another, the companion spoke intimately out of silence, mouth to mouth, inspiring speech. Moses no longer learned his aspirations from the Egyptian court, turning instead to his companion.

An alien in the only land he knew, he became a stranger to himself. As an Egyptian of Pharaoh's household, he lived a lie, but he had no other life. He listened, watched.

The aliens were herded into labor camps, worked in harness—as docile as sheep, of less value than scrub oxen, the lowest thralls in a nation of serfs—yet they were called *habiru*—hebrew—the Egyptians' hated name for outlaw nomads.

One day he searched out the *habiru* woman who had been his nurse.

"You are one of us, Moses, if you choose to be, but to know us you must know our story. Begin with these words: *'Arami 'obed 'abi.* 'My father was a cimarron Aramean.'"

She smiled at his puzzlement. "They don't know about cimarrons at Pharaoh's court, do they? Well, just as domesticated animals sometimes go wild, living unherded on whatever the desert provides, man may also cease to be herded by man, being ruled instead by the one who is unconfined to place, season, task, or form." His brow wrinkled with increased bewilderment.

"This isn't something to be grasped, Moses. Don't try to fit it into your mind. There is a source of all forms and deeds who cannot be named, shaped, conceived, or conjured like the settled gods of settled peoples. This is the one beyond all counting who crosses all boundaries. Our father Abraham went cimarron from his father's house, heeding this *habiru* guide who shepherds the gazelle, sows the wild acacia, and shapes words from desert stillness. Don't try to fit this into your mind. Instead, plant these words in your heart: *'Arami 'obed 'abi*. The fruit they bear is your patrimony."

In despair, the old man climbed Mount Nebo to die. He wanted to go on living. His entire life had been beginnings, each leading to a new failure, nothing completed. Now, down there below, in the rich lands out beyond the Jordan, the people would surely grow fat and forgetful, turning to gods of their own shaping who could be kept conveniently in a prescribed place. Out there beyond the Jordan, settled, growing fat, surrounded by owner worship, they would need him more than ever.

He tilted his head sideways as though listening, shrugged, then chuckled. Yes, they would take possession and try to forget, but the guide was no smelted chunk of metal to be set aside in some corner—or left behind in the desert. With or without him, they would remember and return.

The seventh day, seven days of the seventh month, each seventh year, and the year following seven times seven years had been hallowed for remembrance and return. Henceforth, these times must be the people's Sinai.

Like the Egyptians, the peoples beyond the Jordan feared the wildlands that threatened their world of fields and settlements. They labored unceasingly to tame and maintain a place to live, and then they worshiped the work of their hands, called the gods of their tamed lands *"baalim"*—owner-masters—and dreamed of the day when their labor would triumph, all wilderness would be destroyed, and the earth would be wholly tamed. Born in the wildlands, the covenant-formed people would cross the Jordan knowing it is, instead, the man-made world that must be brought into wholeness and harmony—into shalom—with the rest of creation. Renewed by the times of sabbath, they would remember.

> Each seventh day, you shall cease to labor. Instead of working, you shall celebrate the goodness of the creation. Unlike the city-dwelling Babylonians who hide indoors and dare do nothing, fearing the seventh day's untamed powers, you shall celebrate. Remember, return, and rejoice.

Seven weeks from the first cutting of standing grain, you shall give the first fruits of your labor. Children, servants, widows, orphans, foreigners—none shall be excluded from this feast of weeks. Whenever offering first fruits, you shall begin by saying, "My father was a cimarron Aramean." Remember, return, and rejoice.

Each seventh month, for seven days, you shall leave your houses, living in brush shelters as you did in the desert. Each day the ingatherings of threshing floor and winepress shall be a feast. Children, servants, widows, orphans, foreigners—none shall be excluded from sharing in the fruits of your labor. Life is a gift, unearned, unowned. Remember, return, and rejoice.

Each seventh year, you shall cease to live by agriculture, craft, or trade, living instead from the gifts of the uncultivated earth. Slaves shall be freed. Debts shall be canceled. Man shall not permanently subjugate the earth or his fellow man. Remember, return, and rejoice.

Each year of jubilee, when seven times seven years have been completed, you shall live supported by the uncultivated earth. Property acquired by one man from another shall revert, for all are sojourners. No man owns the earth. Life is a gift. The Creation is good. Remember, return, and rejoice.

Out there beyond the Jordan, grown fat and forgetful, they would soon change it to make-believe, one more religion, and that would consummate his failure. Still, even with sabbath reduced to make-believe, events might sometimes unsettle the people. The guide is no smelted piece of metal.

He sat at the base of a pinnacle and leaned back against it, watching the sky fade and darken. Stars emerged, and then they, too, began to fade, and even his pain became obscured. He tried to fix them in his mind, clinging to whatever remained of life, even the pain. But it slipped away.

Where it is observed at all, the sabbath is rarely more than a cultic tradition defined by ceremonial busyness, but as a time free from busyness and diversion—as a temporal analogue to untamed spaces—it was initially established to function as wilderness. The sabbath was instituted to make the attentive stillness of Mount Sinai the focal center for a whole people, establishing a communal place for regularly turning toward the prophetic task—a place that could even survive in periods of exile and decadence, amidst civilizations wholly dedicated to conquering, owning, and consuming the Creation.

Talmudic legend has it that, as punishment for murdering his brother, Cain forgot the meaning of sabbath. That makes sense. As the first tiller of the earth and builder of cities, he probably did value his work so highly that he forgot. It makes even more sense to assume that his offering was rejected in the first place because his work to bend nature to his will had already defiled sabbatical times and places.

For millennia Semitic peoples have called wilderness "God's land," distinguishing it from settled areas possessed and remade to fit human plans. "Behold, Allah's creation is very good," the Bedouin proclaims in words that are as biblical as they are koranic. "Surely in this is a sign for all to see." In seeing the great goodness of wildlands, we realize that the man-made world is not-yet-good, that the earth's human dimension is still inharmonious and uncompleted.

In every culture and in all ages, human beings have turned to wilderness when searching for life's fundamental meanings. Taoism, Buddhism, and Vedanta emphasize the importance of wilderness settings for the cultivation of individual insight, but, because the prophetic faith is rooted in a whole people's response to the revelation at Sinai, prophecy is primarily concerned with the community's revealed task rather than the individual's enlightenment. Israel goes out as fugitive slaves and is reborn in the desert as a covenant people. Out of Sinai's stillness the community hears itself called to complete its part of creation, to become a people that hallows the earth.

Sabbatical times weave Sinai stillness into history, as the warp holding time's weft. The sabbath day is a time to quit grabbing at the world, to rest, and to rejoice in the Creation's goodness. During the sabbath year all are to cease making their living agriculturally, supporting themselves instead from the land's spontaneous, uncultivated growth. Debts are to be canceled and slaves are to be freed. Land ownership also reverts on the jubilee year; no one shall permanently subjugate the earth or another person. Sabbatical times are regularly recurring vantage points from which to remember and renew the community's covenant to actualize creation's goodness in human history.

Settled peoples work relentlessly to remake and possess the earth because they can live only in man-made habitats where they are subjugated and used by whoever controls the land. In contrast, nomads take life sabbatically, as a gift from "God's land." Rejecting Cain's way, the prophetic faith recalls its nomadic origins when making its offering of first fruits, beginning with the words, "My father was a cimarron Aramean" (Dt 26:5). From Tibet to Morocco, Kazakhstan to Baja, nomads identify with the cimarron, the domesticated animal that goes feral, the escaped slave who knows how to be at home in God's land. The cimarron's ability to be at home in wildlands distinguishes pastoral nomads from peasants and other settled folk, opening nomadic consciousness to insights unknown to peoples who worship owner-masters because they can live only within the man-made world's make-believe boundaries.

Sabbath is to the prophetic faith what ritual, creed, and hierarchical control are to the priestly faiths. There is, however, another sabbath that is a time of remorseful constriction rather than joyful affirmation, a cessation of self-willed busyness that is the contrary of the prophetic faith's empowering communion. Even in Moses's time, this other sabbath was known among the descendants of Cain who feared and fought the wild powers that threatened and often destroyed their fields. Each seventh day, the city-dwelling Babylonians stayed in their houses, fearing the untamed forces that were abroad, dreaming of a time when all that was wild would finally be tamed or destroyed.

The Christian sabbath has often been closer to the Babylonian than to the Hebraic observance. In seventeenth-century England, for example, the Puritan Parliament passed blue laws prohibiting all recreation on Sundays. Even going for a stroll was forbidden. This contrasts with the talmudic teaching that only activity to refashion and manipulate is prohibited. Exertion that is appreciative, celebrative, or recreational is in no way ruled out. The Talmud emphasizes that "the sabbath was made for man, and not man for the sabbath."

The first Quakers decisively rejected the Puritan sabbath, but their sufferings testify to the importance they placed on regularly gathering to wait in stillness, ceasing as a community to labor mentally or physically to bend the world to their will. Even more than their words, their works testify to the cocreative empowerment they discovered in these meetings for worship. As for their attitude toward holy days, far from abolishing them, they insisted that all times are to be hallowed. Yet, failing to recognize that meeting in stillness is the seed of sabbath, they rarely sought to discover its wider dimensions. They failed to see that all days will become sabbatical only when the community finally succeeds in observing at least one day as sabbath.

The generation that crossed the Jordan had been born and raised in the wilderness, assuring the integrity of the covenant-formed community's new consciousness. Succeeding generations were given the sabbatical *mitzvot* as their way to retain this consciousness and thereby to resist assimilation into societies dedicated to conquering and consuming the Creation. Much the way individual contemplatives center into attentive stillness by means of meditational disciplines that clear away self-willed, goal-directed busyness, communities that covenant to hallow the earth also gather into attentive stillness. Faith and practice, prayer and guidance, worship and insight, study and Torah: for a covenant people, each is linked to the other through sabbatical bonding. Sabbath ties the "religious" to the "ethical" commandments. Sabbath bridges all boundaries that would limit worship-initiated participation to less than the whole of life. In its various forms, sabbatical bonding is the way a congregation, community, or people becomes presence-centered. Lacking all sabbath, a people would also lack a gathering place in time from which to hallow the earth. The socially involved congregation would then have no alternative to goal-determined community organization that is inherently violative rather than hallowing.

Sabbatical communion also opens a way to bridge divisions between peoples and classes and to transcend humankind's alienation from land and livelihood. It opens a way toward the Peaceable Kingdom that is a nonviolent alternative to the apocalyptic hopes of revolutionary Zealots.

Is this extravagant? Exactly. It goes beyond all established bounds. It is a matter of discovery rather than argument, practice rather than proof, that requires a double trust. Our Buddhas explore a path that they say leads the individual to enlightenment; they invite a single trust, that they have truly explored the path. But our Prophets point out a communal way of hallowing that no people has yet completed. The Prophets teach us to do as a community exactly what the Buddhas teach individuals, that we should regularly cease to busy ourselves with efforts to bend the world to our will.

In the desert, individuals sometimes become single-mindedly self-absorbed and then make a religion of self-seeking. Some return as psychotherapeutic gurus who teach ways to develop islands of personal tranquility in the midst of the violence that dominates society. Their prescription for peace and justice is cumulative self-realization because, starting with a separated self, they end with self—and with the delusion that life is in oneself rather than among us. This is not the teaching of the Buddhas, but it is the lesson heard by many of their followers. The Buddhas teach individuals a way that the Prophets teach communities, but individuals learn detachment where communities learn hallowing.

6

The Civil Imperative

> Politics is the art of associating men for the purpose of establishing, cultivating, and conserving social life among them. Whence it is called "symbiotics."
> —Johannes Althusius

> The specific political distinction to which political actions and motives can be reduced is that of friend and enemy.
> —Carl Schmitt

> Both sayings are very true: that man to man is a kind of God; and that man to man is an arrant wolf.[1]
> —Thomas Hobbes

SLAVES, ALIENS, AND CIVIL SOCIETY

SLAVERY HAS BEEN ABOLISHED, but Pharaoh still rules. Going cimarron, sabbatically, is a way to go free from Pharaoh. Having gone free from Pharaoh, a cimarron community must discover how to

---

1. Johannes Althusius, *Politics*, tr. with an introduction by Frederick S. Carney (Boston: Beacon Press, 1964), 12.
Carl Schmitt, *The Concept of the Political* (New Brunswick: Rutgers University Press, 1976), 26.
Thomas Hobbes, *The Citizen: Philosophical Rudiments Concerning Government and Society*, in *Man and Citizen*, edited by Bernard Gert (Garden City, N.Y.: Doubleday, 1971), 89.

participate in civil society without being resubjugated. Civil but unsubjugated, the cimarron community insists on a free society based on equal rights of association and agency. Yet, as a matter of empirical fact about human behavior, civil association disintegrates in the absence of a governmental police force entitled to use violence to subjugate the populace.

All of us sometimes and some of us most times must be coerced into civility. All of us in civil society need police protection from one another. And, for a nation-state to exist at all, governmental organization must maintain the national borders by repelling attackers and excluding unauthorized aliens. How can a cimarron community, which refuses to give fealty to any human ruler as its lord and master, live under a national government? Under a modern nation-state, which demands the fealty and obedience of its subjects as though it were the supreme sovereign, who could be free to be faithful, other than those who make Pharaoh their god?

Anyone who sees the difference between obeying the government and obeying the law can also see how to remain free and faithful in civil society, but the way is hard, disreputable, and dangerous. That's why most citizens take governmental command as their law—and therefore see no way, within civil society, to be either free or faithful. That's also why community covenanting to establish a free society that is based on human rights is easier to understand as a pioneering task on ungoverned frontiers than as a peacemaking task in the borderlands between "the people" and "the aliens."

Bible in hand, Anglo pioneers on the American frontier generally understood their task in terms of the primal covenant at Sinai. They were the Israelites founding a new Jerusalem in the wilderness. But, apart from the Mormons and the Puritans, they had no intention of establishing a theocracy, in imitation of Moses. Few pioneers were lawyers, but from the time of the American Revolution until the early twentieth century, some among the first to form frontier settlements would usually have the foresight to bring along Sir William Blackstone's four-volume *Commentaries on the Laws of England*, to fill the gaps in the Ten Commandments.

For pioneers who lacked most of the machinery of government,

THE CIVIL IMPERATIVE

Blackstone's explanation of the common law, as the unwritten or customary law of the English people, had the special virtue of marginalizing legislation and emphasizing the need to *discover* the law in community traditions and covenants. The common law he described from the inside is an exemplar of the customary law that anthropologists describe from the outside—a consensual community practice rather than a written code.

To understand how community-grown law can establish civility beyond and between governments, we'll do better to consult Blackstone than the Bible. Then, when we consider the prophetic task of establishing civility in spite of the nation-state (for which the Bible *is* particularly instructive), the auxiliary role of community-grown law should be clear. The relation between the conservative civil task and the creative prophetic task can be tentatively preconceived as follows: Civility is only one side of a human social order. *Religio* is the other. Both sides of a social order are concerned with the law—and therefore with associated questions of legitimacy. In most societies, religion legitimates the existing order, but the prophetic faith also delegitimates a society, whenever the society's ways break *religio*'s covenanted bonds.

POLICE POWERS AND THE STATE OF (HUMAN) NATURE

In the fifties, I was tending cattle on the Flying H, my family's ranch in the Huachucas, when a prospector who lived on U.S. Forest Service land at the base of Hunter Canyon, Max Baumkirchner, began sabotaging the cattle-watering facilities at Lowry Spring. Three decades before, when the Boquillas cattle company had the ranch, he'd been chased off the spring by one of the New Mexican gunmen they'd brought to Arizona after the Lincoln County War. He then dug a water tunnel below the spring to supply his home.

Baumkirchner had also tried to fence and hold all of Hunter Canyon, but the Forest Service made him give up everything other than the area below the spring where he'd built his house. When

89

he'd come from Bavaria to Cochise County about forty years before, claiming and holding mining prospects, grazing, and waters on unpatented land had more to do with one's territorial drive than with governmental entitlements, and he still had plenty of drive.

Our first problem with him was that he dynamited and burned the ranch's spring house at Lowry Spring. The deputy sheriff who investigated found him ripping out the pipeline to the water trough. But Baumkirchner's sons, who ran a bar and trucking company thirteen miles away in Sierra Vista, had political pull in Cochise County, particularly with the sheriff, so nothing was done about it. The deputy was reprimanded for reporting that Baumkirchner admitted dynamiting and burning the spring house, and his report was never filed.

The Cochise County Sheriff's Office has always been the most powerful political position in the county. In the fifties, the sheriff controlled payoffs and considerable patronage, linking business, criminal, and governmental activities into a single interest backed by armed force—a link that had been forged several decades before after the Bisbee Deportation, when everyone in the Bisbee area who opposed or was suspected of opposing the hegemony of the Phelps Dodge Mining Company had been clubbed by deputies and goons, loaded in box cars, and then dumped in the New Mexican desert.

An official we consulted in the State Land Department's Surface Water Division recommended that we rely on shotguns; there would be no law enforcement concerning the destruction of our watering facilities at Lowry Spring because the Cochise County sheriff backed Baumkirchner. The official was clearly frustrated and disgusted with the Arizona Land Department's good-old-boy way of doing business, but his suggestion that we use shotguns rather than the law shocked my father much more than the favoritism that permeated Cochise County politics. Weeding out corruption and exposing injustice is a perennial task in any social order, but our water rights at Lowry Spring would cease to be rights outside the rule of law. Outside the law, there can be neither justice nor rights.

The law was my father's religion. In his early twenties, he took

THE CIVIL IMPERATIVE

a mail-order course in law, was accepted into the Missouri Bar, and (as his first practice) was elected prosecuting attorney for Texas County, Missouri. (In the Ozarks during Prohibition, no career-minded politician wanted the job.) When his term ended, my parents left for Wyoming, where a decade later he became chairman of the Judiciary Committee of the Wyoming House of Representatives.

My religious instruction when I was a small child came primarily from my father's dinnertime explanations of the law, as it touched our lives. He might explain, for example, why he had to defend the right of Jehovah's Witnesses to refuse to salute the flag, although in 1941 it would probably cost him a career in Wyoming politics and cause me and my sister to be insulted by other children. As the foundation for justice and basic rights, the law is an eminently practicable, persuasive, and durable religion for a child—one that my subsequent insights and turn-arounds have strengthened rather than nullified. I later found it to be inadequate, as a religion, but also doubt that I could have become Quaker if I hadn't first been taught the law as my family's religion.

But the law as my family understood it ceased to be a constraint when one of Baumkirchner's sons threatened to shoot any of us they ran into in Hunter Canyon. We were far from being in an ungoverned state of nature; nonetheless, with the sheriff backing the Baumkirchners, we were on our own. We pulled the magazine plugs on our shotguns and loaded with buckshot, put 30-06 rifles and extra ammunition in the kitchen and living room, and I began wearing a pistol when I rode.

Of the nine people then living on mining claims within the Flying H grazing allotment, only one recently arrived couple had never been involved in gunplay of some kind. The most recent killing had been early in the previous decade, when Bill King shot Jim Kelly in Ash Canyon. Kelly himself had shot and killed at least two people, his moonshining partner at their still in the Huachucas and a Mexican in Tombstone.

King and Kelly had been working Kelly's claim, had an argument, and Kelly threatened to kill King. Soon afterward, King shot

Kelly off his burro as Kelly was riding in the canyon. The bullet entered from the side, but everyone who knew Kelly agreed that, if King *had* taken some initiative, it was just a prudent way to defend himself. After King was acquitted, the sheriff, whom Kelly had once humiliated, pinned a badge on King and made him a life-long honorary deputy sheriff of Cochise County. When King then acquired Kelly's Ash Canyon claims and moved into Kelly's cabin, it was considered bad form, but as Charlie Morgan (King's neighbor in the other fork of Ash Canyon) put it, "If he hadn't killed Jim Kelly, everyone knew Kelly would've soon killed him."

Charlie occasionally told of the time he waited in the brush to kill King for mistreating Maggie, his burro. He had King in his sights, but didn't pull the trigger. "I've lived in the Huachucas all my life," he'd brag, "but I haven't killed a man yet." When I took him to town for an X-ray after he'd been injured in a brawl, I learned that he had, nonetheless, been shot. He still had two shotgun pellets in his back, from an incident when he'd been caught rustling cattle. If Charlie Morgan had ambushed Bill King, it would, of course, have been declared self-defense, since King was armed.

For a month or two after I decided to start wearing a pistol, I rode Hunter Canyon three or four times each week without incident. Then, one morning as I approached Lowry Spring, I heard a pickup coming from the Baumkirchner house. I stepped off the mare I was riding and left her in a patch of brush. Before I found a good vantage point, the truck came into sight and stopped about 150 feet away. I crouched only half-hidden behind a little manzanita. It was Baumkirchner and his two sons. One of the sons had a rifle.

Max Baumkirchner was arguing. As he protested, his sons unloaded a galvanized water trough that had our Flying H painted on it. We'd been syphoning water into it from the dynamited water box, but it had been stolen. Baumkirchner was angry with his sons for returning it.

And I was angry with myself for getting into such a fix. The mare might nicker, start cropping the brush, or even wander out to graze. Or one of the Baumkirchners might see me half-hidden behind the manzanita. Then we'd be in for it. The one with the rifle was glancing around. If he saw me, he'd instinctively raise his rifle. Should I then assume his reaction was just defensive? Seeing me crouching there, he'd be more likely to shoot.

The mare did move a little, but Baumkirchner's protestations covered the noise. Having returned our stock tank, they got in their truck and drove away. I rode home and put away my pistol.

A few weeks later, Baumkirchner used an automobile jack to break the concrete water trough at Lowry Spring. My mother called the Sheriff's Office in Bisbee to ask that someone come out to investigate and make a report. She said that I'd wait at the spring to show what had happened.

'Bud' Moson, the deputy from Sierra Vista, came in response to the call, along with two men I didn't know who were armed but wore no badges. Bud spent much of his time in the Baumkirchner bar; his nickname reputedly came from his taste for Budweiser beer.

He had no interest in the damaged trough or in taking any notes. He just wanted to know where my gun was. After I told him repeatedly that I had no gun, he searched my truck and looked around for one. Then they left. There would be no report on the destroyed trough.

I learned later that just before arriving at Lowry Spring, Bud had radioed that I was trying to kill Max Baumkirchner and he'd take care of it, assisted by the bouncer from the bar and Baumkirchner's son-in-law. I was glad I'd quit wearing a gun.

A workable political philosophy must start with human nature, as expressed in the interactions of all kinds and cultures of human beings. This is unfashionable; social activists like to think civil society and human behavior are infinitely malleable. They dream up the kind of society they want and then try to remake humanity to fit. Among peace activists, Thomas Hobbes's understanding of human nature is particularly unpopular, "that during the time men live without a common Power to keep them all in awe, they are in that condition which is called Warre." I know myself well enough to see that Hobbes is right in my case and in the case of others like me. (I wouldn't have given Baumkirchner's son the first shot, on the chance that he wouldn't shoot.) In all cultures and classes and throughout human history, there also seem to have been many others like me. It just takes a few of us to make adjudication and police enforcement necessary, in order to prevent civil society from dissolving into a self-defense, contract-enforcement, and entitlement free-for-all.

MASTERLESS CONSOCIATIONS

I'm an unlikely Quaker. I learned to shoot rabbits when I was five, had my own shotgun at nine, and joined the National Rifle Association, had my own 30–06, and began hunting deer and antelope at thirteen. For my eighteenth birthday, my parents sent me a pistol, unaware that in New York State where I was going to school the police and university authorities would disapprove. I've quit using guns, except for humane slaughter, but I still dislike gun-control legislation. I don't think governmental coercion should be used to force others to take the Quaker way when police protection is unavailable or law enforcement turns to murder.

When I was growing up in Wyoming, people still chose sides about the Johnson County War. In 1892, the Wyoming Cattlemen's Association hired several dozen professional gunmen from throughout the West to form a paramilitary unit under the command of Major Frank Wolcott, to kill Sheriff "Red" Angus, his deputies, and about fifty blacklisted homesteaders in Johnson County. Taking too long to kill Nate Champion at his cabin on the Powder River, they were surprised by a four-hundred-man posse, were chased to a stockaded ranch headquarters, and then were besieged until the U.S. Cavalry arrived just in time to save them. They were then held and feted in Cheyenne at Johnson County's expense until the county went broke. A decade later, with the hanging of Tom Horn, the cattlemen's association finally had to cede responsibility for all executions to the state.

The invasion had been planned in Cheyenne with the governor's collusion, and when the plan failed he telegraphed Wyoming's two senators to arrange for President Harrison to call out the cavalry, but the Johnson County War was really between two pre-governmental protective associations, before state government became fully functional. Many Wyoming officials considered lynching a regrettable necessity because at the time there was no other effective way to protect property on the hoof and to enforce the claim of the cattlemen's association through its registration of brands, to exclusive grazing rights on public lands—a defense that was later immortalized in Owen Wister's *The Virginian*, in which "Judge Henry" is actually Frank Wolcott, Wister's host and close friend.

Accounts of the invasion focus on Nate Champion, who single-handedly held off the "invaders" while word reached Buffalo. The myths of the American West usually focus on individual gunslingers and delete positive notice of mutual-aid associations, which always formed as the need arose, much the way neighborhood councils apparently spring up, unplanned, whenever a government collapses. (The myth would have the homesteaders scattering and hiding while Champion manages on his own—or maybe with the town drunk—to kill the association's gunmen.) Posses and other protective *consociations*—voluntary, self-governing associations of unsubordinated partners—often turned to vigilantism, extortion, and massacre. Yet they, rather than quick-draw gunmen, were the peacemakers in the West.

Elsewhere, the early evolution of protective associations among human beings has usually been a mixed tale of family expansion and conquest; the "rules" of association have been tribal traditions and the enslavement of conquered neighbors. But in the settlement of Anglo America, society-forming understandings were often explicit compacts. In the West, individuals who met as neighbors often came from extremely diverse backgrounds. Many were also highly resistant to hierarchical social organization. This meant that to function as social animals—to have a round-up, build a school-house or bridge, or form a posse—they constantly had to make and keep promises that bonded them into a society as partners.

Few peoples are as individualistic in their settlement patterns as the hill-country Anglos of the American West. Prospectors, cowboys, and sheepherders may also be self-selected extremes. Yet, "individualism" is a one-sided description of this independence. Hill-country Anglos often function as social animals by means of agreements, where others might rely on status, command, and hierarchy, but they are as actively social in seeking a workable consensus as are other people who know their place in society in terms of a chain of command or inherited roles. In the sixteenth and seventeenth centuries, as feudalism waned, "masterless men" who had no fealty to any human lord became numerous throughout northern Europe and constituted the bulk of the migrants to North America. Until the twentieth century, the frontier was their natural habitat. Consensual association was the only way settlers could live as social beings and still remain masterless, under a system of equal rights for all.

In the early nineteenth century, Alexis de Tocqueville's *Democracy in America* reported that "In no country in the world has the principle of association been more successfully used or applied to a greater multitude of objects."[2] Tocqueville was born into an aristocratic family shortly after the French Revolution. He saw American democracy in relation to the French Revolution's disintegration into tyranny, and he hoped to discover a way that European liberty might grow out of the leveling of lord and liegeman. Living under lordly patronage during the English Revolution, Hobbes had fashioned a replacement for the broken feudal bond of protection and obedience, but Tocqueville searched for a way the civil condition could thrive in spite of masterless equality. He found it in the thriving consociations of the American frontier.

> Governments . . . should not be the only active power; associations ought, in democratic nations, to stand in lieu of those powerful private individuals whom the equality of conditions has swept away.
>
> . . . In democratic countries the science of association is the mother of science; the progress of all the rest depends upon the progress it has made.

---

2. Alexis de Tocqueville, *Democracy in America* (New York: Random House, 1981), 101.

Among the laws that rule human societies there is one which seems to be more precise and clear than all the others. If men are to remain civilized or to become so, the art of associating together must grow and improve in the same ratio in which the equality of conditions is increased.[3]

Quakers, too, were predominantly masterless men and women. Refusing to remove their hats in obeisance to anyone but God, to use the formal "you" of subordination, to exclude anyone from ministry, to give any oath of fealty, to submit to coercive command or to use armed force, or to permit majorities to dominate minorities in decision-making, the first Quakers systematically broke the hierarchical social bond of protection and obedience. As feudalism waned and increasing numbers of masterless individuals discovered social space outside the lord–liegeman relationship, Quakers and other communitarian dissenters sought a radical reformation of society that was based on consociation rather than subordination.

Whether nonviolence can completely replace obedience in maintaining human society depends on whether human consociations can live unprotected by government. If they can't, the next question is whether obedience is sufficient for maintaining and extending the civil bond. If not, then unsubjugated nonviolent communities of some kind are likely to prove essential for us to become a society that excludes no human beings as aliens, even if these nonviolent communities remain quixotically inadequate for the preservation of the civil condition among those of us who are usually competitive and often (quite humanly) covetous, bellicose, and domineering.

The cimarron community that tries to practice civility as nonviolence must concede that we are all participants in civil society and therefore the beneficiaries of the armed force that must be used to preserve it. If we are a peaceful people that refuses to take up arms to protect ourselves, someone else will do it for us.

This is painful. This is where saints steeled for crucifixion flinch, shut their eyes, and flee to make-believe. And it's where civil

---

3. Tocqueville, *Democracy in America*, 407–408.

initiative must make its case that obedience to governmental masters is incapable of substituting for nonviolence in maintaining and extending the civil bond.

UNCIVIL OBEDIENCE, DISOBEDIENCE, AND CIVIL INITIATIVE

Hobbes insists that everyone who is protected by government has, in accepting its protection, promised to do virtually anything it commands:

> . . . He that upon promise of Obedience hath his Life and Liberty allowed him is then Conquered and a Subject; and not before. . . . If he live under their Protection openly, hee is understood to submit himselfe to the Government . . .[4]

This analysis is the cornerstone of Carl Schmitt's case against peaceful peoples:

> A people which exists in the political sphere cannot, despite entreating declarations to the contrary, escape from making this fateful [friend-enemy] distinction. . . . A private person has no political enemies. . . . If a people is afraid of the trials and risks implied by existing in the sphere of politics, then another people will appear which will assume these trials by protecting it against foreign enemies and thereby taking over political rule. The protector then decides who the enemy is by virtue of the eternal relation of protection and obedience.[5]

---

4. Thomas Hobbes, *Leviathan* [1651], 391.
5. Carl Schmitt, *The Concept of the Political* (New Brunswick: Rutgers University Press, 1976), 51–52. Schmitt's note to this passage: ". . . No form of order, no reasonable legitimacy or legality can exist without protection and obedience. The *protego ergo obligo* is the *cogito ergo sum* of the state. A political theory which does not systematically become aware of this sentence remains an inadequate fragment. Hobbes designated this as the true purpose of his *Leviathan*, to instill in man once again 'the mutual relation between Protection and Obedience. . . .'"

THE CIVIL IMPERATIVE

In May 1933, Schmitt followed his understanding of protection and obedience to its logical terminus, becoming (at Martin Heidegger's urging) the Nazis' preeminent academic ideologue. (At the time, no other German equaled his international influence as a twentieth-century political philosopher. Maybe none does now, although giving him credit is considered bad form.) The truth in his explanation of the protection-obedience relationship is embittered by our knowing where it led him and the German people. Nonetheless, it is a rigorously realistic understanding of the political situation in which we all find ourselves, a situation that cannot be wished away. It is the theoretical basis for the national security state. It is the ground for the disciplined solidarity of revolutionary struggle. Every form of antiindividualist collectivism carries it to a totalitarian extreme.

Conceding to the state the power to mold the social order by making the law, Henry Thoreau insisted that the conscientious individual should resist unjust statutes. Thoreau's civil disobedience directly contradicts Schmitt's protection-obedience relationship, pitting individual conscience or a purported higher law against human law. It recognizes no obligation to justify disobedience within the established governmental process. As a result, civil disobedience is often indistinguishable from revolutionary disobedience to dissolve the legal order and replace the government. "This is, in fact, the definition of a peaceable revolution," Thoreau explains, "if any such be possible. . . . When the subject has refused allegiance, and the officer has resigned his office, then the revolution is accomplished."[6] He observes that legislation usually deals with questions of expediency resolved according to the will of the majority (or whatever grouping happens to be most powerful). To submit judgments about what is right to statute-makers who are guided by majority rule turns the social order into a coalitional free-for-all of partisan interests. But he then consigns questions of principle and conscience to private practice, aban-

---

6. Henry Thoreau, "Civil Disobedience" in *The Portable Thoreau*, ed. Carl Bode (New York: Viking, 1964), 123.

doning the public realm to the pursuit of partisan (including private) interests.

> Must the citizen ever for a moment, or in the least degree, resign his conscience to the legislature? . . . It is not desirable to cultivate a respect for the law, so much as for the right. The only obligation which I have a right to assume is to do at any time what I think right.[7]

Thoreau's contrast of respect for the law and respect for the right actually distinguishes between two meanings of the word "law," society-forming right and government-made statutes. For the most part, the two basic meanings of "law" reflect the practical difference between a society's constituting principles and a government organization's policies, but they are most readily distinguished by the fact that the one usage, as in "the common law," has no plural. "The law" as right is a single, intra-active, evolving order. 'Laws' or statutes are chronically in need of interpretation, testing, and adjudication to determine how and whether they fit into the law; *a* law is not *the* law, nor is it necessarily a part of the law. Converting this difference into a radical opposition between *public* policies and *private* principles leads to the ideal of conscientious disengagement—of the few who "live aloof from [the state], not meddling with it, nor embraced by it, who [fulfill] all the duties of neighbors and fellow men."[8]

Thoreau seems uncertain about whether his civil disobedience leads to conscientious withdrawal or a peaceable revolution, but his successors have developed it as a tactic for changing society. Conscientious objection disengages; civil disobedience actively resists. As a tactic for social change, civil disobedience may disrupt the established social order to force government to mend its ways. Or it may, if too weak to be a real threat, still serve as ritual disorder that adds emphasis to dissent. Or it may be an auxiliary to revo-

---

7. Thoreau, "Civil Disobedience," 111.
8. Thoreau, "Civil Disobedience," 136–137.

THE CIVIL IMPERATIVE

lutionary warfare. In each case it is conceived as resistance that in one way or another disorders the established system.

Statesmen and legislators "speak of moving society, but have no resting place without it. . . . They are wont to forget that the world is not governed by policy and expediency."[9] The Archimedean fulcrum outside the established order from which Thoreau would move society is individual conscience. For others, it is contracivil revolutionary organization. In either case, the key assumption is that the law is an obstacle to the formation of a just social order, that the law must be destroyed or disrupted to clear the way for beneficial change. Civil disobedience of this kind is unarmed civil war. Symbolically or actually, it fractures the civil condition by stepping outside the legal order's procedural framework.

"Government is an expedient by which men would fain succeed in leaving one another alone." For example, it is expedient to drive on either the left or the right side of the road and to enforce the decision. We can then avoid getting in each other's way, but there is nothing better, in principle, about driving on the left or the right. Yet, this utility reaches farther than Thoreau indicates. Government is an expedient by means of which we come to count on one another. Thoreau is as desirous of being a good neighbor as he is of being a bad subject, but because government is an expedient that allows us to count on one another, bad subjects are also bad neighbors—unless they disobey the government from within the enforced social order in a way that supports the rule of law.

Sometimes one must choose between obeying the law and obeying the government, as in the case of the human rights violations that were duly enacted and commanded by the German government under the Nazis. Sometimes our neighbors count on us to obey the law rather than the government, as in the case of the efforts by the community of Le Chambon to save Jews from Vichy officials and the Nazis.

Often, though, disobeying the government is like failing to keep a promise. We do count on one another not to keep promises under some circumstances—for example, if unforeseen compli-

---

9. Thoreau, "Civil Disobedience," 133.

cations mean that complying would kill someone. But when I fail to keep a promise I owe an explanation. I am not to be the sole or final judge determining whether I am justified by the injury I think has been avoided. The legal issue in such cases is usually conceived as "necessity," which refers to moral rather than physical "compulsion." Every legal system has a place for lawful noncompliance under exceptional circumstances.

Under a Third Reich, civil initiative would necessarily retreat to churches or other communities where some residue of the rule of law remains. One wouldn't notify the Nazis of efforts to protect Jews, but one would go to cocommunicants, friends, and neighbors to form consociations to protect them. Far from being dependent upon constitutional government, civil initiative is most clearly practicable and necessary on friend-enemy frontiers, wherever the rule of law is lacking or destroyed, or when governments collapse. When governmental powers are used to destroy the rule of law, civil obedience and civil disobedience both fail to institute, maintain, or extend civil association under the rule of law. Nonviolent civil initiative by covenant communities is then *the* way human beings preserve and develop societies based on consent, in which the rule of law, as distinguished from the rule of commanders, is necessarily grounded.

Civil disobedience opens no way to obey the law rather than the government when one's government violates basic human rights. Civil disobedience has no conception of the public conscience as a community practice of the law—a community practice that is capable of acting within the legal system while remaining unsubordinated to the state. As a moral agent, I am, as Thoreau insists, obligated "to do at any time what I think is right." As moral agents, covenant communities are also obligated to do what they think is right. Politico-military organization is incapable of assuming moral agency for individuals and communities; moral agency can't be delegated. But as members of civil society, we are also accountable to the established governmental process for any failure to keep agreements or to obey the government.

Relinquishing the claim to judge and impose coercive enforcement is the linchpin of civil association. Judges are agents of

THE CIVIL IMPERATIVE

politico-military power; they are as devoid of moral authority as jailers and hangmen. Jurisprudence must therefore separate law from morality whenever looking at the law in terms of judicial practice rather than community practice. With regard to criminal law, judges' moral agency must even be specifically restricted; under the rule of law, judges must not outreach valid statutes to enforce moral judgments. Many puzzlements about jurisprudence sort themselves out if one keeps in mind this distinction between the limited, highly specialized court practice of the law and a community's practice of the law. As the enforced social order, the law is understood, cultivated, and practiced primarily by communities rather than judges and lawyers.

In his forties at the time of the Second World War, my father tried to enlist in the army, but he was rejected because he was blind in one eye. Foreseeing the legal issues that would come up in connection with Nazi atrocities, he particularly wanted to serve in Europe with the allied military government. When the war crimes tribunal at Nuremberg was convened, its proceedings were therefore the main topic of our dinnertime conversations.

He could see the political point of killing Nazi leaders, as ritual retribution to channel and defuse passions for vengeance, but ritual vengeance wasn't the law as he knew it. Prior statutes that have jurisdiction over a defendant must define crimes and prescribe punishments. If not, criminal sanctions become a kind of state vigilantism. When used as the basis for criminal sanctions, unwritten or customary law readily becomes Owen Wister's justification for lynching rustlers. The executions of Nazi war criminals were state lynchings.

But the Nuremberg tribunal's rulings *were* declared and therefore explicitly recognized by the United States government and the other allies to be the law, henceforth. At the heart of the rulings was the insistence that individuals—not just states—are obligated to obey international law, regardless of their government's orders, statutes, or rulings to the contrary. Particularly in the case of governmental violations of basic human rights, everyone must obey the law rather than the government. "This principle of personal liability is a necessary as well as logical one," Justice Robert H. Jackson argued in the prosecution's opening statement at Nuremberg, "if International Law is to render real help to the maintenance of peace. An International Law which operates only on states can be enforced only by war because the most practicable way of coercing a state is warfare."

The sentences of the allies' war crimes tribunals were shams—vengeance masquerading as justice; but the Nuremberg rulings raised the first supports for a new tier of law above the national level, to overarch city, county, state, and federal legal systems. My father knew that federal courts would quickly nullify the rulings, as soon as vengeance had been taken on the prisoners of war whom the victors selected for trial; no citizen of the United States would be allowed by a federal court to hold the United States government accountable for its violations of human rights in its conduct of foreign affairs. In such cases, the courts routinely rule out the rule of law.

If international law is to govern persons when it is violated by their government, it must take root at the local level in community practice and grow in the absence of an enforcing police power. It must be rooted in unsubjugated civility—nonviolence rather than obedience. The institution of basic rights for all humanity now depends on the growth of a truly common law that bridges national borders.

Civil initiative maintains and extends the rule of law—unlike civil disobedience, which breaks it, and civil obedience, which lets the government break it. The heart of a societal order guided by the rule of law is the principle that the nonviolent protection of basic rights is never illegal. These basic rights and their matching obligations constitute standards of just conduct that government counter-enforcement is unable to nullify, short of destroying the societal order itself. While openly submitting to the trials and penalties imposed by government, the free community refuses to be coerced into collaborating with violations of the law (that is, of right). Rather, it exercises its rights and protects the violated. This is how liberty grows and free societies form.

THE CIVIL IMPERATIVE

The body of right evolves in much the same way as a body of science, except that the law is concerned with an order based on consent and obligation rather than physical necessity and prediction. Communities and individuals who insist on doing what they believe is right are essential to the life and evolution of law, just as researchers who refuse to falsify their data to fit established theories are essential to the life and evolution of science. The law would freeze and atrophy if intimidation and blind obedience replaced its active consensual core.

The quest for truth (as science) and for right (as law) is the quest for communion (as religion). Science, law, and *religio* each seeks reconciliation, integration, and coherence rather than the denial or elimination of the Creation's unbounded variety and unending change. Each is concerned in its own way with discovering what Mohandas Gandhi called "Truth," to which any genuinely nonviolent way of life is dedicated.

When I seek truth, right, or communion rather than victory, my adversary is precisely the teacher I need. For Gandhian nonviolence—*satyagraha*—my own position's greatest truth-deficiency must be corrected with the truth to be found in my adversary's position. As I correct my position's deficiencies, it becomes more coherent and more nearly complete, requiring a new response from its adversaries, which in turn may yield further gleanings for still another position. Inquiry into the natural order already takes this method for granted; scientific verification is actually a rigorous attempt to refute, case by case (cumulatively but never conclusively). For community-grown law, the discovery of societal right takes essentially the same form as the scientific community's discovery of the natural order's truths—that is, the adjudication of conflicts is integrated case by case, in the course of time, into a community's discernment of a coherent body of norms.

CIVIL INITIATIVE AND POLITICAL JUJITSU

Gandhi's *satyagraha* is a form of what I will be calling *"religio,"* a "rebinding" into an open society that is a communion. *Religio* is much more social and civil than politics—or, to be precise, politico-military organization is just the shadow of the distinctively human form of sociality and civility, communion.

Gandhi comes close to formulating civil initiative rather than civil disobedience, but he misses at the crucial point, by seeking punishment for having protected human rights "in violation" of the law. By asking to be punished for violating the law, he is forfeiting recognition that basic human rights *are* the law.

With this proviso that Gandhi was wrong in pleading guilty to violating the law, Gandhian civil disobedience could serve as a procedural guide for civil initiative: Civil initiative must be societal rather than organizational, nonviolent rather than injurious, truthful rather than deceitful, catholic rather than sectarian, dialogical rather than dogmatic, substantive rather than symbolic, volunteer-based rather than professionalized, and based on community powers rather than government powers. Each of these characteristics of *satyagraha* contrasts with the way civil disobedience is usually done these days, as "mass political jujitsu," a tactic for community organizing developed by Saul Alinsky. As a widely known practice, direct action that involves a community's open insubordination to government will now take the form of Alinsky's political jujitsu rather than Gandhi's *satyagraha,* because virtually all professional organizers and other social activists now consider it *the* form of community direct action—that is, a community's direct action will take the form of political jujitsu *unless* the community has thought through and agreed beforehand on an alternative such as *satyagraha* or civil initiative. Contrasting *satyagraha* with Alinsky's political jujitsu is the clearest way to identify the pivotal choices that decide whether direct action is civil initiative.

Where Gandhi rejects management by objective, Alinsky and his followers insist on it. "Every organization known to man, from government down, has had only one reason for being—that is, organization for power in order to put into practice or promote its common purpose."[10] "The man of action views the issue of means and ends in pragmatic and strategic terms. . . . He asks of ends only whether they are achievable and worth the cost; of means, only whether they will work."[11]

The paradigm for management by objective is military mobilization, a human order dedicated to achieving a common cause that overrides normative constraints. Alinsky's political jujitsu therefore requires a radical friend-enemy polarization. "Before men can act, an issue must be polarized. Men will act when they are convinced that their cause is 100 percent on the side of the angels and that the opposition are 100 percent on the side of the devil. . . . There can be no action until issues are polarized to this degree."[12] Alinsky summarizes these procedures in his Rule Thirteen: "Pick the target, freeze it, personalize it, and polarize it."[13] He admits that this kind of polarization falsifies human relations but insists that it is necessary to generate the resentment needed to motivate active hostility. The "first step in community organization is community disorganization. . . . The organizer dedicated to changing the life of a particular community must first rub raw the resentments of the people of the community; fan the latent hostilities of many of the people to the point of overt expression."[14]

For political jujitsu, civil disobedience is used for its effect, regardless of its direct relevance to the protection of basic rights that the government is violating. For example, civil disobedience

---

10. Saul Alinsky, *Rules for Radicals* (New York: Vintage Books, 1972), 52.

11. Alinsky, *Rules for Radicals*, 24. The contrast with Gandhi is stark: "When there is no desire for fruit, there is no temptation for untruth or *himsa*. Take an instance of untruth or violence, and it will be found that at its back is the desire to attain the cherished end." (Cited in Joan V. Bondurant, *Conquest of Violence* (Berkeley: University of California Press, 1965), 116; from Mohandas Karamchand Gandhi, *The Gospel of Selfless Action: The Gita According to Gandhi,* translated from Gujarati and edited by Mahadev Dasai (Ahmedabad: Navajivan, 1946), 129.

12. Alinsky, *Rules for Radicals*, 78.
13. Alinsky, *Rules for Radicals*, 130.
14. Alinsky, *Rules for Radicals*, 116.

might be used to block a freeway, which would violate local statutes, in order to protest a federal policy that violates human rights. In contrast, civil initiative to preserve and extend the rule of law must necessarily reject this vigilante kind of civil disobedience that uses the violation of legitimate governmental activities in order to coerce the government into changing its illegitimate ways. For civil initiative, all basic rights are matched by governmental obligations that must be assumed by the individual or basic community if, *but only if,* these rights are violated by government officials. The community that practices civil initiative disobeys the government only when there is no other practicable way to obey the law. Because the citizens of a society under the rule of law can choose to obey the law rather than the government, the consent of the governed is a real rather than fictitious foundation for governmental legitimacy.

For those who seek politico-military power, Alinsky opens a way. For those who seek communion, Gandhi opens a way. The choice between the two is radical: between friend-enemy politics and covenant-formed religion; between conquest and communion. There's no way to choose both. The history of the prophetic faith reveals a great deal about this choice between "being faithful" and "being effective"—and about the perennial pursuit of coercive power in the name of communion.

THE CIVIL BOND, SLAVE MORALITY, AND UNSUBJUGATED NOBILITY

The frontier problem in the West was the institution of civil society among diverse individuals and groups. The frontier problem now, worldwide, is the institution of an international society based on human rights. In the borderlands between nations, classes, races, religions, and ideologies where "the people" meets enemies and aliens, the need now is for nonviolent protective associations that covenant to exclude no one from the basic rights that constitute the substance of civil society.

Social contract philosophers such as Hobbes and Locke use the

THE CIVIL IMPERATIVE

idea of the society-forming covenant retrospectively, as a mythological explanation of the civil condition's origins. The covenant community uses it prospectively, as a way to overcome friend-enemy divisions. Covenanting across the divisions that separate "the people" from "the aliens" is the way to establish universal human rights, which national governments will then, eventually, have to recognize.

Covenanting to treat no one as an alien institutes basic rights under the rule of law, establishing rights through community cohesion that displaces governmental coercion. This kind of nonviolence—civil initiative—supports established government by strengthening and extending civil association, even as it refuses to comply with government efforts to exclude some human beings from the basic rights that are essential to civil association. Granting that man to man is a wolf, particularly when he forms a state, civil initiative refuses to leave the formation, maintenance, and extension of civil society to the state. It actively extends the social order's civility to enemies and other aliens—as basic rights that the community covenants to protect, nonviolently, from government officials.

Civil society emerges and evolves from humanity as it is, and most human beings adhere to a slave morality that precludes participation in a covenant community. Only those who go free can form a consociation that is capable of practicing civil initiative to preserve and extend basic rights.

For the subjugated—those compelled to civility by their fear of punishment—"obeying the law" is synonymous with obeying the government's orders. For the vast majority who can be governed by fear, obedience rather than nonviolence is the key requirement for civil association; their nonviolence is derivative rather than generative. In a conflict between the rule of law and government commands (that is, if those who obey the law are punished by the government), the vast majority in most societies will obey the government rather than the law. At humanity's current stage of cultural evolution, this is the way it must be; civil association would dissolve

109

if very many human beings ceased to be subjugated. For each person who would risk execution to save Jews from a Nazi government, many would kill, rape, and pillage.

But for a few people much of the time and for all people sometimes, pride and even love are stronger than fear. Although unsubjugated human beings may turn to crime, some are actively civil. As nobility, unsubjugated pride may even be required to sow civility where violence prevails. "That which gives to human actions the relish of justice is a certain Nobleness or Gallantness of courage (rarely found), by which a man scorns to be beholden for the contentment of life to fraud or breach of promise. This justice of Manners is that which is meant, where justice is called a virtue."[15] But "this is a generosity too rarely to be found to be presumed, especially in pursuers of wealth, command, and sensual pleasure; which are the greatest part of Mankind."[16]

Although the human animal is its own kind's most fearful predator, it is a species whose members must live in society. Granting that civil security and harmony among human beings must evolve out of Leviathan, the covenant community seeks Leviathan's further evolution rather than its extinction; covenanting seeks the evolution of the rule of law out of subjugation to commanders. Politically, covenanting is concerned with hallowing pride, as the nobility of those who refuse to be subjugated but for whom justice is a virtue.

But why not see what love rather than pride can do?

As a *political* virtue, love fails because saints who can love everyone they meet are too late-blooming, rare, and scattered to form an established consociation. Saintliness is far rarer than the "nobility of courage" for which justice is a virtue. Nobility just requires that consociates do justice to those they hate and disdain,

---

15. Thomas Hobbes, *Leviathan* (1651), 74.
16. *Ibid.*, 70. For the key explication of the place Hobbes assigns to the moralization of pride as an auxiliary support for civil association, see Michael Oakeshott, "The Moral Life in the Writings of Thomas Hobbes" in *Rationalism in Politics* (New York: Basic Books, 1962), 288–294; and also in Michael Oakeshott, *Hobbes on Civil Association* (Oxford: Basil Blackford, 1975), 119–125.

not that they love them. Love also fails because it must know the other. Nobility does justice, unknown, to others it may never meet. And love inevitably fails to establish the civil condition among humankind because it overshoots the mark; to seek everyone's good the way a mother seeks the good of her child leads to breakdown rather than civility. Nobility simply upholds fairness: equal basic rights for everyone. Pride resembles and may excel love in courage, particularly when one must risk life, liberty, and the well-being of loved ones to protect the basic rights of strangers. It sometimes approximates love in magnanimity.

Nobility's role in extending civility and governing government is an application of the Quixote principle: To open the way, a cultural breakthrough need not involve masses of people but must be done decisively by someone. Prior to the Third Sally, Quixote did, in fact, advocate this kind of solution to the political problems of his day, that the knights-errant be assembled from their wanderings, to form a consociation for confronting Christendom's threats—from which the priest and the barber concluded he was still mad. Could errantry, as an established institution within civil society, now bring Leviathan to maturity, to promote peace rather than war among the earth's peoples?

Errantry was much more common in Quixote's Christendom than the priest and barber thought. They just failed to recognize the form it was taking: following Jesus of Nazareth according to the Franciscan Rule. Four centuries before Quixote, Francis of Assisi sallied out, at first to crusade for Christendom and then, when that venture aborted and he discovered his true Mistress, to live a religious order into actuality.

Hagiography extols his humility but tells of quixotic pride. "I will yet be venerated as a saint," Thomas of Celano quotes young Francis, "throughout the whole world".[17] Seeking a name and destiny by serving Conquest, Francis first ventured out at arms, but

---

17. Thomas of Celano, *The Second Life of St. Francis* in *St. Francis of Assisi, Writings and Early Biographies: English Omnibus of the Sources for the Life of St. Francis*, Marion A. Habig (Chicago: Franciscan Herald Press, 1983), 364.

on his subsequent sally in the service of Poverty he discovered true errantry. True nobility—masterless morality—means ceasing to live by possession, because possession is the key that locks one into civil society's master-slave morality. Joining the beggars in Rome, kissing a leper, stripping off all his clothing in court, Francis hallowed pride, as true nobility, which opened the way for love. As the Franciscan Rule, the way he opened became a covenant that allowed the faithful to go free without leaving the still-captive Catholic Church.

WITHERING BOUNDARIES AND THE TRANSNATIONAL CHURCH

For the modern nation-state to function as the form that contains civil society, *religio* had to be brought under national control. "*Religio*," the word from which "religion" is derived, traces back to the idea of binding together. It is related to words such as ligament and obligation. Conceptually, it is the substance of covenanting.

In laying the conceptual foundations for the modern state, Hobbes and the other political philosophers of his day therefore wrote at length about church-state relations. The church was considered the organized form of *religio*, just as the state was seen as the organized form of civility. For postfeudal governments to establish modern nations, they either had to bring *religio* under state control or else exile it from the public realm reserved for the state, to a private, personal realm where it would be out of the way.

Religio and the civil bond have been separated, conceptually, in the course of separating the church from the state, which has left political theorists trying to conjure civil authority and obligation from their concept of the state and its coercive powers. Each generation arrives at its truly modern answer, in light of which all previous efforts to explain civil obligation are seen to have been confused.

Religio has never completely atrophied during the era of the nation-state because it was never dispensable. Civil society always needs at least a sustaining remnant of the unsubjugated for whom

THE CIVIL IMPERATIVE

justice is creative activity rather than coerced passivity. (Hasidic tradition tells of this need in terms of a remnant of just individuals, but creating and sustaining a just order among human beings really has to do with community covenanting.) All governments strive to overcome the limits on their control and initiative, which means the rights of the governed must be sustained and constantly re-created by the governed themselves from within their communities, as *religio*.

What about the separation of church and state?

To become modern nations, European states had to bring church organizations under their rule. The churches were subordinated to the state by a radical segregation of religion's inner, private domain from civil society's outer, public domain, by the creation of state churches headed by the national sovereign, and by making constitutional government the sovereign protector of religious pluralism. In the political realm, human rights can only be conceived negatively, as constraints on government action—so, where *religio* promotes communion, classical liberalism promotes negative political rights.

The church-state accommodation during the era of the nation-state has depended on nationalism's being the real religion. Co-communicants kill each other, as enemy aliens, at the state's command. The emergence of a post-Constantinian, decentralized, transnational, fully ecumenical church that no longer subordinates the practice of its faith to the dictates of national governments is a cause as well as a consequence of nationalism's waning—which means that at this point transnational *religio* is fueling its own emergence. Hindus, Jews, Moslems, Buddhists, Christians—the people of peoples gathering as "church" is united by no creed or ritual but by a shared covenant to honor and protect basic human rights. This separates church and state more definitively than has ever before been the case; church and state are independent agents whose interaction is instituting a fully human civility that knows no aliens.

The covenant to recognize universal human rights converts participating faith communities into peace churches; the covenant to consider no one an alien or enemy is the historical substance of pacifism. As an independent agent protecting human rights from violative governments, the church puts a government's sovereignty at issue; by merging obligations to the body politic with obligations to humankind, the post-Constantinian church decisively rejects the sovereignty of the nation-state. Unable to conceive of what is happening, government officials fail to see that civil bonding can no longer be contained within national borders. Even if national governments remain necessary and world government remains unlikely, the nation-state, as the form into which civil society fits, is withering away.

7

Discovering the Church

> He disarmed the principalities and powers and made a public example of them, triumphing over them in the cross.
>
> —Colossians 2:15

Tucson, May 12, 1981

Dear Friends,

Imagine a moonless night and a group of about fifteen fugitives who are groping their way through country that's terrifyingly alien to them. Two carry infants. Three are small children who clutch at their parents' hands and try not to cry.

The blinding stare of spotlights suddenly freezes them in place. An amplified voice blares orders. Uniformed men close in.

They will be sent back, maybe to be tortured or killed—at the very least to live under the daily threat of being assaulted or killed at the whim of any soldier. . . .

—Vichy France? It did happen there, as it has happened so many places before and since, but I'm writing to you because it's happening now, here in Arizona. . . .

Leaving Nogales for Tucson May 4, a friend picked up a hitchhiker who said he was from El Salvador. They came to the Border Patrol checkpoint almost immediately. The Salvadoran had no papers.

GOATWALKING

That evening when my friend came by, we talked about it. Another friend said he'd heard about a whole planeload of deportees who were shot as they arrived in El Salvador, right at the airport. We felt bad about the anonymous Salvadoran. If he'd just known how to avoid the Border Patrol. . . .

MY TWO FRIENDS were Friends (that is, Quakers), and the May 12 letter about the Salvadorans who were pouring into the borderlands was written to Friends; I sent about five hundred copies to meetings and individual Quakers throughout the United States. A mailing of that size wouldn't go far among most denominations, but in the United States there are fewer than 35,000 unprogrammed Quakers, which is the kind of Quaker I am.[1]

In the letter I explained why I was writing to Quakers:

. . . If Central American refugees' rights to political asylum are decisively rejected by the U.S. government or if the U.S. legal system insists on ransom that exceeds our ability to pay, active resistance will be the only alternative to abandoning the refugees to their fate. The creation of a network of actively concerned, mutually supportive people in the U.S. and Mexico may be the best preparation for an adequate response.

—A network? Quakers will know what I mean.

This letter is addressed primarily to Friends because their history presents them with special responsibilities. If the time does come when Quakers are once again being jailed in the U.S. for helping refugees, the implications will be clear to everyone. This

---

1. During the revivalist enthusiasms of the nineteenth century, many American Quakers adopted pastoral forms of worship and came to be called "pastoral" or "church" Quakers. They are unambiguously Christian—something like Methodists without formal baptism. *Unprogrammed* Quakers are the kind that have no pastor and meet in silence, with no "program" of hymns, prepared prayers, or homily. Some are Christians, and some aren't. Quakers who get in trouble for peace, civil rights, or other social "testimonies" are frequently of the unprogrammed kind.

is one reason the U.S. government is usually reluctant to jail Quakers for conscientious resistance and may sometimes even modify oppressive policies in order to avoid creating a confrontation, but this special consideration entails an obligation not to abandon the victims of war and oppression, even when active resistance with all its risks becomes the only alternative to passive collaboration. . . .

That letter to Friends addressed the only faith community I knew. I soon learned that full-time involvement with refugees meant full-time involvement with the church. A "new underground railroad" formed almost immediately to protect Central American refugees, the foundation for which was the ecumenical church. Suddenly, I was spending much of my time in churches and was working closely with the vocationally religious, and my two closest friends were Catholic priests. I was even "Padre Jaime"—Father Jim—to the *comandante* and jailers at the penitentiary in Nogales, Sonora, where Central American refugees were held by the Mexican government for deportation to Guatemala. My next letter would be addressed to "friends." Many of the friends I addressed in this letter would share my ignorance about the church and my aversion to organized religion, so I wrote as an evangelist whose eyes had been opened.

Tucson, July 6, 1981

Dear friends,

Nearly two months have now passed since I wrote many of you about the Salvadorans seeking refuge in the U.S. I can't report that we've had many notable successes. Of the [approximately fifty] refugees mentioned in the May 12 letter, we managed to reach less than half. Unless one knows a refugee's name, the Immigration and Naturalization Service blocks access. Hidden, unknown, and unnoticed, they are herded through jails run by a variety of governmental, business, and social service organizations in communities like Tucson, Pasadena, and El Centro, then are quickly shipped to whatever fate awaits them. The INS takes extreme measures to prevent the public from learning about them and about the atrocities to which they are being subjected in El Salvador.

Because the refugees are here, the war against the people of Latin America is being waged here as well. Yet, because the refugees are among us, the basic communities capable of waging the peace can also emerge here. Such communities are not merely possible, they are essential if our stand for peace is to be more than just another petition addressed to those who command the war machine. . . .

Let me put it more specifically.

Lupe [Castillo, coordinator of the Manzo area council's legal aid program], often warns those who volunteer for work with the refugees that part-time involvement is difficult. It's as though a battle were raging here in Arizona and the other borderlands; the problem is not how much to do but how to allocate the little we can do in order to be most effective in reducing casualties. Each week we must turn our backs on refugees who desperately need help but for whom there's just not enough time or money. And there are hundreds of thousands in El Salvador whose agonies far exceed the sufferings of those reaching the U.S. "If a man has enough to live on, and yet when he sees his brother in need shuts up his heart against him, how can it be said that the divine love dwells in him?"

Please don't take this as a pitch for donations. The issue is much more fundamental and has to do . . . with communion rather than with the giving of money. There's no way for us to take our stand with the refugees while retaining the privileges and immunities the war machine provides us. . . . If we do give up our position of privilege, a place to stand with the dispossessed and serve the Peaceable Kingdom can only be found in a special kind of community that dedicates itself to such service. During recent weeks I've been discovering this catholic church that is a people rather than creed or rite, a living church of many cultures that must be met to be known. Out of these meetings, a meaning has opened to me that I'd like to share.

. . . Recently, as I struggled to cope emotionally with having

DISCOVERING THE CHURCH

become a peripheral witness to the crucifixion of the Salvadoran people, a suspicion grew that the cross opens a way beyond breakdown—as revelatory depth meaning rather than salvationist egoism. This is the kind of meaning one discovers only in meeting those who share it, much the way a language lives among a people rather than in a dictionary's afterthoughts. It is also the kind of meaning that binds the generations and diverse cultures into one people and that is accessible to children and the unsophisticated, a meaning that is here among us, historically and communally, rather than being the invention of clever minds or the discovery of a gnostic elite. . . .

The decision to murder Archbishop Romero probably resulted from the following appeal addressed to soldiers, national guardsmen, and policemen: "Brothers, each one of you is one of us. We are the same people. The campesinos you kill are your own brothers and sisters. When you hear the words of a man telling you to kill, remember instead the words of God, *Thou shalt not kill.*" . . . Monseñor Romero reached out in fellowship to win them from the way of violence, and that constituted a far more radical threat than a call to armed insurrection. . . .

—So as the Monseñor celebrated the mass, "This is my body which will be given up for you. . . . This is the cup of my blood . . . shed for you . . ." they fired a bullet through his heart.

But it doesn't end there. . . . In the midst of this agony, underlying defeat, is fulfillment and renewal—neither a noble fiction nor the rhetoric of consolation, but the lived reality of the Kingdom of Love. The ways of the violent may prosper, but they are like a dream when one awakes. . . .

The peoples of the cross I was meeting turned the world as I'd known it inside out and upside down. Seeing the world's principalities and powers politically, as the substance rather than the shadows of human empowerment, I'd thought there was no alternative to resistance, in reaction to the rule of violence. Meeting the church, I saw that political countermeasures are a shadow's shadow; the powers could neither darken nor disempower the lovingkindness of the many Panchitas who are the redemptive flesh and blood of the church.

Panchita was the cook at the Santuario Guadalupano in Nogales, Mexico. A widow who only occasionally wears the black rebozo, in her late sixties at the time, quite thin and no more than five feet tall, she's a shy woman who rarely forgets to hold her hand over her mouth when she smiles, to hide the gaps. When refugees came to the church, she fed them. Learning why they were fleeing and what was happening to them in Mexico, she began stopping them on the streets and even searching them out under bridges. She soon became as good as the best immigration agents at recognizing them.

Years of caring have etched compassion into her face, so when she talked to them they trusted her and would tell where they came from and why. She then brought them to the church or to her tiny one-room adobe. Once, she found twelve Salvadorans hiding under a railroad trestle and took them home with her. That night she slept at a neighbor's.

Panchita's little adobe is perched high on a steep hill, accessible only by slippery paths, about forty yards from the border fence. It overlooks downtown Nogales and one of the holes in the fence that has been a major entryway for decades. (Sometimes the hole is patched, but someone will always open it again within a day or two.) From Panchita's doorway, the refugees could look down on the patrols on the Arizona side as they made their rounds. They could also signal one another when the way was clear.

Panchita was quite fearful that Mexican Immigration or U.S. Border Patrol officials would learn she was helping refugees, but she kept at it, sharing all she had. She even took in and mothered a fifteen-year-old deserter from the Salvadoran army who would have been shot if caught and returned. This pattern prevailed throughout Mexico; it was usually the poor who helped and the rich who put their faith in fences. On Mexico's other border, on the slopes of Mount Tacaná, I once asked a peasant catechist, who had a large family but was sharing his small home with an even larger Guatemalan family, why so many of the people on Tacaná had opened their doors to refugees, while down below, on the coastal plain around Tapachula, people called them illegals and rarely took them in. "Down there," he explained, "they're too rich to afford it."

Outside the church, even an uncompromising Quaker dedication to serving the Peaceable Kingdom reaches no farther than disconnected acts of charity and resistance. In meeting and knowing the church as a living, visible people of peoples, I found myself among basic communities that are truly empowered to fulfill the covenant in the tasks that actually confront them. After having been Quaker for almost two decades, I decided to seek formal membership in my meeting, in order to join the church. (Many people who consider themselves Quaker and are actively involved in the life of a meeting are "attenders" who never seek formal membership in their meeting.)

Until I began discovering the church, I had no intention of becoming a member because I thought of denominational membership as separative rather than unitive. Unprogrammed Quakers don't think they have a unique or special kind of religious insight. Rather, the insight they find in silent worship is equally accessible to all human beings of all traditions in all ages. Until I began to know the church, membership in meeting seemed separatively sectarian. When I began to know the church, formal membership in my meeting was clearly the way for me to join the church. Just as there's no generic form of marriage that transcends and precludes marriage to someone in particular, there's no generic form of membership in the church I'd come to know. Confirmation came mostly through conversations with my close friends and coworkers, Father Ricardo Elford, a Redemptorist priest in Tucson, and Father Dagoberto Quiñones, a parish priest in Nogales, Mexico.

That they would enter into genuine conversation and share the work of the church with me, as equals, was itself the confirmation that led me to seek formal membership in my meeting. I'd always thought of Catholic priests as the professional guardians of official doctrines and rituals, perennially at odds with the prophetic faith and Quaker heresies; but these two priests—and others I soon met—turned out to live as prophetically as anyone else I'd ever known and to judge all doctrinal professions and cultic practices by the overriding criterion for church membership that Jesus proclaims:

> Lord, when did we see you hungry and feed you, or thirsty and give you drink? And when did we see you a foreigner and welcome you, or naked and clothe you?
> And the King will answer them, Truly, I say to you, as you did it to one of the least of these, my brethren, you did it to me (Mt 25:37–40).

I was meeting the visible, historically specific church formed by distinct traditions and particular people. Father Ricardo, Pat, and I would often banter about our Judeo-Quackolic Church, and in Mexico, where Catholics and Protestants rarely work together, Father Quiñones would introduce me to the archbishop and other priests as a *cuáquero muy católico*—a very Catholic Quaker. In meeting the visible, fully catholic church, I saw that my universalism, which had seemed to stand in the way of formal membership in any specific congregation, was a chimera rather than an obstacle—a lifeless abstraction.

Whatever the truth may be about events reported from Jerusalem two thousand years ago, I learned the truth of the cross because I was there:

Tucson, January 24, 1982

Dear friends,

In Nogales on the afternoon of December 24, I sat with a baby in my arms, hoping he would continue to sleep until his mother arrived, wondering what I would do if she were captured. Christmas crowds provided ironically appropriate cover for the grim game of cat-and-mouse taking place, a game played daily in which refugees try to evade the Border Patrol.

In this case the fate of the young mother and her child hung on the outcome. As family of a man known to be opposed to El

DISCOVERING THE CHURCH

Salvador's military rulers, they would run a high risk of being tortured and then murdered if caught and deported to El Salvador. For almost a year, the woman had been in hiding, nurturing her firstborn, waiting for this chance to run the gauntlet of Mexican and U.S. *migra* in order to reunite the family. . . .

I couldn't help remembering, from two weeks earlier on Mexico's Guatemalan border, the grief in Mother Elvira's eyes as she told of a baby boy, nine months old, whom Guatemalan soldiers had mutilated and slowly murdered while forcing his mother to watch. Only at the risk of wounding the mind can one learn about the methodical torture of dispossessed peoples that the U.S. is sponsoring in Latin America.

The victim might have been the baby in my arms. And it might yet be. As a Salvadoran refugee, he is called an illegal and hunted as a fugitive by the people of power who sponsor the military terror that drove his family from their home.

Flushed with excitement and relief, his mother rushed in and hugged him to her. By nightfall she would once again be with her husband, in a little barrio home in Tucson that a chicana family shares with the refugees (a home sometimes so crowded that cars parked in back must be used as sleeping quarters).

A few miles away from the reunited family, Tucsonans were gathering at the Federal Building for the forty-fifth weekly prayer vigil for social justice in El Salvador and Guatemala. It was a good place to be on Christmas Eve, with Pat and among friends. . . .

It chanced that I was asked to read the passage that begins, "She gave birth to her firstborn son and wrapped him in swaddling clothes and laid him in a manger, because there was no room for them in the place where travelers lodged. There were shepherds in that region, living in the fields and keeping night watch . . ."

The trip to Chiapas and Guatemala November 11 to December 17 went well. Channels of communication with refugees at the Mexican-Guatemalan border—including refugees deported from Sonora and other parts of Mexico—are now open. A cooperative effort to provide needed services for Central American refugees has been initiated.

GOATWALKING

Here are some conclusions from the trip that may come as a surprise: 1. For many migrating Central American refugees, economic and social opportunities are better in Mexico than in the U.S. 2. Although individuals and special interest groups are aiding some refugees, the church is the only institution that can make a sustained effort to aid undocumented refugees in Mexico. Any other foundation for refuge or for an underground railroad will be destroyed by Mexican Immigration, which has become an agent of the U.S. government. 3. In common with most borders, the Mexican-Guatemalan border cannot be closed, so even with Mexican Immigration enforcing U.S. policy against the refugees, many refugees will continue to arrive in the U.S. 4. If efforts to aid Central Americans who are arriving in the U.S. are not to have a Pied-Piper effect that is detrimental to the refugees' long-range interests, aid must be combined with a concerted attempt to provide migrating refugees with accurate information about their choices. 5. To formulate programs in terms of "aiding refugees" is, in addition to encouraging a patronizing attitude, highly misleading. In solidarity with the oppressed peoples of Latin America, Anglo America needs to build the church, and in the U.S. that includes defying government prohibitions against helping undocumented refugees evade capture. . . .

I don't know how to tell you, in writing, about the trip to the Guatemalan border. The trip was people rather than scenery, but writing some of the names and settings would be a betrayal. As a priest in Guatemala said, anything in writing is dangerous. Yet, secrecy is first cousin to the lie. Lies sever community; secrecy smothers it. . . .

Here's a selection from my notes:

Nov. 21–25: —Looked around Tapachula and took bus trips to the two border crossings (Talisman and Ciudad Hidalgo), to the coast (Puerto Madero), and up into coffee country (Cacahoatán and Unión Juárez). Talked openly with priests (only two of whom were open with me) and as a tourist with others (most of whom bring up the Central American refugee situation in the course of

DISCOVERING THE CHURCH

conversation without being led beyond an initial "Do you think touring Guatemala is advisable?").

In one village, a campesino surprised me by asking if I was from Guatemala and then acting knowingly doubtful when I said I wasn't. "Near here, where I live, there's one of your class who came from Guatemala to avoid being killed."

—And what kind of Guatemalan fugitive would I, an ascetic-looking loner of blue-eyed European extraction, appear to be? — Of course! [One of the foreign priests, many of whom are Spaniards.] But if the *campesino* thought so, what will they think in Guatemala? I'll have to work on my cover—and definitely leave my little maroon, imprimatured Bilbao *Biblia* behind in Mexico with my other subversive documents.

. . . *The Diario del Sur* [a Tapachula newspaper] quotes the Procurator of Justice for Chiapas as saying that "the majority of the illegals have a criminal record and only come to commit crimes." Also, "the flow of illegals brings with it unemployment and the increase of delinquency," so "stringent action is needed to control the border with Guatemala." . . .

Nov. 26–Dec. 1: Padre X tells me that none of the refugees starve in Mexico, that they can always find some kind of work, if they're at all capable and willing. One of the problems is that they work only long enough to get some money and continue northward in search of something better, so it's hard to find them work requiring stability, even when they're highly qualified. Padre Y tells me that at least 2,000 Salvadorans are working in Tapachula in construction. One educated guess is that 30,000 to 40,000 undocumented Central Americans are in Tapachula on any given day. The freight yards are swarming with migrating men.

And what about women? Because they're not hired for most jobs and can't mix readily into railroad jungles, many are trapped. . . . Although all of us dealing with refugee problems in the U.S.–Mexican borderlands know that destitute young refugee women farther south in Mexico—especially in the Tapachula area—often have no alternative to prostitution, I tended to think of it as a temporary expedient they might use to get bus fare. I failed to consider that a large and constantly replenished supply of highly exploitable young women would become enmeshed institutionally in the same profit-taking patterns that we see in the creation of a highly exploitable class of laboring "illegals"—except that all of the worst features are accentuated in the case of prostitute "illegals." Think of a way that undocumented workers are exploited, and undocumented prostitutes will be even more exploited because they are an even more vulnerable excluded class.

On the Guatemalan border at Ciudad Hidalgo, women carrying loads on their heads casually wade the river at a ford a few hundred yards downstream from the bridge across the Suchiate River. Customs and Immigration are nuisances they can do without. Upstream, truck-tire pontoons cross passengers. (One optimistic entrepreneur tried to sell me a return trip to Guatemala.)

Why don't Mexican Immigration and Customs force the traffic to move farther away from the bridge? Then it would be harder to watch. There's no way the rugged jungle border between Mexico and Guatemala could be closed. . . .

I asked a woman who lives next to the river whether it is true that bodies sometimes float by. She said it happens all the time. She pointed at a shoe next to us and said, "This shoe came off when they pulled one out a day or two back." I said it must have been a Salvadoran. (Arnulfo had explained how to tell Salvadorans by their shoes [which often have a distinctive composition sole manufactured in El Salvador].) She said that, indeed, it had been.

Most of the local people thought it would be safe enough for me to go across to Guatemala. According to Padre Z, six people were killed on the other side of the river a couple of days ago, but they were involved in the upcoming elections. (A civilian puppet party is permitted to field candidates, but the military reportedly feels this is a good time to exterminate their civilian collaborators and thereby forestall Washington's deciding on a Salvadoran-style "reform coup" to replace undisguised military rule.)

Padre Z has been housing and feeding refugees. . . . [He] is brimming over with Christian joy and generosity, but he's not the least bit fuzzy-minded about it. He knows, for example, that an active community is necessary to respond to the refugee situation. . . . He invited me to speak at a retreat [of local Catholics involved in the charismatic movement]. I spoke poorly, but the gathering was prepared . . . The way the organizing session jumped into issues where governmental authority would be defied is noteworthy. In the U.S. these issues would have elicited hot debate and much soul searching. In contrast, everyone at the retreat knew what the Law is and that the Mexican government is violating it, so the question of obedience wasn't even raised . . . With an initial base of about 150 people, the group can minimize individual risk while magnifying the dissuading influences that can be brought to bear on government officials who do consider initiating sanctions . . .

. . . Most people in Southern Chiapas will soon know that the active Christians are trying to protect the refugees. I wonder if the government will hesitate to persecute the Christians for acting the way everyone thinks they ought to act. (Local politicians are sensitive to that sort of thing, especially since their wives are often active. After the meeting, I was invited out to a ranch where I was introduced to the governor's brother.) If Mexico City orders a crackdown, there will, indeed, be a crackdown of sorts, but local sentiment could keep it from being more than a brief show of force to please Washington . . .

Dec. 5 [Malacatán, Guatemala]: A few moments ago I was in the plaza, sitting and watching the evening promenade, when there was a burst of pistol fire from the police station about fifty yards from me. Everyone scurried for cover, and businesses quickly shut their doors and turned off inside lights. I walked over to a place where a bus driver and passengers were peering from the corner of a building. There were lots of ideas about a guerrilla attack, but no one really knew why the police started shooting. I had to cross the plaza area to get to the hotel, which faces the police station across the small plaza, but I figured it'd be best to get in. They had the door locked and the lights off but let me in when I knocked.

Soon the Guardia de la Hacienda (green uniforms), Guardia Nacional (blue uniforms), and secret police were in the plaza in force. The hotel owner said it wouldn't be good for me, a stranger in town, to go out. She also said that if any shooting started, all those submachineguns would be very dangerous—that they usually killed a lot of bystanders when they opened up. . . . So I guess I'll spend the evening in the hotel.

One of the government's dilemmas seems to be that military terrorism is most effective in cowing a populace when it's publicized, yet publicity is bad for the tourist trade (which, of course, is nonexistent where I've been; I'm the only person registered at the hotel tonight, and their register shows no gringos during recent months—just Salvadorans and Guatemalans). The daily paper has six stories about eleven disappearances and three stories about seven recovered corpses, all written in ways that indicate the death squads got them ("tortured-strangled-was intercepted by various unknown men"). The guerrillas burned four buses on the Interamerican Highway last night, but didn't hurt anyone. (As the bus burns, they often hand out leaflets to the passengers.)

Many of these stories are tucked away among ads in back pages, like fillers. The death squads are clearly working all over, not just in insurgent strongholds, reports of disappearances being from every part of the country. In Escuintla, a crowd of people is reported to have turned up to see whether five people murdered yesterday were family members who had disappeared, but no identification was made. (People do still identify the corpses in Guatemala, by the way.)

It's surprising how many evangelical-pentecostal churches are in even the smallest towns here. The Mormons are also quite strong.

The surrounding country is almost all pastureland—large holdings with well-bred Brahman, Gyr, Indo-Brazil, and *Bos indicus* X Brown Swiss. Planted areas are mostly forty or more acres and in forage crops. It'd be quite good cow country, if people didn't have to suffer so much for it.

Dec. 6: The morning-after story is that two women from the cantinas had been picked up and put in jail. A drunk Green Guard, out of uniform, approached, maybe to join in the "fun." Maybe he made a threatening gesture. In any case, he was armed and wasn't known by the men on guard, so he was shot dead.

DISCOVERING THE CHURCH

—Went to the bridge at Talisman today and talked at some length with a couple of the Green Guards manning a checkpoint. They say we can go into the cattle business cheap, a solid $3 million finca selling for only $1 million. (One was burned a few kilometers away a couple of weeks ago.) When I wondered about the risk of being killed, they said, in common with everyone else, "There's no problem, if you don't get involved in politics." —But the East is where they recommended for cattle ranching. "There were guerrillas, but it's completely cleaned out now, empty and ready for cattle." . . .

—Had dinner with a couple of Salvadorans tonight, young men who were "just traveling in Guatemala" and said they planned to return to El Salvador in a couple of days. They were unusually interested in the route north. They may have thought I was unusually well-informed about Salvadoran refugee concerns, for a retired rancher. . . .

"Now that you can scarcely find a priest in El Salvador," one of the Salvadorans outside the door says, "we learn religion from any preacher who comes along." In all their talk, they've been strictly individualistic. To the degree that religion is identified exclusively with soul saving, the renewed church in Latin America may find itself addressing a remnant. Whatever might be happening concerning armed struggle in Latin America, the prospects for real revolution may be preserved or destroyed according to the ascendancy either of religious egoism or else of communion. From what I've seen in Guatemala, a fundamentalist Bible Belt is well on the way to taking form . . .

I hope to return to Chiapas in March—to work with others there on a booklet-with-directory for Central American refugees, but especially to attend a training session for catechists in one of the highland pueblos.

Am I converting to Catholicism, then? Well, not in a sense that would make me less Quaker. I've been discovering the Catholic Church, not by studying Catholicism but by meeting Catholics. Whatever our creedal differences, we meet as one people by virtue of our allegiance to one Kingdom. And my discovery is that the church is truly catholic, a people of peoples that incorporates not only a multiplicity of nations and cultures but also divergent beliefs, rites, and perspectives. . . .

. . . Good news is reaching us from the pueblos of Latin America. . . . The good news is the formation of basic communities capable of going free. Returning now to the earlier comment that, in solidarity with the oppressed peoples of Latin America, Anglo America needs to build the church, our response to the refugees has not yet developed beyond programs for welcoming them to Babylon. We may cry solidarity and write it on signs, but we aren't yet living it, nor have we even realized that we, too, are living in exile. . . .

8

Pilgrims' Progress

> When a foreigner sojourns with you in your land, you shall not do him wrong. The foreigner who sojourns with you shall be to you as the native among you, and you shall love him as yourself; for you were foreigners in the land of Egypt: I am the LORD your God.
>
> —Leviticus 19:33–34

BECAUSE THE ARIZONA-SONORAN borderlands are where I feel most at home, I once came close (while looking for work in 1959) to applying for a job with the Border Patrol. Instead, I found work on the border with the U.S. Forest Service, at Canelo, and then with the U.S. Park Service, at the Coronado National Memorial. Until the refugees began arriving, the only time I ever went over the fence was to stop a grass fire in Mexico.

I knew, of course, that it was bad form for a federal employee to go over the fence while on the job, and I was reprimanded afterwards for making an "unauthorized incursion into Mexico," but the circumstances were exceptional. Rapidly widening as it moved north through dry grasslands, the fire would have formed a front at least a mile wide by the time it reached the tinder-dry chaparral at the border, and would then have chimneyed up steep canyons, kiln-hot and explosive, to the top of the Huachucas.

Nor did I have any quarrel with U.S. immigration officials, before I learned what was happening to arriving refugees. At my family's ranch in the Huachucas, we always hired Mexicans, because Anglo and Mexican-American cowboys are usually practicing (on ranch livestock) for the next rodeo, but we never hired a Mexican without papers. We would give food and a place to sleep to Mexicans who passed through after coming over the fence; we told them where they might find work; but we refused to hire them.

I never met another rancher or farmer in Arizona who followed the same policy. It was expensive to immigrate a cowboy and his family, and then he was free to find work anywhere, which meant that our wages and working conditions had to be competitive.

The morning after that Salvadoran hitchhiker was taken from my friend by the Border Patrol, I woke knowing I should find out whether anything could be done for him, but I had only vague notions about how to go at it. I called the Border Patrol; then, the INS; but in each case they made it clear that they weren't in the business of putting concerned citizens in touch with refugees who might need help. Then I called the Manzo Area Council, the Tucson barrio organization that provided legal aid for the undocumented, and was told I should talk with Father Ricardo, who in turn offered to bring me a form G-28 for the refugee to fill out, if I could somehow manage to reach him. But I couldn't find him without some cooperation from federal officials.

My name is the same as that of a former mayor of Tucson, now the clerk of the superior court. I phoned the appropriate immigration official and, using a strictly business, Alpha-male voice, said, "This is Jim Corbett, here in Tucson. I need the name, A-number, and current location of a Salvadoran male you picked up at the Peck Canyon roadblock yesterday afternoon." He checked his records and told me, and I was soon on my way to the Santa Cruz County Jail with the G-28—a little less naive about what I could expect from government officials but unaware of what I was getting into. It would be years before I'd find time for much else.

My being invited by the National Council of Churches of Christ (NCCC) to be the "resource person" on Salvadoran refugees at their nationwide immigration consultation the following January indicates how limited the response was to Central American refugees, two years after tens of thousands of Salvadorans began arriving in search of safe haven. Before hearing about the Salvadoran hitchhiker who'd been taken from my friend by the Border Patrol, I couldn't have named Oscar Romero, the archbishop murdered there the year before by death squads. Nine months later I was asked to be the resource person on Salvadoran refugees at a consultation that brought together about four hundred clergy and professionals for whom refugee assistance was a full-time career.

I soon discovered why. Few professionals in the field of refugee assistance wanted to have anything to do with the Salvadorans and Guatemalans who were crossing the U.S.-Mexican border in search of first asylum. It would threaten their federal funding for resettling Vietnamese, Soviet Jews, and Cambodians, or for assisting first-asylum Cuban refugees who had federal approval, or for operating programs for first-asylum refugees overseas.

The official government position was that the Salvadorans and Guatemalans arriving in the United States were "illegals" rather than refugees, that they were just coming to the United States looking for jobs, that no refugee-causing violations of human rights in El Salvador and Guatemala were causing the influx. Anyone who assisted them in any way with food, shelter, transportation, communications, or concealment was therefore, according to federal officials, committing a felony punishable by up to five years' imprisonment for each act of assistance—and up to ten years for conspiring to do so.

The United States had ratified a United Nations treaty and enacted a federal law committing itself never to return a refugee to a country where he or she had reason to fear persecution—that is, to provide safe haven for first-asylum refugees, regardless of their nationality, political opinion, social class, race, or religion—so when the U.S. government returned the Salvadorans and Guatemalans it claimed they were "illegals" rather than refugees. By international declarations, customary international standards, ratified treaties, and federal law, if the returnees were genuine first-asylum refugees, they had a lawful right to be in the United States, regardless of the way they entered the country or whether they had visas or other documentation. If they were refugees, returning them would be a grave violation of international human-rights law, called *refoulement*.

Elliott Abrams, head of the U.S. State Department's Human Rights Office at the time, would repeat the official position time and again with the same words: "Legally and morally, the distinction between economic migrants and political refugees matters greatly. The United States is legally obligated and morally bound to protect refugees, but not to accept for permanent residence every illegal immigrant who reaches our shores." He was also in charge of drawing up periodic certifications that there were no human rights abuses in El Salvador that would make U.S. military assistance to its government unlawful.

The NCCC consultation was an excellent opportunity to develop nationwide networking and a workable strategy for counteracting the INS tactics that prevented legal aid from reaching detained refugees. At my urging, the consultation also approved a resolution calling for the National Council of Churches' member denominations to take direct action to assist undocumented Central American refugees. But no one there offered to become part of the relay network or even asked me about the plans for congregations to declare themselves sanctuaries for first-asylum refugees, as invited by the written statement I distributed.

NCCC WITNESS TO IMMIGRATION
National Council of Churches of Christ
Consultation on Immigration
Washington, D.C., January 28–30, 1982

Preliminary statement concerning Salvadoran refugees,

BY JIM CORBETT

Most of the undocumented refugees currently reaching the U.S. by way of Mexico are from El Salvador. No one knows how many are in the U.S., but they must number more than

100,000—probably closer to 200,000—that have arrived since January 1980.

Among them are people fleeing from military and death-squad violence, from guerrilla violence, and from what might be termed bushwhacker violence, but the situation's generative feature is that their government has instituted a program of systematic terrorism calculated to traumatize the populace into acceptance of established patterns of rule. In much of Latin America, similar programs of military terrorism exist and are being further developed under a unifying U.S. sponsorship that combines massive arms buildups, extensive military training, advanced intelligence technology, regional integration of military forces, and destabilization of governments considered politically incompatible. Consequently, the Salvadorans are probably only the first wave of an influx of Latin American refugees fleeing this military terrorism who will reach the U.S. through Mexico during this decade.

For the most part, the U.S. public will see the fundamental moral and religious issues posed by this refugee influx only if the institutions and public figures to whom Americans commonly look for moral and religious guidance do assert, in action, the right of conscience to aid anyone fleeing from torture and murder. Specifically, public awareness and sympathy depend on the willingness of clergy and religious organizations to defy U.S. government prohibitions against aiding undocumented refugees.

. . . The refugees are right here at the door, pleading for help. The most urgent need of the vast majority of Salvadoran refugees in the U.S. is to avoid capture. Actively asserting the right to aid fugitives from terror means doing it—not just preaching at a government that is capturing and deporting them, not just urging legislation that might help future refugees. With people in our midst being hunted down and shipped back, denouncing the terror while ignoring the victims simply teaches the public how to live with atrocity.

. . . If the churches continue to ignore the Salvadoran

refugees' desperate need to avoid capture, the American public will continue to see the refugees rather than their persecutors as illegals. Refugee advocates' court victories will continue to be seen as a weakening of U.S. defenses against the Brown Peril. TV coverage of new arrivals will continue to be seen as documentation of the need for more repressive immigration laws. A failing economy and the government's desire to increase its police powers at the expense of civil liberties will also, almost certainly, result in the targeting of undocumented Latinos as scapegoats for the nation's ills. This trend may still be reversed if even a few of the mainline churches act decisively to awaken public awareness of the situation's moral and religious dimensions.

In short, much more than the fate of the undocumented refugees depends on the religious community's participation and leadership in helping them avoid capture. If the right to aid fugitives from government-sponsored terror is not upheld in action by the churches—regardless of the cost in terms of imprisoned clergy, punitive fines, and exclusion from government-financed programs—the loss of many other basic rights of conscience will certainly follow. . . .

During the first stages of sanctuary network formation, the group that was most involved with helping refugees cross through the Arizona-Sonoran borderlands to Tucson was a goat-milking cooperative. We called ourselves "Los Cabreros Andantes," which could be translated as "the goatherds errant."[1] We'd just completed a three-year exchange with seminomadic goat ranchers in the South Baja sierras.

The Cabreros Andantes weren't a religious organization, but we were "church" in the societal sense. Few groups could have been better prepared, bonded together, and predisposed than the

---

1. *'Cabrero andante'* is a multiple play on words that pokes fun at our kinship to the archetypical *caballero andante* or "knight errant," Don Quixote de la Mancha.

Cabreros Andantes to help the refugees get through. Errantry shifted from goat herding to refugee aid.

The goat-milking cooperative made it possible for me to be gone most of the time, since others would milk my goats, as part of the common herd. By the end of 1981, the Cabreros' refugee aid had branched off into the Tucson refugee support group, and I was rarely in town for the Cabreros' weekly meeting in our home. By 1984, when the goat-milking cooperative dissolved into another of its offshoots (The Goat and Garden Group, Inc.), Pat and I didn't even have a goat. Instead of shifting toward a land-centered livelihood that cultivated a biocentric ethic (as we'd intended), we'd shifted toward a city-centered way of life that depended on Pat's job as a plant science technician to support my volunteer activities with the sanctuary movement.

As a cowboy, horse trader, Park Ranger, Forest Service GDA (General District Assistant), teacher of wildland symbiotics, and goatwalker, I'd come to be at home in the Sonoran desert. From the New Mexican line to Organ Pipe, Tucson to Guaymas, I knew much of the land and some of the people. No one else was ready to do my border-bridging part of sanctuary networking, but everywhere in the borderlands church members who came in touch with Central American refugees were doing what they could, at the sacrifice of other concerns. Most of those involved were active members of churches, because Central Americans who are lost, broke, hunted, or in despair generally go to a church to seek both divine and human support. Whatever the need, a volunteer could be found to do it. In Tucson, hundreds of people opened their homes to the refugees. Housewives were on call to go into Mexico and drive back with refugee children, claiming them as their own. Two border-wise Quaker women who lived in a retirement community near Douglas, one in her late seventies and the other in her eighties, used their camper to cross refugees who were too sick, injured, or elderly to cross on their own. Doctors risked their licenses to remove bullets and treat torture wounds without notifying the police. Even the police and sheriff's deputies began helping refugees to avoid detention and reach help. On some occasions, even Border Patrol officers helped refugees evade capture.

The pastor of Southside Presbyterian Church, John Fife, soon emerged as the natural spokesperson for the churches' refugee aid in Tucson. In addition to being by far the best speaker among us, he had the patience, determination, and toughness to do the grueling organizational and diplomatic chores that held sanctuary together through the crucial stages when it would otherwise have spun apart. His congregation at Southside became the nucleus for local growth and the base for nationwide ecumenical networking. He also informed, lobbied, and connected the Presbyterian Church in the United States, so that it became the primary national support network for the growth of sanctuary. And, even more important for the continuation of our daily work, he was the only one who had the patience and skills to keep the Tucson Ecumenical Council's Task Force on Central America working with the Manzo Area Council, the terminally overloaded, Alinsky-style barrio organization that was the sole source of INS-accredited legal aid (until it went under in 1985 and the Tucson Ecumenical Council established its own legal aid office).[2]

On March 24, 1982, the second anniversary of the assassination of Archbishop Romero, Southside Presbyterian Church declared sanctuary in Tucson, loosely coordinated with sanctuary declarations by about twenty-one other churches in Berkeley, Los Angeles, Washington, D.C., and several smaller cities. A few days before the declaration, *The Tucson Citizen* ran a headlined, multipaged report by Randy Udall on the help Central American refugees were receiving from Tucson churches, focusing on my border crossings. Before the report, the Tucson refugee support group reached consensus that we should be open about what we were doing and that Randy should be free to identify me as the person crossing refugees. (With thousands of refugees carrying my name and phone number,

---

2. See Ann Crittenden, *Sanctuary: A Story of American Conscience and the Law in Collision* (New York: Weidenfeld and Nicolson, 1988), and Miriam Davidson, *Convictions of the Heart: Jim Corbett and the Sanctuary Movement* (Tucson: University of Arizona Press, 1988), for accounts of sanctuary's development in Tucson.

it wasn't really a secret, in any case.) I refused, though, to make myself available for a news photo.

The head of Mexican Immigration in Nogales had begun to receive reports about me and Father Quiñones from the U.S. Border Patrol, so I expected to be intercepted soon on a border run, but I thought my odds for lasting several more weeks or months would be better, the fewer the people who could recognize me. I was also concerned about my weekly visit, as Padre Jaime, to the Nogales penitentiary. At the press conference for the sanctuary declaration, I sat on the far edge of the dozen participants, partly behind a pillar, and made my statement quite short, in hopes that I could keep a low profile. But, as it turned out, the "CBS Evening News" used my statement to report on the churches' declaration of sanctuary, and the CBS coverage was in turn picked up by the Western Hemisphere's most popular Spanish-language TV news program. My low-profile days were over.

When Father Quiñones and I went to the penitentiary in Mexico the day after, we were surprised to find that the *comandante* and most of the jailers had seen me on television but that it had enhanced rather than destroyed my credibility, even with the *comandante*.[3] As Padre Jaime, I walked a blurry and sometimes comic line between openness and cover. The jailers wondered why, instead of giving the sign of the cross and blessing the prisoners when I left, I would just say "good luck" and wave good-bye, so I explained that I was a different kind of *padre*. When they then wondered about the order to which I belonged, I said I was with the *Sociedad de los Amigos*—"the Society of Friends," the formal

---

3. Four years later, on Good Friday, 1986, the jailers still called me "Padre Jaime" and let me persuade them to open the penitentiary in the evening after lock-down, without the *comandante*'s knowledge, for an unscheduled concert by Joan Baez. An all-points pickup order for me had gone out from Gobernación—the Interior Ministry—two years before; a local law-enforcement official had let Father Quiñones know that if I turned up on the Mexican side of Nogales I wouldn't be leaving; and both the national and Sonoran press were covering the sanctuary trial daily, particularly in connection with Father Quiñones and Socorro de Aguilar. My credibility as Padre Jaime turned out to have more to do with coverage than cover.

name for Quakers. (When one of the jailers met Pat and me in the big Nogales department store, and, not remembering where I'd met him, I introduced her as my wife, his astonishment indicated he thought it must, indeed, be a peculiar order, even after Vatican II.) As far as Father Quinones was concerned, Quakers adhere to the equal priesthood of all believers, and that was good enough to make me Padre Jaime, as long as I didn't give any sacraments.

Because Mexico's constitution prohibits the wearing of clerical dress in public places, my lack of a collar raised no questions. (Father Ricardo suggested that I wear black pants and a white shirt. "Then everyone'll assume you're either a priest or a waiter.") Constitutionally, priests are in a class with prostitutes and convicted felons, denied the vote and other rights of full Mexican citizenship, so the requirement that I be a *"padre"* in order to visit prisoners had to do with practicalities and Mexican traditions rather than legalities. Without church involvement, the Nogales penitentiary (officially called the "Center for Social Re-Adaptation") would have become more of a refugee torture center than a collection point for deportation.

In Mexico, family members are usually expected to provide many of prisoners' basic needs, and the church tries to fill in where family support is lacking. Our regular routine in the prison was for Father Quiñones and Socorro de Aguilar, the parish prison volunteer, to distribute the blankets, bubble-plastic packing sheets (to use as mattresses and blankets), food (usually hard-boiled eggs), plastic butter bowls, and clothes I brought from Tucson. Then they would celebrate mass with the Mexican prisoners while I stayed with the Central Americans to do counselling, collect phone messages and letters to family and friends, and distribute a leaflet that explained legal procedures and nominal rights for first-asylum refugees who reach the United States. The leaflet also listed sources of legal aid for refugees in Arizona and California and gave my name and home phone, in case the deportees made it back and needed help.

During 1981 and into 1982, conditions in the penitentiary were atrocious. On one occasion, the chief of Mexican Immigration even called Father Quiñones and me to prevent a riot by the Central Americans. The *comandante* had been having refugees beaten at random and had also thrown tear-gas canisters into the men's holding tank when they were asleep at night. (Mexicans have had ample opportunities to learn from the U.S. Border Patrol about this way of deterring return, which is often summed-up with a slogan: "If you catch 'em, you ought to clean 'em and fry 'em yourself"—as INS Western Regional Commissioner Harold Ezell put it when speaking to U.S. Border Patrol officers under his command.[4]

The Central Americans had a ration of two corn tortillas and less than twelve ounces of watery soup daily, for which they had to scrounge Styrofoam cups from the prison garbage (hence the plastic butter bowls churches in Tucson were collecting for them). Mexican prisons commonly starve prisoners, but the *comandante* especially wanted to encourage any with money to buy food from his "restaurant," which he sold at a markup of much more than one hundred percent.

In Nogales, winter nights are often subfreezing, but the Central American men, who were provided with no blankets or other bedding and often lacked jackets or extra clothing, were held in an open-air concrete "tank" that had no beds or other furniture. (It was designed to be hosed down when the refugees were shipped out, except that the drain was ordinarily clogged.) Central American women were held in common with the Mexican women prisoners in a large room that opened into an exercise yard separated from the men's side. The *comandante* allowed Father Quiñones to provide the women's side with mattresses discarded by local motels, and the Mexican prisoners also kept the guards from stealing the blankets we brought, but young women were sometimes sexually abused by the jailers and were occasionally taken to the men's side at night, to be auctioned. Boys over six were usually held in the men's tank and on rare occasions were left behind when their parents were deported. Medical care was virtually nonexistent;

---

4. Harold Ezell, quoted in Ed Magnusen, "Immigration's Happy Warrior," *Time*, 27 January 1986, 23.

many of the refugees were sick; some had untreated war and torture wounds; and even aspirin had to be smuggled to them.

Throughout 1981, ordinarily about eighty refugees—and sometimes more than two hundred—were bused from Nogales each week to the Guatemalan border, where they would be expelled from Mexico onto one or the other of the two bridges over the Suchiate River, near Tapachula. After talking their way into Guatemala, most would start north again, so the leaflet I distributed at the prison soon spread through Central America and Mexico. By the time sanctuary was declared in 1982, I spent most of my waking hours responding to calls, counselling refugees in Mexico, and bringing some of them through to Tucson. I was so exhausted that the prospect of a year or two in a U.S. penitentiary didn't seem much of a threat.

GOING NORTH

From late 1981 until July 1984, I traveled throughout Mexico to help with church networking, to counsel refugees, and to accompany those who most urgently needed help. I also spread information about routes and roadblocks, methods and risks, which was more important than accompaniment. If refugees know how to avoid roadblocks and slip through borders, hundreds can get through for each of them who can be personally guided to safety. There's no way to maintain a closed, secure system while helping refugees solely on the basis of need, so I simply shared what I knew about the ways to get through, assuming I'd have to keep updating as immigration officials instituted countermeasures. Surprisingly, the controls and countermeasures remain essentially the same in 1990 as they were during the 1980s. Even the holes in the border fence remain much the same.

In the United States and Mexico, sanctuary volunteers commonly call migrant refugees "pilgrims" (*peregrinos*), so the notices and news I distributed concerning the routes and risks soon acquired a name: "Pilgrims' Progress."

PILGRIMS' PROGRESS

November 1982

The Tapachula area in Chiapas, Mexico, is the crossroads of Central American refugee migration. Most Salvadorans and Guatemalans who reach the U.S. have passed through this area. In addition, all Salvadorans and Guatemalans deported from central and northern Mexico, such as the prisoners we see in Nogales, Sonora, each week, are forced into Guatemala at two bridges near Tapachula. Many of these deportees simply cross the Suchiate River and start north again. . . .

In spite of its focal position, the Tapachula area has been ignored by all agencies dealing with Central American refugees. Total aid during the last two years probably amounts to no more than $5,000, counting about $2,000 donated by the Tucson refugee support group, which also donated a Ford van. Last July, the bishop of Tapachula established a diocesan organization to provide refugee services, and some outstanding volunteers have been attracted to the effort, but it remains virtually unfunded.[5]

. . . One of the basic principles of counterinsurgency is that sanctuaries bordering the area to be controlled must be eliminated. Refugees are indistinguishable from guerrillas. Therefore, the refugees and all who help them must be targeted by military and death-squad incursions while the host government is pressured to expel them.

Guatemalan intelligence and commandos operate routinely in Chiapas and maintain cooperative relations with some Mexican authorities . . . The U.S. government can call on agents throughout the Mexican law enforcement agencies that have been trained and equipped under U.S. drug-control programs. Israeli advisors, including Israeli Intelligence, have also had considerable influence on the development of Guatemala's counterinsurgency program. In Chiapas, when refugees or those working with them are mur-

---

5. Bishop Porcayo Uribe started the refugee program of the Tapachula Diocese in response to the murder of his close friend, Father Cervantes, and placed Father Antonio Steffani in charge. Bishop Uribe and two nuns were killed in an automobile accident north of Tapachula the following June. Father Steffani died suddenly of an unexpected embolism a few months after the bishop's death.

143

dered or disappeared, or when a refugee camp is attacked and dispersed, one often doesn't know whether Guatemalan or Mexican agencies are involved or on whose behalf they are acting.

The most important tip about refugee accompaniment is never to act like prey. In Mexico, it's also helpful at times to seem to have official connections. Carry a list of government notables, with their phone numbers. Never threaten; never show contempt for a corrupt functionary; avoid all gringo arrogance. Just move with the confidence of one who belongs. The appearance and manner of clergy is often a good model. Instead of pretending to be invisible when you meet those who are hunting you, be sociable and seek positive interaction. When they might be of help, ask.

I once took the passport of a missing sixteen-year-old Salvadoran girl to the head of Mexican Immigration in Ciudad Hidalgo, to see whether they had any record of her being deported. I explained that she'd disappeared in Mexico City when she'd gone out to mail a letter—that her distraught parents, whom I'd met at the hotel, wanted me to check at the deportation points to see whether she might have been picked up and deported by Mexican Immigration. For several years, the papers Immigration filled out when Central Americans were deported through Ciudad Hidalgo had been tossed into cardboard boxes, and he said I could look through them if I liked. The other Immigration and Customs agents puzzled over me as I took my time shuffling through their records, but they never asked who I was, assuming I must be with the CIA. Afterward, when they'd see me on the banks of the Suchiate, they'd just nod knowingly and wish me *buenas tardes*.

Gobernación (which is, roughly, the Mexican equivalent of the U.S. Department of Justice) assigned two agents to watch me in Mexico City when it was moving refugee camps from Chiapas to Campeche (July 1984). The two agents took a room next to mine at the Hotel Edison, left their door open, and would sit smoking cigarettes and watching. If anyone visited me, one of them would stand outside my door to listen—nothing high-tech or even subtle about these two. At the same time, a number of church refugee workers were kidnapped and threatened in Chiapas, and in Mexico City a noted journalist who dared to write about events in Chiapas was also picked up by unidentified men and held overnight, kept blindfolded in a room where Guatemalans were being tortured. I was reasonably sure the two agents were there to spy on me (not to warn me), since Gobernación is never subtle about warnings, either. (About two years later, in the same area of Mexico City, Mexican agents pistol-whipped one of our Tucson sanctuary volunteers—in the park across the street from the Hotel Oxford.)

During this same period, I needed to slip in and out of Tapachula without being noticed. The head of Immigration was already watching for me. When I made a late-night visit to Tapachula's director of the Protestant program for refugee relief, I was therefore concerned that the man who was leaning against a telephone pole outside, watching the program director's second-floor apartment, might recognize me. I could go in with my back to the stakeout, but then he'd be waiting, trying to identify and maybe photograph me, as I came out. The apartment had just the one entrance.

A reporter and a photographer from *The Sacramento Bee*, Dale Maharidge and Michael Williamson, were in Tapachula, working on a series about Central American refugees,[6] and they'd arranged to meet me on the street outside. Seeing the situation, they parked a few yards from the stakeout and sat staring at him. When I joined them after about ten minutes, the stakeout seemed too distracted to notice much about me. If he did identify me, it probably enhanced the rumor among the local *migra* that I was from the CIA.

April 1983

Refugees who are able to get a Mexican tourist visa must usually bribe their way into the country at Talismán or Ciudad Hidalgo, at the checkpoint on the southern outskirts of Tapachula, at the

---

6. See "Escape from El Salvador," a 36-page special report, (*The Sacramento Bee*/from a series published Aug. 26–30, 1984).

checkpoint immediately north of Huixtla, and at the checkpoint at Juchitán (south of Tehuantepec). The Colón busline, which is the only line that runs from the Guatemalan border to Mexico City, is closely checked. The local buses from the border to Tapachula are only checked occasionally; from 7:30 to 9:30 A.M. they're usually too crowded for Immigration to bother. Between the border and Mexico City, inspection is most thorough at the Huixtla checkpoint. In Mexico City, bus, train, and air terminals are watched, and immigration or other officials often rob and sometimes assault the refugees. Refugees on Colón buses should get off before reaching the terminal. . . .

Refugees who don't have visas usually cross into Mexico by wading the Suchiate below Ciudad Hidalgo-Tecún Umán. One common route involves taking a local van-bus at the market in Tecún Umán to Limones, crossing to Libertad, then going to Ciudad Hidalgo or Puerto Madero and catching a local bus into Tapachula. Below Tecún Umán, the mosquitoes will usually keep officials indoors and out of the way in the evening, especially where there are mangroves.

Refugees often walk around the Huixtla checkpoint, which is the toughest roadblock in southern Mexico. The railroad parallels the road on the west but is often watched. (The residence of the local immigration chief overlooks it.) Apart from the railroad tracks, the west side is swampy and should be avoided. The east is pastureland and brush—the best way to go. For anyone who can borrow or rent a car, the easy way is to follow a Colón bus, preferably one coming from the border. The agents at the checkpoint will be so eager to get at the Central Americans in the bus that the car can pull around and pass uninspected. When going through a checkpoint, slow almost to a stop, smile, and then nod, wave, and drive on as though someone had signaled to go ahead.

If Salvadoran or Guatemalan accents can't be disguised, it's best to look for a priest to buy bus, train, or plane tickets in Mexico City. Children are bound to use their Central American dialect, so it's better to travel with them at night when they're more likely to sleep. With children, buses are better than trains, since most children will run around in railroad cars and talk to others. Trains do have an advantage for alert adults, in that one can simply get off at stops to buy a taco from a vendor, when Immigration officers get on to check papers, then board the car again from the side the officers entered. Remember that bus drivers, conductors, and hotel desk clerks sometimes split the take from shakedowns, and many are on the lookout for young women to be forced into prostitution. Air travel from Mexico City to Hermosillo, La Paz, Chihuahua, or Monterrey (but not to border cities) is often the cheapest as well as the safest way to go.

Local lines and oblique routes should always be used when approaching the border. Reaching Tijuana by the West Coast route is the most difficult approach. Those who need to reach the California border are currently doing best by going to Obregón, Los Mochis, or Guaymas and catching a local flight to Constitución or Santa Rosalía, then taking a bus up the peninsula. Ferries also cross the Sea of Cortez, but immigration checks are common, if superficial. Immigration agents are sometimes on duty at the Santa Rosalía bus stop. . . .

The easiest route is currently Matamoros via Monterrey. There's an in-bound checkpoint at the Nuevo León–Tamaulipas border where border-bound traffic is only occasionally checked, and there's also an immigration checkpoint twenty-one kilometers west of Matamoros that rarely inspects eastbound traffic. Mexican Immigration often checks arrivals in Reynosa and Matamoros, so take one of the three daily *"directos"* to Matamoros that bypass Reynosa, then get off on the main intersection of the *Periférico* (the outer boundary road), where other passengers will usually be getting off shortly before arriving at the terminal.

One of the most popular crossings is at La Canasta, about eight kilometers east of downtown Matamoros. It's the site of an old cable crossing over the Rio Grande where large boulders bridge the river—and is a popular picnic area on weekends, where people gather, swim, and mix from both sides of the river. Some of the Anglos who live to the immediate east report walking Hispanics to the Border Patrol, and one woman sometimes shoots near them to frighten them away, so it's best to follow the little road that goes past the county equipment shed northward to the levee and paved

147

road, then north and west about three kilometers to Good Shepherd Church, which is on the Brownsville bus line.

From Laredo to the Gulf, most of the Rio Grande can be crossed with little risk of detection, but the river itself is quite dangerous. Much of the time one can wade across, no more than waist-deep, where silt bars form at the tip of each bend, but the river is deep and fast whenever a large volume of irrigation water is coming through. Children should always wear life jackets designed to hold them on their backs, with an adult who is a good swimmer pulling them. To reduce the risk of inadvertently dunking them, pull them with a line attached to the neck of the life jacket. After entering the water but before starting across, hold them and show how you'll pull them, until they become reassured about floating. Provide reliable floaters of one kind or another for all adults. (Locals often use innertubes, but department stores in Brownsville carry a variety of inexpensive beach and boating accessories that work better, inflate quicker, and are more portable.) Take a plastic garbage bag to keep your clothes dry, and tie it so it also works as a floater.

One of my closest calls came on the Matamoros *Periférico*. I'd arranged for the refugees with me to sit in various places in the bus, since they all looked Central American. When I stood and moved forward to get off at the stop before arriving at the bus terminal, they stood and took their luggage to follow.

"We're not stopping this time," the driver told me. "Not until we reach the terminal."

We returned to our seats and sat down again. His only reason for refusing to stop had to be that he intended to turn us in for a reward of one kind or another. He probably wanted the young woman who was in the group, whom he'd been watching and sizing up. But a few blocks farther there'd been a serious accident, and the way was blocked by vehicles, a crowd, and ambulances.

"Since we're stopped anyway," I told him, "we'll get off here."

He frowned but opened the door, and the Salvadorans followed me single-file through the crowd and down the street—the perfect picture of a *pollero* with his *pollitos*.[7]

June 1983

The Mexican government's role as a U.S. agent is most obvious in northern Mexico, where all major road and rail approaches to the United States are guarded at strategic points. The checkpoint at Benjamin Hill, one-hundred-eighteen kilometers north of Hermosillo, is typical of these refugee interception points. Only northbound Latinos are normally checked. Mexicans with southern accents are often detained and sometimes deported, but Anglos driving cars with U.S. plates are usually waved through uninspected. Years ago, the USDA established an agricultural checkpoint here, financed by the U.S. government but staffed by the Mexican Secretariat of Agriculture and Hydraulic Resources (SARH). This arrangement continues, but a second inspection has been added for Central American refugees, staffed by Mexican Immigration. (A joke circulating in Hermosillo has it that the gringos consider it logical to add Latin Americans to their list of undesirable insects.) On the outskirts of Hermosillo, a prison camp has now been built for processing the refugees who are caught. It looks like an INS detention center, is designed to process and deport up to 23,000 annually, and is scheduled to begin operation in about a month. Similar refugee prison camps have recently been completed outside other Mexican cities near the U.S. border.

In cities where the border is a fence rather than the Rio Grande, most of the holes in the fence have been used for decades. (Outside

---

7. *Pollero*—"chicken tender"—is a term for a smuggler of people that is less insulting than '*coyote.*' On a country crossing, the *pollero* will be seen with the people he is guiding following him single-file, like chicks (*pollitos*) following a hen. "*Coyote*" is commonly used to refer to *polleros*, but a *coyote* can be almost anyone who does shady things for money. For example, in the proverb, "The *coyote* must have his bite (*mordida*)," "*coyote*" refers to government officials.

towns and cities, the border fence is usually just a barbed-wire stock fence.) The most-used holes are usually within sight of a port of entry and surveillance from Border Patrol and Customs offices. The U.S. patches the fence now and then, but the holes reopen in a day or two. They're actually advantageous to almost everyone: those who cross regularly soon learn when and how to go through without being caught, and the Border Patrol doesn't have to work so hard at getting its body count. (In the late eighties, cameras mounted on high poles, designed to make twenty-four-hour video recordings, were added in many border cities, but they seem to have made no difference, as far as use of the holes and apprehensions are concerned.)

To be of use to the Border Patrol, a hole must be left open enough of the time so people will continue to use it instead of going farther away where catches are harder and take more time. The Border Patrol baits holes by leaving them untended some of the time, thus assuring continued large catches at other times. Children who live along the Mexican side of the fence make a game of probing the Border Patrol defenses; give one a quarter and he'll ordinarily prefer to spend it on the U.S. side, for the adventure of going across, so Mexican children who live along the fence almost always know when the holes are open and whether the safe times have changed.

Even in areas such as South Texas or El Paso that have checkpoints on all major highways leading away from the border, the Border Patrol almost always leaves a *coyote* run free of road blocks in order to catch trucks and vans that try to take large groups north. These will be round-about routes with mostly local traffic. The trick is to work out a profile that lets you slip through. Use a local car (economy models are best) with clear windows. Move no more than three refugees at a time, always during daylight, accompanied by several passengers who are readily recognizable as Anglos. Blonde is better than brunette; female is better than male; old is better than young.

The Lower Rio Grande Valley between Laredo and Brownsville is by far the easiest place to cross the U.S.–Mexican border. The land is flat, with no natural barriers or surveillance points. Mesquite and salt cedar make a dense jungle on both sides of the river, which snakes back and forth in mile-long bends toward the gulf. Because the river can't be covered, the Border Patrol concentrates on preventing the undocumented from driving north out of the valley, but it's easy to walk in any northerly direction and find good cover and water. One just needs to avoid the roadblocks on U.S. 281 and U.S. 77, near Falfurrias and Sarita, but the highway rest stops immediately south of checkpoints should *not* be used as drop-off points. (Much of this area belongs to the King Ranch, the management of which tries to keep track of what's happening and also cooperates with federal agencies, so don't make unnecessary tracks, especially around stock waters.) The *coyote* run out of the valley is Texas 1017 through Jim Hogg County to San Antonio, which has an intermittent checkpoint immediately north of the junction with 2686. Just south of Hebbronville, a surveillance patrol often positions itself on an embankment from which to look down into passing vehicles.

Since most residents of the Lower Rio Grande Valley are Hispanic, and Spanish is the most common language, streetwise refugees dressed like middle-class North Americans can often walk past the Border Patrol at the Harlingen airport, but they need thorough training about how to act and what to expect. One woman—a model of middle-class North American respectability—breezed right by the Border Patrol at the security gate, but then she decided, seeing that she had to walk about seventy yards to the plane, to carry her luggage on her head.

THE FIRST SANCTUARY ARREST

On February 17, 1984, Stacey Merkt was arrested in Jim Hogg County, along with a nun and a reporter, while accompanying three Salvadoran refugees from McAllen to San Antonio. I flew to the Lower Rio Grande Valley, where several sanctuary workers met for five days to organize a legal defense system for the area's sanctuary volunteers. The experience of being arrested shattered the nun, who had been the driver. She went into seclusion and decided to plea bargain and to be a prosecution witness if called. Since the legal defense of the reporter's right to cover sanctuary was necessarily separate from our defense of sanctuary, we were concerned with assuring legal aid for Stacey and the three refugees, including the bond needed to get the refugees out of detention.

Early in 1983, Stacey had phoned me from Colorado to find out how she could help with sanctuary work, so I'd met her in Mexico City and she began accompanying high-risk refugees to Matamoros, near the mouth of the Rio Grande. When she was arrested for the first and only refugee run she made in the United States, she'd become a full-time volunteer for Casa Oscar Romero, a refugee shelter operated by the Diocese of Brownsville. I'd also done the preliminary counselling in Mexico City for Brenda and Mauricio, who, with Brenda's infant daughter, Bessie, were the Salvadorans detained.

When I'd first met Stacey in Mexico City, I immediately asked how old she was. On the phone she'd impressed me as a highly intelligent woman of mature judgment, but she looked no older than eighteen: small, fragile, un-self-consciously beautiful—one of Fra Angelico's Umbrian angels. Not the kind of person I'd ordinarily choose to lead hunted fugitives through an underground of terror, extortion, betrayal, and rape (the world through which Central American refugees must move in Mexico). She turned out to be about ten years older than she looked—and dependably tough. Only minutes after we met, a Guatemalan woman who was on the edge of hysteria arrived looking for me, accompanied by six frantic young children. They'd been on the road several days and had suffered all the usual extortions, indignities, and deprivations. While I talked with the woman, Stacey talked with the children, using the few words of Spanish she knew. Within minutes, the children became calm and almost joyful. Clearly, Stacey would be able to help, as few of us could.

Brenda really was about nineteen, but she'd already survived much worse. In Mexico City, I'd told her she wouldn't be tortured if captured by the Border Patrol, but I hadn't considered the psychological torture that's routinely used by law enforcement agencies in the United States, which can be as effective as physical pain for extorting statements, confessions, and "voluntary departures." (All torture is, of course, aimed primarily at the psyche.) We learned that the Border Patrol interrogators were threatening that they'd take Bessie away and put her up for adoption as an abandoned child, that Brenda would never see Bessie again if she refused to answer their questions and make a statement, so it came as no surprise when she failed to remain silent until they let her attorney see her, as I'd counselled. She told them she was Mexican and had no connection with sanctuary, thinking that would protect those who assisted her and would keep U.S. Immigration from sending her back to El Salvador. (Within minutes after taking her into custody, they knew perfectly well she was Salvadoran because she matter-of-factly bared a breast to nurse Bessie.)

When I'd seen Bessie in Mexico City, she'd been sick. A doctor said she was also anemic, so they'd remained there several weeks before going on, for Bessie to recover and gain strength, but she remained quite frail. She was probably about eighteen months old, which many of us who worked with refugees had noticed is an age when children will often cease speaking for a year or more—and some may even seem to become autistic—after seeing a parent tortured, raped, or violently "disappeared." We were therefore particularly concerned with what might be happening to Bessie as the Border Patrol used her to pressure information and statements from Brenda. Informed of the urgency, sanctuary congregations in Santa Fe and Seattle quickly raised the high bailbonds that were set for the Salvadorans' release, but the Border Patrol and INS managed to keep them in custody and block adequate legal counsel for several days.[8]

---

8. Soon joined by her husband, Pedro Farela, Brenda became one of the Lower Rio Grande Valley's most active and articulate defenders of Central American refugee rights. Bessie seemed to have no lasting ill-effects from the hardships and terrors of their journey north; she's a remarkably happy child who's usually delighted with the world. After four years of legal proceedings in which the INS rejected their application for political asylum, they came dangerously close to being deported in September 1988, but appeals turned

GOATWALKING

McAllen, Texas
February 20–25 1984

for Good Friday

"*¿Dios mío, Dios mío, por qué me has abandonado?*"

Greed rules.
Murder prevails.
Love dies on the cross.
Another purported messiah has come and gone, and the Creation remains unredeemed.

The cross I admire is a work of art bejewelled with noble fictions. But art will never transmute the agony of real crucifixions, nor can future times undo the breach they tear into eternity.

I first looked carefully at the stations of the cross while waiting on the border for two Salvadoran refugees. My meeting the refugees and my discovery of the church have been simultaneous and intertwined. The human figure in those pictures has the face of people I know.

The figure from long ago could be the lead character in a docudrama about triumph born of defeat. But when the face is real, a person one knows, nothing will make it right. To hear of the grief, the pain, the degradation just wounds the mind and poisons the heart. Art may substitute a therapeutic fantasy. It can never salvage the reality.

YHVH gave Job double what he had lost and replaced his first daughters with three who were the most beautiful in the land.

---

the decision around and they were granted safe haven in the United States.

Since 1982, sanctuary providers and nonprofit legal-aid programs have been quite successful in preventing the return of high-risk refugees such as Brenda and Bessie. The strategy has been to bail them out of detention (when necessary), exhaust all appeals (which usually takes three or four years), and then, for the vast majority who are denied political asylum in the United States, find safe haven in one of the countries, such as Canada, that comply with the requirements of international refugee law.

That's how to set things right in the storyteller's land of Uz. But in our world it is Pedro and Olivia forced to watch as the National Guard rapes their three daughters and then takes two away to be tortured to death. In our world Job wanders the garbage dumps of El Salvador, searching for pieces of his daughters. Could even YHVH now still the screams of silence when Job's eyes meet those of his wife or of the surviving daughter?

Greed rules.

Murder prevails.

Faith rooted in belief dies on the cross.

Is the agony justified if it serves to end the rule of greed and redeem future times? Then give us Barabbas, the liberator who knows the beneficial uses of human sacrifice. Sweet, suffering Jesus teaches Sunday school classes the highest ideals, but in this world of last resorts violence is society's underlying bedrock. When easier answers are stripped away, even the church calls for Barabbas.

Rejoice at the fall of El Paraíso![9] The fifteen-year-old boy soldier whose sex education was torture sessions now lies like a limp doll where the mortar round threw him. What can sweet Jesus do for Pedro and Olivia to match Barabbas' heroic service? Outside Sunday school, everyone has always known that the Christ is a warrior in the line of David who is willing to sacrifice more than self to redeem his people. The crowd knows his name and chooses him.

Consider old Comandante Barabbas, who, having murdered even his closest *compañera* for the future's sake, comes to the time when liberation finally requires that he turn his pistol against himself.[10] He is truly hope's martyr, giving all he meets—his entire present—for the sake of the time to come. The trouble with Jesus

---

9. El Paraíso—"Paradise"—is a stronghold of the Salvadoran armed forces that, during the eighties, fell twice to guerrilla forces.

10. In April 1983, the leading guerrilla comandante in El Salvador, Cayetano Carpio, ordered the murder of his second-in-command and very close friend, Comandante Melida Anaya Montes, because she advocated a strategy opposed to his. He tried to disguise the murder as a CIA operation, but his responsibility was uncovered, so he "executed" himself.

is that he calls for the hallowing of this every meeting with merciful service rather than sacrifice, insisting redemption must be now as well as future. The trouble with Jesus is that he refuses to sacrifice enough to make room for hope.

Murder prevails.

Faith rooted in hope dies on the cross.

Is this, then, the image of God? —Despised, in final agonies, stripped of all but loyalty to the creative task, that even this may be the fulfilled present on which the whole earth and all time turns.

THE TUCSON PASSOVER

On April 13, 1984, Jack Elder was arrested in San Benito, Texas, and charged with transporting three Salvadorans from Casa Oscar Romero to the local bus station. As director of Casa Romero, Jack routinely gave Central American refugees rides to the local bus station, hospitals, and churches, regardless of their documentation—as openly and routinely as employers throughout the area gave rides to their undocumented employees. The refugee aid program of the Brownsville Diocese was clearly the real target, so sanctuary workers in Tucson immediately began consulting with refugees and alerting volunteers to the possibility that this could be the beginning of a nationwide crackdown on sanctuary.

We were particularly concerned about a special Freedom Seder for refugees that had been scheduled for April 18. To attend the seder, refugees would go to Southside Presbyterian Church to meet volunteers who would then take them to Temple Emanu-El (Tucson's Reform synagogue). For the three counts of "transporting," Jack would face a maximum sentence of five years per count. If this was the beginning of a crackdown, everyone who helped refugees reach the seder would risk facing the same counts for each undocumented refugee given a ride.

Canceling the seder would have taken sanctuary underground, which would have been the same as declaring its end; sanctuary that isn't open and aboveground ceases to be sanctuary. We had only five days to prepare, but by telephone and at Sunday worship services we explained the risk and invited refugees and volunteers to go to the seder anyway. Assembling at Southside, we would plan for a nonviolent protective response in the event federal officials tried to detain the refugees, then form into a caravan to go to Temple Emanu-El.

If only a few sanctuary volunteers came, those who did would presumably be much more vulnerable than if, say, as many as sixty came. At 5:00 on the evening of the seder, the time when supporters had been asked to begin assembling, only four or five refugees arrived. By 5:15, we were still less than a dozen, mostly refugees. Then, about 5:20, others began arriving, and more kept coming until there was no longer room inside and new arrivals crowded around the doors and windows. Soon, traffic jammed the surrounding streets. More than seventy Salvadorans and Guatemalans came, and the caravan that took them to Temple Emanu-El was two miles long.

From that day there would be no further question that refugees would find protection within the community and that efforts by the government to crush the practice of sanctuary would, instead, stimulate its growth. Since then, the Freedom Seder has become a holy day in the Tucson sanctuary congregations' liturgical year, a formal assembly and communion to renew the sanctuary covenant that gathers us into a people of peoples. It is a remembrance of Passover that weaves the present experience of refugees and sanctuary congregations into an awareness of more than three millennia of exile, oppression, and liberation. In the Arizona-Sonoran borderlands where the First and Third Worlds meet, sanctuary for Central American refugees is—in a limited but decisively practical way—weaving Isaiah's prophecy of the gathering of peoples into history, as a fulfillment. Whatever else this gathering of peoples may be or become, as a communion it *is* sanctuary for the violated.

9

Weaving Sanctuary into the Social Fabric

> My house shall be called a house of prayer for all peoples.
> Thus says the LORD, who gathers the outcasts of Israel,
> I will gather yet others to him besides those already gathered.
>
> —Isaiah 56:7–8

THE BIBLICAL MATRIX OF THE BASIC PROPHETIC COMMUNITY

TAKING THE BIBLE AS an *unquestionable* source of guidance for present choices misconstrues the way it works. Only as a free agent that takes full responsibility for its decisions and agreements can a covenant community (or its members) practice the prophetic faith. Biblical guidance is necessarily open to the unrepeatably unique place in time and space that conditions every decision by a responsible agent.

Above the imprimatur for the *Latinoamerica* translation of the Bible, we are advised that to receive the Bible's teaching we must seek together with our brothers and sisters, participating in a Christian community. Congregational study is the way Torah is clarified and vitalized because Torah is addressed to the community and must be heard and done by the community. When this process is relegated to the select few or to private hours, the most liberating teaching becomes an instrument of domination and alienation. But the seeking community need not be composed exclusively of those who follow Jesus. Nor can a church that is truly catholic exclude unbelievers. This may be of limited practical relevance for most Latin American *comunidades de base*, but it is crucial to the growth of similar communities in Anglo America. Helder Camara's invitation to "Abrahamic minorities" opens the way:

> Jews, Christians and Muslims know the story of the father of believers . . . Will those who are not Jews or Christians or Muslims allow us to give Abraham's name to those minorities who are called to serve? Of course other races and religions can use an equivalent name, which is more appropriate to their tradition. And you, my brothers and sisters who are atheistic humanists, don't think you have been forgotten. Translate what I say in my language into your language. When I talk of God, translate, perhaps, by "nature," "evolution," what you will. If you feel in you the desire to use the qualities you have, if you think selfishness is narrow and choking, if you hunger for truth, justice, and love, you can and should go with us.[1]

In a concrete, historical sense, when I joined the church through membership in my Quaker meeting, I became a Christian. That's the kind of Jew I am, the kind Paul grafted onto Israel as church. I choose to do without Paul's theological splints, just as Quakers do without ritual and ceremonial splints such as baptism, liturgy, and the Eucharist. Where the graft has taken, churches resemble the Palestinian congregations that had James as their rabbi: Already Jewish, they needed no theological splints to become that kind of Jew—just a willingness to follow the way of fulfilling the law and the prophets that has been opened by the cross.

To find guidance from the Bible, I first had to learn how to wrestle and argue with it. To take it seriously enough to wrestle with it, I also had to learn to honor it, listening attentively to what its ancient voices actually say in their own way. The faithful must

---

1. Helder Camara, *The Desert is Fertile* (Maryknoll, New York: Orbis Books, 1974) 13–14. Helder Camara is the retired bishop of Recife.

argue for justice, as Abraham and Job did, even against God Himself. It's certainly no breach of the prophetic faith to argue with the Bible, wherever it promotes what we see as injustice. Rather, anyone who fails to argue with the Bible on behalf of the covenant isn't taking the Bible seriously. "It is not in heaven, that you should say, 'Who will go up for us to heaven, and bring it to us, that we may hear and do it?' Neither is it beyond the sea, that you should say, 'Who will go over the sea for us, and bring it to us, that we may hear and do it?' But the word is very near you; it is in your mouth and in your heart, so that you can do it" (Dt 30:12–14).

THE PROPHETIC FAITH AND POLITICAL SOLIDARITY

By 1984, the relation of sanctuary to the politics of revolutionary solidarity had become *the* issue dividing the sanctuary network. The Chicago Religious Task Force on Central America (CRTF) led the effort to politicize sanctuary. Specifically, the CRTF wanted to exclude refugees from the sanctuary network if they chose not to speak out, if they had the "wrong" political outlook, or if they were of the wrong nationality. (For example, from this perspective Nicaraguan conscientious objectors who were fleeing conscription by the Sandinistas had the wrong politics and nationality.) The CRTF also wanted to mobilize sanctuary along majoritarian centralist lines, to become the infrastructure for mass political jujitsu.

No more than one in twenty of the Salvadoran and Guatemalan refugees in need of safe haven wanted to go public, so the politicized version of sanctuary would have been highly selective, even among refugees who had the "right" politics and nationality. There was no way that sanctuary on the border could have been politicized in this way, even if we'd wanted to do so. On the border, arriving refugees set the agenda; only in the hinterlands could congregations conceive of mail-ordering a refugee according to politicized criteria.

As far as organization under a national management was concerned, virtually none of the sanctuary congregations would delegate decision-making about faith and practice. Most Quakers reject centralized managerial decision-making on principle. Most Catholics think one pope is enough.

Federal officials were also eager to promote the politicized understanding of sanctuary, since they knew the movement would then quickly self-destruct. There probably weren't ten congregations in the whole country that would prune their advocacy of human rights to fit the strategies of revolutionary warfare, but many thousands did want to respond charitably to refugees while conscientiously evading the prophetic side of sanctuary, which entails a public stand by the congregation that empowers refugees to speak truth to power. (Anyone who doesn't struggle to evade the prophetic side of covenant faithfulness isn't entirely sane. All genuine prophecy is disreputable, breaks ranks and undermines in-group solidarity, alienates friends, and jeopardizes family.)

In September, I traveled to a number of regional sanctuary meetings in order to share a discussion piece that presented "a view from the border" that corrected the politicized misconstruction of our practice of sanctuary, the first four paragraphs of which were adopted by the Tucson Ecumenical Council's Task Force on Central America and then circulated throughout the sanctuary network as its policy position:

A View from the Border

There is no sanctuary movement apart from the covenant peoples that the Christians among us customarily call "the church." Churches and synagogues must decide whether they will adhere to the prophetic faith they proclaim, not whether they will become members of still another ecumenical organization. As Bishop Lona of Tehuantepec puts it with reference to Latin America's base communities, this is not a movement within the church; rather, it is the church on the move.

The covenant to become a people that hallows the earth has always entailed that the beneficiaries of oppression relinquish their allegiance to wealth, privilege, and domination, taking their stand with the poor and persecuted in the face of established oppression. Sanctuary for Central American retugees happens to be the most prominent way this covenant requirement presents itself to congregations in the United States at this point in our history. Whenever a congregation considers becoming a sanctuary for the persecuted, Israel stands at Sinai, deciding to be Israel; having heard the cock crow, the church is now deciding to be the church. Functionally, providing sanctuary is the congregational analogue of the baptism of individual Christians: an initiating act of incorporation into the covenant peoples.

This view contrasts fundamentally with the interpretation that would convert the growing network of sanctuary congregations into a mass movement that is defined by its political objectives and distinguished by its religious identity. The sanctuary covenant community that has formed in Tucson could never assimilate into such a movement because we provide sanctuary for the persecuted regardless of the political origins of their persecution or of their usefulness in promoting preconceived objectives. We are convinced that whenever the covenant community's decision to stand with the oppressed is understood to mean it must place itself in subordinative alignment with any creed, ideology, hierarchy, platform, armed force, or party, its prophetic role is betrayed and its reconciling role is abandoned. We disagree with any interpretation of sanctuary that would shape it selectively into a factional instrument.

The poor and persecuted we meet are living human beings, not an abstracted class that includes only those of the poor and persecuted who fit partisan criteria. Our personal and community ties to the peoples of Central America originate in and are vitalized by our meeting and knowing Central American refugees; we could not now restrict our response according to the refugees' usefulness in promoting a set of objectives. There is, nonetheless, plenty of room within the sanctuary network for faith communities that place factional restrictions on their participation. Our disagreement is with those who would exclude us from the sanctuary network, not with the inclusion within the network of those for whom sanctuary is shaped by religious or political objectives.

WEAVING SANCTUARY INTO THE SOCIAL FABRIC

The contrast between our view from the border and the view that would convert the network of sanctuary communities into a movement defined by its objectives is rooted in the difference between two kinds of faith . . . There is a faith that is primarily belief. This kind of faith calls for definitive doctrines from which guiding objectives and priorities can be derived. And there is a faith that is primarily trust. This kind of faith expects to be guided by a unifying presence that enlivens each moment, breaks all borders, gathers us into communion with one another, and addresses us in all we meet. . . .

Instead of responding to arriving refugees according to their needs, we might restrict our response in ways that would make us refugee medics—for the U.S. government or for Salvadoran and Guatemalan armed revolutionary movements. We might also limit our response in ways that would take the refugees' presence solely as the occasion for organizing media happenings directed against U.S. intervention in Central America. All of these responses would have a bearing of one kind or another on the U.S. government's policies; none is apolitical. Our experience indicates that a full-dimensional involvement with the refugees does far more to build a community base for action and to oppose U.S. intervention in Central America than would programs that focus solely on political objectives such as extended voluntary departure status for Central Americans and opposition to intervention. When mistaken for the position of the sanctuary network, such limitations only damage our credibility. . . .

Two incidents during the summer of 1984 underlined the immediate need to distinguish covenant-based sanctuary from goal-directed sanctuary: After a meeting in Tucson in June concerning legal defense strategies, at which everyone except representatives of the CRTF agreed that sanctuary should be practiced and defended as civil initiative rather than civil disobedience, the CRTF published an issue of their magazine (*BASTA!*) that made it appear that sanctuary providers favored Alinsky-style civil disobedience. To make it seem that even I now favored the CRTF approach, they pruned the following clause out of a carelessly constructed sentence I'd written: "Law-abiding protest merely trains us to live with atrocity."[2] Then, in Washington, D.C., Philadelphia, New York, and Chicago, a series of closed meetings took place among a handful of self-selected leaders of the "National Sanctuary Movement" (most of whom were actually representatives of prorevolutionary political-solidarity organizations), at which it was decided that the sanctuary movement's campaign of civil disobedience would be launched in San Diego, targeting the Catholic bishop with demonstrations and sit-ins. The spokesperson for sanctuary activities in San Diego, Sister Louise MacDonald, was horrified when she learned of their plans, writing the CRTF that the proposed "National Sanctuary Action" had no support among local sanctuary volunteers and that it would wreck sanctuary in San Diego. Receiving no reply, she called the CRTF and was informed that the matter had already been irrevocably decided on the national level.

When Tucson sanctuary groups heard about it and weighed-in with Sister Louise, the NSM organizers modified their plans; instead of sitting-in at the diocesan offices they would climb over the fence at Camp Pendleton, recruiting participants primarily from political-solidarity groups in Los Angeles. As a media happening, it turned out to be an inconsequential fizzle, but the dam-

---

2. In my NCCC statement, I'd emphasized that, "with people in our midst being hunted down and shipped back, denouncing the terror while ignoring the victims simply teaches the public to live with atrocity." Speaking at Austin, in October, 1982, I carelessly rephrased this point: "When the government itself sponsors the torture of entire peoples and then makes it a felony to shelter those seeking refuge, law-abiding protest merely trains us to live with atrocity." My point was that people should help refugees rather than engage in merely symbolic reactions, which would also have ruled out the kind of media-oriented civil disobedience favored by the CRTF; but, when the first clause was deleted, it gave the CRTF the categorical assertion it wanted, to cite me as a supporter of their revolutionary opposition to the legal system. Numerous INS, Justice, and State Department memos and public statements about the sanctuary movement then made this the government's favorite quotation from me; it was exactly the kind of polarizing concession from sanctuary providers that federal officials wanted at the time, that we rather than they were the ones breaking the law.

age to our credibility was much worse than any of us anticipated. In spite of a close friendship with the archbishop of Hermosillo, the archbishop of Tijuana would later prevent the college of Mexican bishops from supporting the refugee aid of Father Quiñones and the Archdiocese of Hermosillo, on the ground that it was entangled with the U.S. "National Sanctuary Movement," which the Tijuana archbishop said was dominated and directed by Marxist organizations that were more concerned with winning revolutionary wars in Central America than with the protection of human rights.

After the two kinds of sanctuary went their separate ways in 1984, efforts to politicize the covenant-based, congregational practice of sanctuary that prevails in the borderlands have been chronic but inept. Because we've kept the differences between covenant-based and politicized sanctuary out in the open since 1984, politicized sanctuary has been more of a nuisance than a serious threat to our efforts to weave sanctuary into the social fabric. Most sanctuary congregations now know that politicized sanctuary would be no more than a mirror-image of the U.S. government's violations of refugee rights.

ORDEAL BY INANITION: THE ARIZONA SANCTUARY TRIAL

Federal officials were preparing a much more concerted attack on covenant-based sanctuary during these same months, code-named "Operation Sojourner." On January 14, 1985, indictments were served on fourteen sanctuary volunteers and two Salvadoran refugees, initiating what came to be known as the Arizona sanctuary trial. After the government dropped charges against two nuns (Sisters Ana Priester and Mary Waddell), and the two refugees and one of the volunteers plea bargained, eleven of us stood trial: two Catholic priests (Fathers Dagoberto Quiñones and Tony Clark), a nun assigned by her order to aid refugees in Phoenix (Sister Darlene Nicgorski), a Presbyterian minister (John Fife), the United Methodist Border Ministries missioner in Arizona (Peggy Hutchison), the director of religious education for Sacred Heart Parish in Nogales, Arizona (Mary K. Espinosa), the director of the Tucson Ecumenical Council's refugee services (Phil Willis-Conger), a Unitarian volunteer in Phoenix (Wendy LeWin), a lay worker for the Santuario Guadalupano in Nogales, Mexico (Socorro de Aguilar), and two Quaker volunteers (Nena MacDonald and me). Nationwide, more than forty nuns, members of the clergy, and lay workers were named as unindicted coconspirators.[3]

Federal officials deliberately packaged the Arizona sanctuary trial as a contest between church and state. Initially, the INS had launched "Operation Sojourner,"[4] in response to pressure by Senator Barry Goldwater, who was outraged that "60 Minutes," *People* magazine, *USA Today*, and numerous documentaries, newspaper series, and TV news reports were covering my border crossings, with no apparent intervention or deterrence by the government. The initial objective was to catch, convict, and jail me and John Fife, but then the investigators discovered sanctuary really had become a nationwide activity of churches, religious orders, meetings, and synagogues.

The government strategy shifted, to target the church. Yet, the trial was most noteworthy for its irrelevance to the church-state issues that sanctuary raised. With the indictments, the prosecutor, Don Reno, included motions to rule out any mention before the jury of refugees or refugee law, other international law or human rights issues, events in Central America that were causing people to seek refuge, INS and Border Patrol violations of refugee rights, and sanctuary as a faith-mandated religious practice. The case was to be presented to the jury as a simple conspiracy to smuggle aliens, unrelated to any other considerations—which would have been a workable tactic for targeting and jailing two individuals but just

---

3. For the behind-the-scenes details concerning government strategizing in the Arizona sanctuary trial, see Ann Crittenden, *Sanctuary: A Story of American Conscience and the Law in Collision* (New York: Weidenfeld & Nicolson, 1988). For a detailed report on the trial, see also Miriam Davidson, *Convictions of the Heart: Jim Corbett and the Sanctuary Movement* (Tucson: University of Arizona Press, 1988).

4. The INS name for its Arizona operation to infiltrate sanctuary was inspired by the recurrent biblical commandment to protect the widow, orphan, and sojourner—which can also be translated "foreigner" or "alien."

made the trial a pointless sideshow when the church itself was selected as the government's target.

The federal district judge, Earl Carroll, outdid the prosecution, framing his rulings to strengthen the government motions. The prosecutor then found himself obliged to object to the jury's hearing the tape recordings made by government infiltrators (which was to have been the core of the government's evidence), since the tapes revealed what had actually been happening. The trial began in October 1985. The prosecution rested on March 7, 1986. The defense rested on March 14 without presenting any testimony, precluded by the judge's rulings from making a relevant defense.

Don Reno later explained that the government's primary objective was deterrence, that by targeting so many church people federal officials expected to discourage the further growth of sanctuary. He may have realized he'd miscalculated the church reaction when, shortly after the indictments were served, he moved to drop charges against Sisters Ana Priester and Mary Waddell; they told their lawyers to argue against it because they wanted to go to trial with the rest of us. Instead of acting as a deterrent, the indictments and trial elicited an outpouring of support for sanctuary and the defendants, in Europe and Latin America as well as nationwide. Volunteers sponsored by mainline denominations, religious orders, and many congregations poured into Tucson to assure that all aspects of our aid to refugees would continue. Donations for legal aid exceeded the $1.2 million defense costs by more than $200,000. Congregational declarations of sanctuary multiplied, joined by many colleges and universities, over twenty cities, and the state of New Mexico. Even denominations that had been unconcerned about the refugees' plight were outraged to learn that the government had sent informers into worship, Bible study, and confessional gatherings.

They were even more outraged as the details became known. The infiltrators the INS selected for Operation Sojourner were two petty criminals who sold information by the item; one of whom continued to supplement his income as an informer by pimping; the other, by gun-running. The INS case agent's first field work on Operation Sojourner was in response to a complaint by *coyotes* that the churches were hurting their business. Accompanied by the pimp, the case agent had a conference with the complaining *coyotes* in Hermosillo's Hotel Sonora, notorious as *the* place in Northern Mexico where organized white slavers forced Central American women into prostitution. "You can't get choir boys to do this sort of thing," Prosecutor Reno explained the choice of informers when even Judge Carroll expressed concern, but in Dallas an FBI officer devised a plan for using nuns, by having one of his infiltrators try to seduce them on camera. (The shocked informer, Frank Varelli, refused to consider the possibility and later exposed the operation.) Throughout 1985 and 1986, a nationwide rash of church break-ins and vandalism was symptomatic of the government's practice of contracting out much of the field work for its investigations to petty criminals.

No one involved in providing sanctuary thought the government could intimidate the church into ceasing to protect first-asylum refugees, but everyone could see that we had to reach some shared understandings about sanctuary principles and procedures, particularly with regard to secrecy, partisanship, and communications. Our position in Tucson continued to be that the church isn't and can't be a secret society, that its protection of human rights can't be politicized into a mirror image of government violations, and that networking had to be open, horizontal, and consultative rather than closed, hierarchical, and managerial. Our emphasis was that the time had come to assure that sanctuary would continue as a firmly rooted institution within our society, regardless of the nationality or politics of anyone who needed protection from human rights violations, and that the only way for sanctuary to become an established institution is by the aboveground, societal practice of our covenant to protect the violated—unpoliticized and unpolarized.

Although the indictments stimulated rather than deterred support for sanctuary, the government's use of infiltrators and its bugging of meetings and phone conversations was effectively poisonous. In many sanctuary churches across the country, congregants even expressed fears of using the telephone or church facilities to discuss personal problems. Many sanctuary congregations wanted to develop screening and security procedures for identifying spies, coding communications, and securing phones and facilities from government bugging, which would have turned sanctuary into a kind of secret society within the church—and the sanctuary church into the kind of conspiratorial organization the government said it was. The antidote was obvious: flood the government with more information than it wanted and prepare to jam the courts with sanctuary cases.

Those of us who had been indicted were in the crucial position for setting the standard. To the dismay of our attorneys, the eight of us who were arraigned in Tucson therefore used our arraignment (on January 21, the first full day of the Tucson Sanctuary Symposium)[5] to take our stand for openness, at the risk of having our release on our own recognizance canceled. In the Federal Courthouse entryway immediately after arraignment, I read our statement to the reporters and supporters who crowded the street:

> . . . As active members of our faith communities, we intend to continue to engage in sanctuary ministry, but we have signed our release agreements under the conviction that our faith *is* consistent with the laws of our country. Nothing we have signed at our arraignment is to be construed as an agreement to apostatize. . . .
>
> After the Second World War, our government committed itself by law never again to expel or return refugees to any country where they would face persecution. At Nuremberg and Geneva, our government also established that everyone has both the right to protect refugees and the duty to obstruct the commission of state crimes. Consequently, providing sanctuary for refugees is not an act of civil disobedience. Rather, the need to provide sanctuary for refugees demonstrates that,

---

5. A sanctuary symposium and consultation had been scheduled in Tucson for January 20–26. See Gary MacEoin, ed., *Sanctuary: A Resource Guide for Understanding and Participating in the Central American Refugees' Struggle* (San Francisco: Harper & Row, 1985), for the proceedings of the Tucson sanctuary symposium.

in its violations of human rights both here and abroad, the present administration lacks legitimacy.[6]

KEEPING AGREEMENTS AND MAKING LAW

Initially, members of faith communities in the United States and Mexico simply took it for granted that they could count on one another to protect refugees whose right to safe haven was violated by government officials. Sanctuary for the persecuted was tacitly understood to be part of what it means for the church to be the church, and coworkers usually knew each other well enough to need no formal agreements that stated how they could count on one another. Then, as an explicit declaration, sanctuary was the foundation for networking among congregations that had only distant or indirect contact with one another. And then, as needs multiplied for us to interact with unknown congregations, to assimilate new volunteers, and to engage the administrative, legislative, and adjudicative activities of government, our practice of sanctuary had to be stated as principles and procedures to which participants formally agreed.

Before the Arizona sanctuary trial, we issued policy statements such as "A View from the Border," but we tried to make-do without explicit principles and procedures. Requiring that sanctuary volunteers understand and agree to abide by a written contract before we would work with them seemed dangerously close to the formulation of a creed. But after the indictments we could no longer put off the formulation of explicit understandings. For example, if we failed to be explicit about the agreement that no sanctuary volunteer would plea-bargain, some of the many newcomers would do so, and then everyone would feel betrayed—those who plea-bargained, because we'd failed to let them know we expected them to choose trial rather than concede any violation of law; those who

---

6. This paragraph came from a statement signed by 143 of those who accompanied refugees to the Tucson Freedom Seder April 18, 1984.

stood trial, because the integrity of their stand in support of human rights had been compromised.

Close friends know implicitly how they can depend on one another, but trust among casual acquaintances is impossible if they don't know explicitly what agreements they are trusting one another to uphold. Suddenly, newcomers constituted more than half of the Tucson refugee support group, with more volunteers turning up at most of our weekly meetings, so in addition to considering case reports from counselors, reviewing border geography, and making the plans for the week's crossings, our meetings during the trial were concerned with reaching consensus on principles and procedures, which evolved into a seven-point agreement required of each participant:

Seven Principles and Procedures that Guide
the Sanctuary Practices of the
Tucson Ecumenical Council's Task Force
on Central America and the
Tucson refugee support group (Trsg)

[New volunteers are asked to agree to these principles and procedures before joining in the sanctuary work of the Tucson refugee support group.]

1. Only persons who are fleeing persecution or life-threatening conditions of armed violence and who cannot safely remain in Mexico are helped by the Tucson refugee support group to cross the borderlands, but social and legal services are provided for arriving Central Americans by the Tucson Ecumenical Council Task Force on Central America, regardless of documentation or refugee status.
2. All refugees who need sanctuary services are helped, regardless of their political alignment or nationality. None is pressured to go to publicly declared sanctuaries or to speak

out. All are informed of available options, provided with legal counsel, and allowed to choose their course.
3. The INS district director is informed by mail whenever Trsg helps refugees cross the borderlands. The nationality, age, and sex of refugees is provided, but not the name.
4. Trsg will neither buy help from *coyotes* nor link its sanctuary services to individuals or organizations that smuggle or hide undocumented refugees for financial or political profit.
5. In the event that Trsg volunteers are indicted for helping refugees, they agree to do no plea bargaining and to insist on a jury trial.
6. Volunteers agree to refuse to testify if called before a grand jury. (Refugees need to trust counselors; Mexican coworkers need anonymity; we would therefore betray our sanctuary ministry by secretly testifying about these matters to the very officials that are violating refugees' rights to safe haven and volunteers' rights to protect refugees. Also, we are open and ready to stand trial to establish the lawfulness of our activities, and our sanctuary procedures and activities are published and available, so calling sanctuary volunteers before a grand jury to betray refugees and coworkers would just be a political device to imprison subpoenaed sanctuary volunteers without trial.)
7. As changing circumstances require new adaptations, the evolution of Trsg/TEC sanctuary services is guided by principles of civil initiative, protecting human rights within rather than outside the law. (If federal officials continue to violate refugees' right to safe haven, the INS must now either validate sanctuary by failing to challenge our open practice or else put the church on trial until the courts finally rule that, as civil initiative, sanctuary is lawful. In any case, the sanctuary church will outlast presidential administrations and partisan judges.)

Many of us also sought agreement that sanctuary volunteers would henceforth depend on government-paid, pro bono, or pro se legal aid—that all donations for sanctuary legal aid would be used for the defense of refugees rather than sanctuary workers. We failed to reach consensus on this point, largely because several volunteers who were ready to risk imprisonment weren't ready to risk losing their homes to pay legal fees. We did agree that the choice would remain open, regardless of defense strategies, and that those who did choose to hire attorneys and solicit donations would see to it that the separation would be clear to donors. In light of the rulings by Judge Carroll that make a relevant defense impossible, a pro se defense may turn out to be the best way for future sanctuary defendants to make themselves known to a jury, at least in the Ninth Circuit where Judge Carroll's rulings have all been upheld (by a panel of Reagan appointees).[7] Fortunately, the government has given us no occasion to test our ability to mix self-representation (pro se) with a professional defense.

THE MERKT RULING: ESTABLISHING A PRACTICABLE DEFENSE

The Trsg requirement that the INS district director be notified whenever refugees are assisted to cross the borderlands is closely related to the Fifth Circuit Court's reversal of the 1984 conviction of Stacey Merkt for transporting: "By definition, a person intending to assist an alien in obtaining legal status is not acting 'in furtherance of' the alien's illegal presence in this country."[8] The consideration in this case was that affirmative filing for political asylum was permitted by the San Antonio INS office; applicants who voluntarily came in to apply for political asylum would be released on their own recognizance during the adjudicative process; but any Salvadoran or Guatemalan who filed in the Brownsville area would be imprisoned. According to the Merkt ruling, transporting undocumented people to San Antonio to file for political asylum would be lawful.

Notification of the INS keeps our sanctuary aid both fully en-

---

7. *United States v. Aguilar*, 871 F.2d 1436 (9th Cir. 1989).
8. United States v. Merkt, 764 F.2d 266 (5th Cir., 18 June 1985).

gaged and honestly accountable. In Phoenix on May 15, 1985, Pat and I went to lunch with Ruth Anne Myers, the INS district director for Arizona, and Mark Turner, a reporter for the *Arizona Daily Star*. In the course of our discussions, Ruth Anne Myers agreed that the INS would detain no affirmative asylum applicants in Arizona. To apply affirmatively, they would have to go to the INS office in Tucson or Phoenix,[9] since asylum applications at ports of entry on the border are under the direct control of officials in Washington, D.C.

That August, Trsg learned of two Salvadoran refugees making their way north to the border who wanted to apply for political asylum and to speak out when they reached the United States, which meant we had the case we needed to put both the Merkt ruling and the affirmative filing policy to the test. I met the refugees at the border fence, and at about the same time Bates Butler, one of the sanctuary defense team (and U.S. attorney for Arizona under President Carter), called Ruth Anne Myers to inform her that I was bringing them through to Tucson to file for political asylum. Because I'd become an irritating embarrassment to the Border Patrol (who were often kidded and sometimes berated for their failure to catch me when I brought refugees through), I thought they might make a concerted effort to intercept us, so I took the refugees on a three-day walk north through the New Mexican side of the Peloncillo Mountains, which had been Geronimo's favorite place for hide-and-seek with the U.S. cavalry and Mexican *rurales*—rough country where there was little risk of being seen and where pursuers could only run us to ground with well-trained bloodhounds. An NBC camera crew accompanied us from the border fence through the mountains, and our journey was later reported on network news. The refugees also held a news conference shortly after arriving in Tucson.

This was exactly the kind of crossing that had Barry Goldwater calling for my head and Border Patrol officers eager to take it as a trophy. What was the point of shaking a red cape at federal

---

9. For details, see Mark Turner, "Defendant, INS Officer Break Bread Together," *The Arizona Daily Star*, 28 May 1985.

officials? We wanted to leave no room for doubt that this kind of civil initiative to help refugees is lawful, as the Fifth Circuit Court had ruled. If not, the prosecutor had no need to seek an indictment or prove his case. He could just ask the judge to cancel my release pending trial. If he thought my helping the refugees was illegal, that was also what his oath of office required. The prosecutor raised an objection to my publication of an op-ed piece in the Sunday paper, but no one made any public objection to my bringing the refugees through the borderlands.

On February 2, 1986, in the midst of the trial, five Trsg volunteers with seven Salvadoran refugees were intercepted and arrested by the Border Patrol while driving to Tucson. The volunteers carried copies of a letter I'd sent to Ruth Anne Myers that morning, which explained that we were aiding the refugees in compliance with the Fifth Circuit ruling. The refugees were trying to get through to Canada, where they were assured safe haven. The letter included the Trsg procedural guidelines for sanctuary assistance, with the following comment:

> The sanctuary trial complicates efforts to refine our sanctuary procedures and reach accommodations with the INS, but we do feel that a sequence of trials will result in our establishing the full legality of our sanctuary services. If the INS would like to test specific issues by initiating further jury trials, we might be able to volunteer the documentation and defendants you want, so please don't hesitate to let us know what you need for any projected future indictments. We do believe that we should be ready to put our practice of sanctuary before trial juries as often as may be necessary, but we would prefer to find less costly and time-consuming ways to resolve the church-state issues involved.[10]

The sanctuary volunteers who had been arrested were released without charges. Nor were charges brought when volunteers were

---

10. Letter, 2 February 1986, available in *Some Sanctuary Papers, 1981–86*, Trsg, Tucson, 193–196.

once again intercepted on June 15, 1987. Nor when another interception occurred on October 4, 1988. In each case, the driver carried a copy of the notification letter that had been sent to the INS district director, which stated that the refugees were being helped "to reach legal counsel in order to determine the best way for them to establish legal status in the United States." In each case, the Border Patrol officers who made the arrests were also quite angry when they received orders to release the arrested sanctuary volunteers. At higher levels, federal officials clearly had no desire to put the Merkt ruling to the test or to try to stop sanctuary with more trials. Every week or two during and after the trial, we were sending what had become a form letter to notify the INS of refugees the Tucson refugee support group assisted to reach Tucson.

On May 1, 1986, the jury for the Arizona sanctuary trial convicted eight of us and acquitted three. With Mary K. Espinosa and Nena MacDonald, I was acquitted. Whatever the jury's reasoning, I'd undoubtedly benefited from the prosecutor's inability to use any of the many videos, photos, and written reports about my activities without a high risk that the jury would realize what the trial was actually about. Judge Carroll made a sour face when he first glanced at the sheet on which the jury had written its verdict in my case, then managed to recover his professional poker-face as he read it. INS Western Regional Commissioner Harold Ezell was less restrained when asked for a statement: "The son-of-a-gun who started the whole thing got off scot-free. He ought to be behind bars."[11]

As it turned out, none of the defendants was jailed. Instead, they were put on probation. The judge wanted them to end their involvement in sanctuary activities, as a condition of probation, but they refused because the sanctuary covenant continued to be integral to the practice of their faith. They would just agree to cease bringing refugees through the borderlands, giving them rides, and helping to plan or coordinate crossings. John Fife explained that

---

11. Ann Crittenden, *Sanctuary: a Story of American Conscience and the Law in Collision* (New York: Weidenfeld & Nicolson, 1988), 325.

his congregation would continue to be a sanctuary church, that the judge's condition would mean leaving his pastorate, and that the only way the judge could force him out would be to jail him. Sister Darlene explained that her order, the School Sisters of St. Francis, is a sanctuary order, that the judge's condition would mean breaking her vows and leaving her order. The church-state issues this would raise were too sticky, even for Judge Carroll. He dropped the condition.[12]

Since then, there has been no further challenge by federal officials to our practice of sanctuary in Tucson. The Border Patrol has agreed not to pursue suspected "aliens" into a place of worship; up to fifty newly arrived first-asylum refugees commonly receive sanctuary in John Fife's church on any given night; and there have been several incidents when hot pursuit has ended in the kind of old-fashioned sanctuary that was common during the Middle Ages. In 1988, for example, Catholic Workers (joined by John and Father Ricardo) stood in the door of Casa Maria, the Catholic Worker soup kitchen, when Border Patrol officers wanted to go in after several men who had taken refuge there. Learning that mass was regularly celebrated at Casa Maria, the officers withdrew—as TV news teams recorded the incident.

---

12. Although John Fife, Sister Darlene Nicgorski, and Peggy Hutchison went on nationwide speaking tours for sanctuary and John and Peggy went to Europe to consult with church groups that began establishing sanctuary there (three times, in John's case), federal officials were surprisingly adept at falsifying history to project the image they wanted. Numerous accounts were soon published by highly credible sources that reported all of us had been convicted and had agreed to end our involvement in sanctuary. Here's a typical illustration:

"In May 1986 the remaining sanctuary defendants at the Tucson trial were each convicted on at least one count; they were given suspended sentences and paroled once the defendants agreed not to participate or publicly identify themselves with the sanctuary movement during their period of parole."

From J. Bruce Nichols, *The Uneasy Alliance: Religion, Refugee Work, and U.S. Foreign Policy* (New York: Oxford University Press, 1988), 249.

LAME DUCKS AND
NEW NECESSITIES

I thought my obligation to do high-profile crossings was over, that with the Merkt ruling guiding both the INS and Trsg, with sanctuary firmly established in the Arizona-Sonoran borderlands, and with our crossings having become too routine to be newsworthy, clergy who had an institutional base should henceforth project sanctuary's image, but the 1986 Immigration Reform and Control Act (IRCA) posed a challenge to sanctuary that could only be exposed and engaged with another public crossing. IRCA includes a provision that makes it a felony to help "aliens" enter by any means other than inspection at a port of entry, even if they have a right to be in the United States. This was designed to target sanctuary assistance in the borderlands, since an honest judge would have had to concede that the old law specified sanctions only for transporting and harboring *"illegal* aliens," and, according to international and domestic law, first-asylum refugees are not illegal aliens. Under the pre-1986 legislation, a sanctuary trial that took the statutory and treaty provisions seriously would have had to begin with a determination that illegal immigrants rather than first-asylum refugees were assisted.

The INS had consistently refused to admit first-asylum refugees from El Salvador and Guatemala at ports of entry, no matter what risks they ran in Mexico, but we thought this policy might change to make the new antisanctuary provision functional. In August 1987, we had a suitable test case. A Salvadoran woman with three small children arrived on the border in Nogales, Mexico. They were trying to join her husband in the United States in order to reach safe haven in Canada, where they had already been admitted, subject to the usual health and fingerprint checks. She'd narrowly averted rape and forced prostitution in Mexico City and was at risk of being summarily deported by Mexico. All she needed from the U.S. government was permission to cross the United States to reach her husband and enter Canada. If she couldn't enter the United States just to reach safe haven in Canada, then we would assume that the INS policy remained unchanged, that no first-asylum Salvadoran or Guatemalan would be permitted to reach safe haven in the United States through a port of entry, and that sanctuary assistance to cross the borderlands would therefore remain necessary for all first-asylum Salvadorans and Guatemalans who arrived at the border and were at risk in Mexico.

The local INS office told us that only the State Department could issue visas to "OTMs" (aliens other than Mexicans). Because the woman lacked a valid visa and could not safely go out on the street or travel in Mexico, I took their passports and the Canadian Consul's letter verifying that they were approved for entry into Canada to the U.S. consul in Hermosillo, Mexico, who refused to issue visas, explaining that, even for transit visas for them to cross the United States, he would need proof that they have a permanent place of residence in El Salvador to which to return. He admitted that this is a catch-22 requirement for refugees but said that the statute is absolute and unambiguous on this point. I asked him to check with the U.S. embassy in Mexico and with officials in Washington, D.C., to confirm his understanding of the statute and to see whether anyone could think of any possible loophole or exception. He did and reported that there was none.

When Senator Dennis DeConcini learned that the woman and her children couldn't cross the United States to reach the safe haven already offered by Canada, he was outraged. Over a period of weeks, I worked with his immigration aide to try to persuade federal officials to let them get through. The one remaining possibility was that Delia Combs, the INS assistant commissioner, Refugee, Asylum and Parole (CORAP), would make an exception in this case and parole the woman and her children into the United States without a visa. She refused. We then gave notice to the assistant commissioner and to the INS district director that we would therefore have to take care of it ourselves. A reporter accompanied me on the crossing, and the story, which included a picture of me crossing with the woman, was published on the front page of *The Washington Post*, October 15, 1987. In my letter to the INS, I explained that, since we had exhausted all possibilities for complying with the new provision in the 1986 Immigration Act, our entry without inspection was lawful because necessary to protect the woman and her children from what would otherwise have happened to her.

Because George Bush took about nine months to replace Reagan appointees who knew they were going out, the INS had almost a year of lame-duck administration after the 1988 presidential election. Before the election, the Justice Department wanted no sanctuary cases. After the election, as lame ducks, the faction within the Reagan administration that was commonly known as the "kamikazes" did want another sanctuary trial. INS Regional Commissioner Harold Ezell (a dedicated kamikaze) still hoped to get me before he left office. I decided it would be a good time to work with Father Ricardo on border networking and response teams that would follow the Trsg principles and procedures but would be entirely independent of Trsg. If I was going to draw fire, I wanted to draw it away rather than toward established groups such as Trsg. The lame-duck period also looked like a good time to offer the kamikazes a clearly defined target. (I may be critical of Alinsky's emphasis on polarization, but I think everyone should know social jujitsu well enough to deal constructively with government kamikazes.)

During the eighties, many Central Americans died trying to cross the Sonoran desert, and we expected the situation to be much worse during the summer of 1989. During the cool months, groups of five to forty indigenous Guatemalans—usually totaling more than one hundred and sometimes as many as three hundred weekly—were walking from the Altar area of Sonora or from the border between Sásabe and Lukeville north to a citrus orchard near Phoenix, where they would then negotiate with *coyotes* to take them to Florida. Many spoke no Spanish, just a Mayan language such as Kanjobal, Quiché, Chu, or Mam. Virtually none read maps or realized what a dangerous and circuitous route they were taking to reach Florida. In many cases, at least one of them had been over the route before, but they often knew the way only from descriptions of landmarks and the names of towns.

We'd seen virtually no indigenous Guatemalans on the Arizona-Sonoran border before General Rios Montt's "Beans-and-Bullets" campaign in 1982–83. Then, after some discovered Anglo America by means of this route, their numbers began multiplying rapidly, because upon arrival back in their villages all of them who were caught and deported had one highly salable skill: personal familiarity with the way north. In the summer of 1989, all previous records for continuous heat on the Sonoran desert were broken, but church efforts in Sonora and the thousands of warning leaflets and posters we distributed seemed to be effective. On several occasions, we did have to pick up some Guatemalans who came close to dying, but it turned out to be a record year of no reported migrant deaths on that stretch of desert. The following summer, Father Ricardo and I intensified our distribution of warning leaflets in Sonora and Guatemala, but we had no calls from O'Odham villages, no deaths were reported, and from June through September the flow of indigenous Guatemalans shifted over to Tijuana. Word had circulated.

In October 1990, Congress halted the deportation of the Salvadorans who were already in the United States and made them eligible for "Temporary Protected Status." Then, on December 19, federal officials conceded virtually everything sought by sanctuary providers in a civil suit (*American Baptist Churches v. Thornburgh*—"the ABC agreement") that had been filed in 1985 as a companion to the Arizona sanctuary trial. Because there was "a real and immediate threat of prosecution of sanctuary providers," the court had ruled that the plaintiffs had standing to bring the suit. Federal attorneys maneuvered from 1985 through 1989 to keep the case out of court, but subsequent rulings just shifted the basis for the plaintiffs' standing. Finally, to avoid having the evidence of federal violations of refugee law presented in court, the Department of Justice agreed to halt the deportation of in-country Guatemalans as well as Salvadorans and to readjudicate any Guatemalan or Salvadoran political asylum application that had been rejected during the eighties. At least 500,000 undocumented Salvadorans and Guatemalans would be eligible for temporary safe haven, and more than 100,000 asylum cases could be readjudicated under new, reformed procedures.

In effect, we'd won. Adequate supervision and legal aid would still be needed, but the violation of Central American refugees' right to safe haven *within* the United States had ceased to be an entrenched federal policy. At the same time, though, the U.S. government intensified its antirefugee program in Mexico; U.S. ports of entry remained closed to Central American refugees; and the U.S. government's program to intercept drugs in Mexico fused with its program to intercept refugees. The Mexican government's count of deported Central Americans soared to about 100,000 in 1990 (many of whom were repeaters who tried until they got through). Even Iron Curtain ruthlessness couldn't control the U.S.-Mexican border (or even give the market price of drugs a significant boost), but the political need to find a new Evil Empire and establish a reverse Iron Curtain is making the borderlands much more dangerous.

Ten days after the ABC agreement was signed, on the verge of 1991, I had to bring a torture-scarred Guatemalan through the borderlands to Tucson. Neither the need to avoid the Border Patrol nor the ways to make a "run" had changed much since 1981. The ABC agreement was a notable victory for the sanctuary movement—yet, just an agreement signed by a government that continues to sponsor gross violators of human rights in Central America and that routinely violates its own statutes and treaties. The sanctuary movement's real victory during the decade had been the development of sanctuary as an enduring institution within the fully catholic church. Particularly in the borderlands, sanctuary congregations now have the experience and networks to continue, regardless of government countermeasures. For these churches, synagogues, and meetings, providing sanctuary has become integral to being faithful.

10

Going Up to Zion: The Extension of the Sanctuary Covenant

> True freedom lies where a man receives his nourishment and preservation, and that is the use of the earth.
> —GERRARD WINSTANLEY, the Digger

FORCED APOSTASY AND THE PROPHETIC COMMUNITY

THE ANTISANCTUARY PROVISION of the 1986 Immigration Reform and Control Act (IRCA) was a relatively unimportant challenge to our practice of sanctuary, compared to the act's central provision, the I-9 attestation. IRCA "requires employers to verify employment eligibility of individuals on [form I-9: Employment Eligibility Verification] . . ." The I-9 makes employers, with the assistance and signed attestation of job applicants, the primary agents for denying employment to the undocumented. Sanctuary congregations and all of their members who are either employers or job applicants are now ordered to enforce the INS policies from which they have covenanted to protect refugees.

When indicted, the Arizona sanctuary defendants declared that they would continue their sanctuary ministry, even at the risk of being jailed while awaiting trial. When eight of the defendants in the Arizona sanctuary trial were convicted, they refused to agree to conditions of probation that would require them to break with their faith communities. But the I-9 requirement goes beyond all attempts to force passive acceptance of the INS violations of refugee rights; it makes job applicants and employers in the United States the primary enforcement agents of INS policies. The INS just oversees employer compliance, and employers enforce employee compliance. Compared to the jail sentences risked by the sanctuary defendants, the sanctions for persistent noncompliance with the I-9 requirement are also persuasively draconian: for job applicants who remain in the United States, a lifetime of unemployability; for employers, prison and the forfeiture of all assets.

The classic Quaker view of the issue raised by the I-9 was stated by John Woolman in *A Plea for the Poor*:

> The Creator of the earth is the owner of it. He gave us being thereon, and our nature requires nourishment which is the produce of it. As he is kind and merciful, we as his creatures, while we live answerable to the design of our creation, we are so far entitled to a convenient subsistence that no man may justly deprive us of it.

> The livelihood of the landless poor depends on their access to the market for their labor. Being excluded from earning a living violates their right to life. With respect to this basic right, no human being is an alien.

In relation to refugees' right to safe haven, which in the case of Salvadorans and Guatemalans is systematically violated by the INS, employers and job applicants who profess the sanctuary covenant and yet require or sign the I-9 attestation are clearly unfaithful. If the profession of the sanctuary covenant means anything at all, it must mean this, that we will not become agents for the violation of the human rights we covenant to uphold. In the United States, the I-9 attestation has become *the* definitive act of apostasy for a sanctuary community and its members. It is the way that the violation of the right to safe haven is now being woven into the social order.

Those for whom compliance with the I-9 requirement would

constitute apostasy are denied the First Amendment free exercise of their religion, but the broader issue here is between liberty and subjugation. The conception of the state as the corporate manager of society is the clearly stated organizing ideal of fascism, but it has become the underlying assumption of all statist politics—majoritarian versions of democracy as well totalitarian versions of nationalism and socialism. Unfree peoples are forcibly held under state management, apart from *excepted* rights such as those enumerated in the first eight articles of the U.S. Bill of Rights. The Ninth Amendment was included in the Bill of Rights to emphasize that a free people never relinquishes the unnamed rights that distinguish it from unfree peoples. A people that is under state management—a citizenry that consists of conscripts or slaves of the state—is unfree, even if it is granted some exceptions to its bondage.

Regardless of the good or bad consequences of imposing employer sanctions in the United States, it's one thing to consider what any government can order its hired agents to do, another to consider what it can rightfully conscript citizens and religious societies to do for it.[1] As armed violence institutionalized, a state and

---

1. Employer sanctions aren't the decisive issue here. For example, I opposed the old Immigration Act's "Texas Amendment," which exempted employers from criminal charges whenever transporting or harboring was integral to the job. (If Jack Elder had been taking those three Salvadorans to harvest vegetables for a Texas grower instead of giving them a ride in connection with diocesan refugee aid, he would have been exempt from the three counts of transporting for which he was indicted.) Living in the borderlands and working as a cowboy, I've seen how the Texas Amendment made undocumented workers highly exploitable, in ways that also promoted racism (especially among other workers). The relation of an undocumented worker to an employer was often that of serf to master.

Most jobs now go south of the border more eagerly and massively than workers come north, and employer sanctions are stampeding jobs out of the United States. Only refugees who must seek safe haven in the United States are truly excluded from the market for their labor, because the labor market is now as international as commodity markets. If labor can't come north to $35 per day jobs, the jobs will certainly go south to $3.50 per day labor, so protectionism just serves to accelerate the massive migration of jobs out of the United States and the eventual equalizing of First- and Third-World wages. Even agricultural work is learning to migrate; as the apple orchards are being torn out of the State of Washington, they're being planted in the State of Chihuahua.

its agents do many things that I and the religious society of which I am a member refuse to do, and if religious liberty is to mean anything at all it must mean that the state is prohibited from conscripting citizens or the church to act against conscience or covenant. The church ceases to be church if it places the practice of its faith under state management.

Most sanctuary congregations are employers who must now choose whether they will comply with the I-9 requirement, and they must also choose how they will respond to the sufferings of members who refuse to comply and to the anguish of members who are coerced against conscience into complying. One might expect Quakers to be among the first to go into the breach the I-9 has torn into efforts to weave sanctuary into the social order, since "testimonies" against this kind of oath or attestation have been characteristic of Quakers. Some Quakers in every generation are jailed and dispossessed for the practice of their faith, so the Religious Society of Friends has developed and maintained institutions to respond to "sufferings" of this kind—which makes faithfulness easier. Yet, Quaker job applicants who, against conscience and covenant, sign the I-9 attestation will probably outnumber those who refuse to sign, just as Quakers who will sign loyalty oaths outnumber those who refuse. Quaker ways have long since evolved beyond the heroic age of the founders, when all Quakers willingly went to jail and forfeited their land rather than take the pledge of allegiance—and even beyond the conformist age of the followers, when any who failed to call their oaths "affirmations" would be disowned. Nonetheless, some Quaker meetings that include many members who will sign the I-9 attestation are also reaching consensus that compliance would constitute a betrayal of the meeting's faith and practice. Here are my own meeting's minutes on the I-9:

> As an employer, Pima Monthly Meeting of the Religious Society of Friends will not require, fill out, or file form I-9 (Employment Eligibility Verification). In common with all other testimonies concerning faith and practice, the Meeting's refusal

to require, fill out, or file form I-9 will be open and public. (Approved, 5-14-89.)

Pima Meeting will not discriminate against job applicants who are undocumented, either in hiring or paying them. (Approved, 6-11-89.)

Some of us will decide on the basis of family obligations, career objectives, or material needs to attest that we are not aliens excluded from employment, in spite of our conscientious opposition to doing so. Some, as employers or administrators, may even compel others to do so. Yet, we all agree that we will refuse as a meeting to do so, as a matter of faith and practice. Is this difference between the practice of members and the declared faith-and-practice of the meeting hypocrisy? It is if we call our unfaithfulness something else. Is it defection? It is if we don't seek diligently to create alternative livelihoods and mutual support that will permit all of us to be true to our covenant.

The kind of basic community that enhances its members' ability to be faithful to the covenant of full communion is radically different from collectives and corporate bodies. Members can't keep the covenant alive if the community turns apostate; the community can keep the covenant alive when its members are forced to be unfaithful. The covenant community opens ways for its members to be true through the community's practice of the prophetic faith, even when they are coerced into being unfaithful in their personal and familial practice.

The church as many of us have come to know it through the sanctuary movement includes all who covenant as primal societies to treat no one as a violable enemy, alien, or inferior. Quakers are among the least numerous of the peoples who constitute this catholic church that is limited by no credal, ritual, sacramental, or organizational forms. Yet, Quakers may seem to be set apart by their insistence on functioning as a religious society rather than a corporate collective. Most other denominations have corporate forms of organization that exhibit all the classic contrasts between moral man and immoral "society"; their freedom to be faithful is inversely related to the extent of their corporate organization. Don't expect a religious order whose members take a vow of poverty to give all of the order's wealth to the poor, in the manner of the primitive Franciscan *society*. Don't expect a church that must keep its cathedrals, government-funded charities, and tax privileges to refuse to comply with the I-9 attestation just because its bishops declare that the I-9 institutes structural injustice. But don't even expect a Quaker meeting that has an eye on substantial corporate holdings to do so.

Quaker insistence on functioning as a religious society is no peculiarity. It just keeps managerial superstructures from obscuring what most denominations now see as church: a people that is present in each of its basic communities, not the ecclesiastical management of religious organizations. Assemblies of Roman Catholic bishops won't act on their denunciations of the I-9, but Catholic communities are going into the breach to uphold the sanctuary covenant, in greater numbers than Quaker meetings. Refusing to make the I-9 attestation is no Quaker peculiarity but simply a matter of faithfully building the fully catholic church, as a sanctuary for all life.

Any state, to maintain the enforced social order, will limit what can be done in the name of religion, but conscripting the church to act as the state's primary agent for enforcing government policy is a radically different matter, *the* fundamental issue for the separation of church and state. If the church can be conscripted to act as the government's agent, then church-state separation and first amendment guarantees of religious liberty are a sham. For sanctuary providers, the I-9 requirement is easily seen to be a complete breach of church-state separation, because it forces apostasy; to become the primary agent of the U.S. government's violation of refugee rights betrays the sanctuary covenant. Yet, the basic issue here is equally relevant to the church's being conscripted to act as its employees' tax collector, to which most religious bodies acceded long ago. In effect, the keystone of church-state separation in the United States has been decisively destroyed, insofar as the church acts as an employer.

For sanctuary communities in the United States, the freedom to be faithful now depends on their members' access to livelihoods in which they make their living rather than earning it, neither giving nor taking hire. This is where Pat and I find ourselves, along with many of our friends.

Pat and I have decided to turn apostate, if put to the full test, which means that in our hearts we've already broken the sanctuary covenant. Maybe we'll find a way to meet our other obligations, such as veterinary care for our animals and medical and dental care for ourselves, without making the I-9 attestation in order to earn money. If so, it will be a matter of good fortune rather than faithfulness—maybe even a side-effect of having played such a prominent part in developing sanctuary for first-asylum refugees in the United States. If we hadn't done and said so much to develop sanctuary, it wouldn't be particularly important for us to name and admit our unfaithfulness. Because we did, it is. Otherwise, our betrayal could be taken as a model—or at least as a way to be true rather than a sign that the way is blocked for some of us.

We're not indulging in guilt, and we don't repent. Guilt would just divert us from the task at hand, and repentance would mean we'd decided not to make the attestation, after all, whatever the cost. We're just confessing that we're currently at risk of being trapped into betraying the sanctuary covenant, along with many others who have entered it in good faith. If this were a matter of saintliness rather than errantry, martyrdom of some kind would probably be in order; but, contrary to some published reports, our quixotism is far from saintly, especially where martyrdom is concerned. As errantry, our practice of sanctuary has spiraled to a full cycle, where Pat and I must, to detour the barrier posed by the I-9, now take an initiative like the decision to let our goats go and postpone concern with livelihood and a land ethic in order to respond to refugee needs. The sanctuary cycle spiraled to a place where we now see the land ethic with eyes enlightened by discovery of the fully catholic church, but it has also spiraled to a dead-end where our old concern with harmonious livelihood can no longer be set aside.

The anguish of being conscripted to betray the Peaceable Kingdom and serve the rule of violence is much the same for those of us who feel it as a loss of liberty as it is for those who feel it as a burden of guilt, but the members of the church-errant seek freedom where professors of sin seek absolution. When the anguish of coerced apostasy neither bogs down in guilt nor ends in martyrdom, errantry remembers and turns toward Zion, where the community can walk its covenanted way freely because it is once again at home, living on its own land. A covenanted way of life must have its home on earth somewhere and sometime, to be a way of life.

DIGGERS AND THE LAND ETHIC

In Lancashire sometime during the winter of 1648–49, while making his living by tending cows on the common, Gerrard Winstanley had a vision in which he was told to proclaim a simple message: Work together and eat bread together and neither give nor take hire.

During periods of stillness, Winstanley had become convinced that "every part of the Creation should lend a mutual help of love in action to preserve the whole." He concluded that a new kind of human community must therefore emerge. The poor are Israel, cut off from the land that would support them and caught in the Egyptian bondage of rulers and landowners, but the time is at hand when Israel will be called forth out of this bondage "to live in tents."

The new community could never grow from the violent overthrow of the powerful, since violence is the way and spirit of existing society and can only establish new rulers.

> Therefore if the rich wil stil hold fast this propriety of *Mine and thine*, let them labour their own Land with their own hands. And let the common-people, that are the gatherings together of Israel from under that bondage, and that say the earth is ours, not mine, let them labour together, and eat bread together upon the Commons, Mountains, and Hils . . .

None can say, Their right is taken from them; for let the rich work alone by themselves, and let the poor work together by themselves; the rich in their inclosures, saying *This is mine;* The poor upon their Commons, saying *This is ours,* the earth and fruits are common.[2]

(In the spring of 1649, Winstanley and the other Diggers moved out onto the commons near Cobham and began planting, but they were soon dispersed or imprisoned. The movement lasted little more than a year.)

For Winstanley, studying how "the whole creation is knit together into a one-nesse of life" is a form of worship, just as working together and eating bread together in ways that support the whole are also worship. Each is a form of active communion. Aldo Leopold calls this conception of communion "ecological conscience."

In *The Land Ethic,* Leopold observes that "There is as yet no ethic dealing with man's relation to land and to the animals and plants which grow upon it. Land, like Odysseus' slave-girls, is still property. The land-relation is still strictly economic, entailing privileges but not obligations. The extension of ethics to this third element in human environment is, if I read the evidence correctly, an evolutionary possibility and an ecological necessity." He goes on to say that "a land ethic changes the role of *Homo sapiens* from conqueror of the land community to plain member and citizen of it."[3]

If we cease to live by conquest and become plain members and citizens of the land community, we give up any claims we may have, either privately or collectively, to possess and use the land as though it were just an object. This is the cornerstone of human economic and legal systems—not only of capitalism, but of civilization. Leopold believed that the land could be included in our

---

2. Gerrard Winstanley, "The New Law of Righteousness" in *The Works of Gerrard Winstanley,* ed. George H. Sabine, (New York: Russell & Russell, 1965), 195–196. All quotations from Winstanley are from Sabine's edition of his works.
3. Aldo Leopold, "The Land Ethic" in *A Sand County Almanac* (New York: Ballantine/Oxford, 1966), 238–239.

ethical system by a simple extension of the same principles that led us to declare that human beings can no longer be owned as property. But this evolutionary extension of rights from human society to the land community entails a qualitative change, too. The nature of civilization itself would change, if basic rights were extended to all life.

For Winstanley, the inner light reveals we actually are knit together into a oneness of life, so we need no grand designs and cunning stratagems that split the world into means and ends. To recover awareness of the divine presence in ourselves and others, we must go free, working together and eating together in ways that support rather than destroy life. Reformers generally insist, to the contrary, that humankind must be still further tamed—that society must be restructured, humanity remade, and deviants redirected because, unreconstructed, we are too greedy. Are human beings really too greedy? Or does greed itself want too little? To settle this issue, there's no need to appeal to the inner light. Watch the advertisements on TV for a few hours. Wander around in a big department store. These are the riches we have plundered from the earth. Could possessing and consuming more and more of *that* be the meaning of life?

The problem is not that modern man wants so much but that he aspires to so little. Once, somewhere, he heard that the sun is a morning star, and he awaits the new dawn, fixing his restless mind on the TV for hours each day in the hope that whatever he awaits will happen. And every day does bring some improvement: a less filling beer, a cookie without calories, a softer toilet paper, a quicker aspirin, a less lethal cigarette . . .

> Here is a man who uses a pearl like that of the marquis of Sui to shoot at a bird at a distance of 10,000 feet. All men will laugh at him. Why? Because the thing he uses is of great value and what he wishes to get is of little. And is not life of more value than the pearl of the marquis of Sui?
>
> —Chuang Tzu, 28:3

Extending the morality of basic rights to include land has nothing to do, initially, with public rather than private ownership or with passing new statutes. It has to do with a community practice that weaves the land's rights into the social fabric. This approach is contrary to the way environmental activism is usually done. In common with other activists, environmentalists generally urge intervention by the state as a cure-all for the greed-driven destruction of land and life by property owners. This faith in the managerial restructuring of society to eliminate private property is fundamentally at odds with covenanting.

Private property is an institutional form of unmanaged freedoms of association and decision-making. It is "the static and relatively less important side of the institution of private contract."[4] Considerable cultural evolution must occur before a pluralistic social order can emerge that is characterized by persuasion, negotiation, and contract among persons with equal rights—a social order in which decision-making is diffused throughout society. Private property is the way individual and community rights of association and agency stabilize, and it is therefore a prerequisite for the emergence of basic communities that covenant to establish biocentric rights as the law of their land. Conversely, to the extent that the human social order that is pluralistically constituted by understandings, contracts, and covenants among equals is collectivized into managerial forms, the prospects are retarded and diminished for the emergence of a land ethic that institutes biocentric rights. Whatever the relative merits of trying to engineer human harmony with the rest of life on earth by means of government management (instead of trying to cultivate it by community covenant), a land ethic that seeks to extend basic rights to the land and its life must take the way of covenanting. If the land ethic visualized by Aldo Leopold is to emerge, the private ownership of land must be hallowed by community covenants, not absorbed into centralized state management.

---

4. Lon L. Fuller, *The Principles of Social Order* (Durham: Duke University Press, 1981), 27.

As covenanting, land redemption is ownership turned around to establish rights rather than uses for the land community. This rights-creating covenanting is no more mystical than any other aspect of a society's law concerning real property. In any society that allows land-owning associations to enter into covenants that "run with the land," a community that acquires land can convert its anthropocentric rights (its ownership) into biocentric rights; the covenanting community itself makes that part of the law of its land. (See *Appendix A*: The Saguaro-Juniper Covenant, for an example.)

THE BASIC COMMUNITY AS A PRIMAL LAW-MAKING SOCIETY

As a partnership rather than a corporate body, a covenant community requires that its members be free agents who retain their personal rights and responsibilities. In contrast to an elemental collective, which seeks to mobilize its members into a manageable mass (to achieve an objective), the primal society seeks to reach consensus on basic rights (to establish a way of life). The covenant community enhances its associates' cocreative ability to live the law into actuality, and this enhanced empowerment is also retained rather than delegated as covenant communities enter into partnerships with other communities and individuals.[5]

---

5. The distinction between societal order and managerial organization is fundamental to understanding the rule of law, but our age of corporate powers often forgets it. As explained by Hannah Arendt, "The mutual contract by which people bind themselves together in order to form a community is based on reciprocity and presupposes equality; its actual content is a promise, and its result is indeed a 'society' or 'cosociation' in the old Roman sense of *societas*, which means alliance. Such an alliance gathers together the isolated strength of the allied partners and binds them into a new power structure by virtue of 'free and sincere promises'." In contrast to a social contract to relinquish one's power of action to a ruler, "the act of mutual promise is by definition enacted 'in the presence of one another'." ". . . A body politic which is the result of covenant and 'combination' becomes the very source of power for each individual person who outside the constituted political realm remains impotent." [Arendt's note: ". . . The idea of covenant presupposes no-sovereignty and no-rule . . ."] *On Revolution* (New York: Penguin, 1965), 170–171; 308.

Managerial organization is essential for human beings to function as social animals; to succeed in meeting many of our needs, we must pursue them by means of directed collective action. But societal order that encompasses and subsumes managerial organization is essential for human beings to function as social animals that pursue diverse and often opposed objectives. Managerial organization becomes the rule of war when it breaks through societal constraints; societal order that subsumes all goal-determined organizations (the rule of law) is the condition for peace among human beings who claim equal basic rights of personal agency in the pursuit of diverse objectives.

By making decisions through unity or consensus, the covenant community incorporates members as coagents; each person retains equal rights of agency. This kind of decision-making is a practice rather than a method or technique; it is learned internally, from within a group that does it, rather than externally, through the abstraction of a set of rules or instructions.[6] Abstractly, as a method, it would mean, first, that the community starts from prior agreements when deciding about its principles and purposes and the way to implement them and, second, that every participant can veto a new decision.

The covenant to hallow the earth has to do with societal linkage rather than base community boundaries. It weaves communities together just as it weaves their members together. It acts horizontally on the faultlines between self and other, friend and enemy,

---

6. For an instructive study of the way Quakers reach unity in decision-making, see Michael J. Sheeran, *Beyond Majority Rule*, Philadelphia Yearly Meeting, 1983. His conclusion indicates my reason for emphasizing that this procedure is a community practice rather than a method that could be learned as a set of rules:

". . . Individualized, atomic man is incapable of community because of the inability to surrender the individual-focused starting point which has been fundamental to Western culture since the beginning of liberalism. Therefore all attempts by a person whose socialization has been locked into the atomic thought-world to achieve the community longed for are doomed to fail, doomed to imitate the externals of a participation based upon communion without ever quite attaining the communion itself that would transform those externals into reality" (p. 115).

"the people" and "the aliens." It therefore starts with whatever faultlines are at hand, not with a model for shaping covenant communities into the building blocks for constructing a pyramid of collective power. Nonetheless, a specific kind of association is essential for vitalizing this fabric of interwoven associations: the gathering that studies, deliberates, and seeks agreement about the meaning and practice of the covenant to hallow the earth, in light of the daily contingencies faced by those who enter into the covenant. Grand inquisitors, corporate administrators, and guerrilla *comandantes* would have us be useful to the organization, but to hallow the earth a people must be *kadosh*—free rather than useful, unassimilated rather than collectivized, active cocreators rather than passive followers.

When associations for worship, sustenance, and service share a land base and unite for deliberation and decision-making, they constitute a primal covenant society that is fully capable of determining and practicing its law. The covenant community is then primal, in the sense that it, rather than constituting members, becomes the key individuality for understanding its interaction with the open network of all communities that covenant to hallow the earth. Calling this open network "the church" is much more indiscriminately catholic than any established usage but introduces no discontinuity. The church keeps discovering that it is more indiscriminately catholic than it thought, which is to be expected of a society that bridges all borders and lives on humanity's faultlines.

In Anglo America, a person's society-forming initiatives commonly involve activities within a variety of worship, livelihood, neighborhood, educational, interest, service, and other associations that are unsubordinated to one another, have overlapping memberships, compete with one another for members and support, and are often at odds about the enumeration of rights that formulate the law or "right." (Right-to-life and pro-choice groups illustrate the diversity to be expected when right is refracted through human viewpoints into numerable rights.) Some Anglo-Americans are even involved in more than one worship group, as in the case of Quakers who are also active Buddhists or Jews. Stewardship of land ties this network of decision-making associations to full-spectrum governance, and it also integrates governance, which is the distinctively human form of cocreativity, into the mutually supportive creative activity that, as Winstanley put it, "knits the whole creation together into a onenesse of life and moderation, every creature sweetly in love lending their hands to preserve each other; and so upholds the whole fabrique."

Covenanting is concerned with interweaving persons and groups into a communion, not with drawing organizational boundaries that segregate one kind of association from another; it has to do with symbiotics rather than analytics. Speaking of *a* basic covenant community is therefore a convenient fiction, in the same way that speaking of a substantially separate self or agent among other persisting selves is a convenient fiction. As a communion for whom no "they" is an alien, "we" has no fixed boundaries. We are empowered and entrusted to be the cocreators of a humanity that hallows the earth, but there is no multiplicity of creators. The catholic communion we form is the body of the boundless.

This is where words darken counsel and all names are blasphemy.

11

Betrothal

> Just as he came, so shall he go; and what gain has he that he toiled for the wind, and spent all his days in darkness and grief, in much vexation and sickness and resentment?
>
> —Ecclesiastes 5:16–17

REWARDS, SUFFERINGS, AND OTHER VANITIES

QUIXOTE WORE HIS WOUNDS as trophies, like an old bull rider. Francis was stigmatized for faithfully following the way of the cross. The wages of errantry are troubles and wounds.

Formal religion and faithful errantry turn away from each other. The religions propose their various ways for followers to cure disabilities, avoid punishments, and reach a final reward; the church-errant serves gratuitously, betrothing itself for better or for worse, in sickness and in health, for richer or for poorer, unto death.

Turning to errantry solves no problems and heals no wounds. It is no substitute for medical care, mind-altering drugs, or massage. It's more like a rodeo cowboy's deciding to switch from saddle broncs to bulls. You can ride out the broncs, if you're good at it. No one rides out the bulls. The best bull riders just know how to last a little longer and hit the ground dodging.

Unlike formal religion, errantry is wanderings and openings, uncertainties and beginnings. From the time I turned Quaker, I've never reached a destination. I know nothing of personal salvation.

I haven't even been cured of chronic ills—just crippled with new ones.

A year to the month after I turned Quaker, while taking my two older children back to their new home at the end of their first summer visit, I came down with a high fever that marked the onset of an autoimmune disease. The doctors couldn't decide on the name to give it. If I survived more than six months, that would make one diagnosis unlikely; if more than twelve months, another name could be tentatively scratched. Whatever the name, my body had suddenly become allergic to itself, as though it were an incompatible transplant.

Sometimes my heart would be the focus of rejection; sometimes, my lungs; sometimes, my kidneys, intestines, or muscles. From one day to another, I never knew what symptoms to expect or whether the rejection would be lethal. A year and a half later, in the midst of a free-speech controversy at Cochise College (where I was head librarian during the school's first, founding year), I came down with another uncontrollable high fever. When the fever broke, the disease had transmuted into ordinary rheumatoid arthritis.

A friend who was being forced out of his Bisbee pastorate for backing my stand against censorship, Father Dick Cantrell, thought I was making myself sick by suppressing anger, that I needed to learn how to scream and break things. He also thought I should take alfalfa pills. I knew I was making myself sick, but probably not because of Anglo reticence. In any case, I'd rather be arthritic than angry, so I never tried screaming and breaking things. I did take the alfalfa pills he gave me, since I thought they'd do no harm.

The flare-ups matched times when I became intensely concerned with externals over which I had no control. I soon learned that I could block the pain and endure almost any stress if I acted from internal leadings, detached from external expectations, misunderstandings, and falsehoods. I could endure and even be at ease if I just did what I really considered obligatory, while grasping for nothing and regretting no losses or mistakes. Taking externals too seriously (not the failure to externalize pent-up emotions) seemed to be the trigger. Instead of trying to undo my Anglo upbringing, I pushed it to a new extreme, beyond propriety, indignation, and guilt.

During childhood, I'd conditioned myself to stoic endurance (because I saw it as my Native American side, which couldn't be expected of my merely Anglo playmates). I don't know exactly when I first decided, in addition to learning how to be at ease with hunger, cold, and pain, to cultivate detachment from social expectations and disapproval, but I remember the generative circumstance: watching the winter stars after taking Mrs. Nolan's seventh-grade astronomy course.

On the high plains, when the wind dies, and the ground blizzards settle, and a moonless night freezes into crystalline clarity, the heavens are more alive and open to communion than life itself. In that society of stars, human history has barely begun and will surely end before many of this midnight's rays reach the earth. In that society, the majestic sweep of interstellar space-time belittles all human plans and swallows all human hopes. And even that society of mortal stars shrinks to an insignificance that is beneath smallness as well as greatness, in the boundless reaches of eternity.

My eighth-grade English teacher advised my parents that I should be put on a vocational track in high school, since I clearly wasn't college material. "He really isn't high school material," she explained. They didn't put me on the vocational track, but my first two years of high school confirmed her evaluation—until, as a sophomore, I was assigned a short story to write, which was the first time I can remember doing a homework assignment. The teacher liked my story so much that she read it to all the sophomore English classes. It was about a man preparing to commit suicide.

I'd appended a resoundingly upbeat conclusion that brought tears to the teacher's eyes (sentiment without substance that didn't touch the case my protagonist made for killing himself). These days, no matter how sweet the concluding sentiments, a fifteen-year-old D-student who suddenly bloomed with a story like that would face a battery of counselors, but it just came as a pleasant surprise to the teacher and my parents, especially since school work began to coincide at times with my interests, once I quit making it a matter of principle to ignore all homework assignments. I also wrote another suicide story that I liked much better but showed no one.

In my junior year, I changed track, becoming a hypercompetitive debater. (Natrona County's high school was nationally known for its debate teams.) My success as a debater and my suddenly high grades won me a scholarship to the Eastern college of my choice, from which I was graduated with highest honors in six semesters.

My mother came to my college graduation and then stayed with me for several weeks as I moved on to graduate school. She seemed clinging and over-protective, which was entirely out of character. Finally, she told me that she'd stumbled across that other story I'd written—in which, after excelling at college in all measurable academic respects, the protagonist kills himself on graduation day.

Unlike the protagonist in my story, I never considered killing myself and didn't suffer a severe depression until my first marriage broke up. I also dismissed the expressions of existentialist nausea that were then fashionable at American and European universities. In clearing away all affirmations of externals, I had no desire to retreat into subjectivity. I just used the suicide story to express the same negation that Koheleth communicates by postulating he's King Solomon.[1]

Logical positivism (which asserts that the meaning of any assertion is identified entirely with the set of verifiable consequences it entails) suited my undergraduate tastes as an unbeliever. Judged

---

1. See *Ecclesiastes* 1:12 through 2:17.
Tradition has it that Koheleth *is* King Solomon because, where we might use a contrafactual conditional, he says "I, Koheleth, have been king over Israel . . .", and then a scribe later gave the book, as a title, what is now the first verse: "The words of Koheleth, the son of David, king in Jerusalem." In Koheleth's world, King Solomon appeared to have reached practical wisdom's historical zenith and to have enjoyed all its fruits (knowledge, public esteem, legal judgment, peace and political power, sensual pleasures, engineering and artistic accomplishments, and incomparable wealth), so Solomon was the best person to testify that all this is vanity and a striving after wind.

in terms of truth consequences, the perennial theological issues evaporate. As unfalsifiable beliefs, religious faiths are less than false; they are meaningless.

Logical positivism particularly suited my undergraduate tastes at the point when, having discredited and swept aside everything else, it turns the universal solvent of its meaning criterion against its own expression of faith as belief. There is no way to verify the assertion that the meaning of an assertion consists of its verifiable consequences. (The unbeliever who believes in his unbelief is preeminently credulous.)

Maybe there's more to my suicide story than I've admitted, since the best way to show the vanity of practical wisdom is the way Koheleth chose—by imagining the highest human achievements, not by narrowing it all down to undergraduate academia's testable microcosm. To coax this insight from John Woolman School students who were preparing to goatwalk, I just asked them to write their obituary, assuming that they would live to be ninety and have the wealth, education, health, and talent to do anything humanly possible. Maybe, as an undergraduate, I felt compelled to live out an experiment in keeping with my suicide story—something concludable even if inconclusive—because I couldn't settle for Koheleth's wisdom, which is only noble enough to expose the emptiness of folk wisdom's proverbial prudence.

Confirmation that all human ambitions are vanity would, I hoped, prove to be just a way station, so I decided against living as an academic philosopher. Although I'd learned I was clever enough to make a comfortable job of it at some university, and I thought that clearing away conjurings is at least as worthwhile as most other jobs (especially where conjurers congregate), I really had nothing to teach. I'd also satisfied myself that, wherever wisdom itself might be found, I wouldn't find it in academia. During the year of graduate study, I coasted through to a master's degree while devoting myself to partying and to reading fairy tales. Then I volunteered to be drafted into the army, to get military conscription out of the way.

Serving out my time as a conscript, starting a family, and then settling into ranching, I thought I could put the search aside. I had no reason to think there actually is a wisdom to match the intimations of my star-gazing childhood. "Just as he came, so shall he go; and what gain has he that he toiled for the wind, and spent all his days in darkness and grief, in much vexation and sickness and resentment? Behold, what I have seen to be good and to be fitting is to eat and drink and to find enjoyment in all the toil in which one toils under the sun the few days of his life which God has given him, for this is his lot" (Eccl 5:16–18). Koheleth's wisdom returns in resignation to Sancho's maxims of creaturely contentment.

Then, my barely formed family broke apart, and something much stronger than those childhood intimations wrenched me around. Yet, being wrenched around didn't falsify Koheleth's insight. Using Zen disciplines, I accommodated my intellect to the prospect that, although we human beings have eternity planted in our minds, I could aspire to no wisdom beyond the mindful savoring of my daily activities.

My mind conceded defeat; I tried to abandon my aspirations and make new ones to fit my expectations; but my body refused, quixotically, to surrender. It began trying to self-destruct whenever I cultivated contentment as an alternative to following my leadings.

Koheleth clears away all hope. In itself, everything is vanity; nothing is meaningful; and there will be no final ending where everyone (or anyone, for that matter) lives happily ever after. But it is here, where every idol crumbles and all hope dies, that errantry lifts up the unsupported standard—the cocreative leading that reflects the eternity planted in the human mind—and carries it into the breach. If Quixote fails to live his chivalry into the Creation, who will? If not now, when will there ever be another Quixote? And he does fail, repeatedly, comically, inevitably—yet, even in his worst defeats, quixotically. And the quest survives.

Koheleth fails to take his unbelief far enough. He sees that everything we could conceivably grasp as the meaning of life is vanity. Implicitly, everything we could conceive and believe to be God is therefore an idol, but Koheleth retreats to resignation before taking this plunge. Depths that he never explores buoy up the ability to see and feel that our idols are idols—depths in which the fruitless quest for meaningful beliefs and works germinates into Abrahamic errantry.

"So important is the matter of idolatry, that whoever rejects it is as though he acknowledges the whole Torah" (Chullin 5a). The prophetic faith rejects idolatry where official religions reject atheism, because atheism just negates the names used for conjuring. (Anyone who breaks official idols is someone's atheist.) Making definitive images of "God" rejects the prophetic faith, not the denial of a definition or doctrine that claims to be an accurate description of God. In the case of the pilgrim people's covenant of steadfast love, verbal tokens that are obviously opaque will therefore continue to be next best to silence, as stand-ins for the Only Name, if we ever think we know it.

> Moses said to God, "If I come to the people of Israel and say to them, 'The God of your fathers has sent me to you,' and they ask me, 'What is His name?' what shall I say to them?"
> God said to Moses, "I am present as I am present." And He said, "Say this to the people of Israel, "I-AM-PRESENT has sent me to you" (Ex 3:13–14).[2]

The revelation at the burning bush breaks all boundaries but is neither evasive nor cryptic. To the contrary, it reveals too much to be grasped: I-AM-PRESENT has no names that can be grasped and used by religion's professional handlers.

The rejection of idolatry means there are no independent beings, powers, objects, goods, or evils that should be either worshipped or destroyed. This can be restated as an acceptance of fundamental unity: I meet in every other the Presence for whom there is no other. "As you did it to one of the least of these, you did it to Me." The ruthless iconoclasm of an Elijah opens into the

---

2. Martin Buber's explanation of this translation of the Hebrew, *Ehyeh asher ehyeh*, to "I am (or shall be) present as I am present" is to be found in *Moses* (New York: Harper & Row, 1958), 48–55.

gospel's affirmation of I-AM-PRESENT. "No man has ever seen God; if we love one another, God abides in us, and his love is perfected in us" (I Jn 4:12).

LEARNING TO SAY THE SHEMA

In the course of attending Quaker meeting for almost thirty years, I've been moved only twice to say a few words of ministry, and I now doubt that I should have spoken then, yet I make it a practice to start Friday evening with the Shema and other passages from the Jewish prayer book.[3] Often, when I'm in town, I join a congregation to say the Kaddish as well (the Aramaic prayer for the coming of the Kingdom, which is to be said only in community). For much the same reasons that Pat and I go, Father Ricardo likes to attend the evening Sabbath service with us, on the rare occasions when he isn't celebrating mass and has no other obligations. Next to the Bible, the Reform Jewish prayer book is Ricardo's favorite source for the ecumenical liturgy he prepares weekly.

A Catholic priest's love of the Jewish liturgy is easier to understand than a Quaker's. Quakers reject all fixed forms of worship and ground their meetings in silence; Jews repeat obligatory prayers passed down from one generation to another, some of which include verses first formulated at the dawn of human history and many of which have been repeated daily for more than a millennium. How can a Quaker consistently join in the fixed prayer of the synagogue, except as an impostor, either in the meetinghouse or in the synagogue?

I don't say the Jewish prayers because I believe in a God who wants praise or answers petitions. I don't say them as personal inspiration or leadings that I feel moved to share with others. I say them to renew the covenant—to betroth myself in the exact words,

---

3. The *Shema* is the Jewish declaration of faith, which observant Jews repeat at least twice daily. In the Reform prayer book, the full Shema consists of Deuteronomy 6:4–9 and Numbers 15:40–41, which deletes passages included in the traditional *Siddur*: Deuteronomy 11:13–21 and Numbers 15:37–39.

insofar as I can know them, of my adopted ancestors who bequeathed the prophetic faith as an inheritance open to all peoples. I say them because the Peaceable Kingdom exists and is established only insofar as a people accepts its sole sovereignty, and in pledging this allegiance I, as a Quaker, am inseparably one with the House of Israel, much as the gospel of steadfast love proclaimed by Jesus of Nazareth is inseparable from the prophetic faith of the Hebrew Bible. I say them, too, because I've seen the fulfillment of the Isaian prophecy of the gathering of the covenant peoples—decisively, as a breakthrough, even if still far from being completed. When I join the congregation at Temple Emanu-El to repeat the Aramaic words once used by Jesus, that the Kingdom may come in our lives and during our days and through the life of the whole House of Israel, I'm also saying silently that this is, truly, a house of covenant-affirming prayer for all peoples. Joining in this age-old rededication of the covenant people to its pilgrimage, I turn toward the week's sabbath and its culmination in Sunday meeting, where insight and ministry out of the meeting's stillness may come as a prophetic leading about my community's present and future practice of covenant faithfulness.

Can a covenant community actually observe a day—or even an hour—of sabbath, if its members are assimilated into industrial civilization? Are its members' houses, furnishings, and food—even covenant congregations' temples and cathedrals, synagogues and meetinghouses—suitable for celebrating sabbath, or are they plunder? Actually, most of the sabbath commandments never have been observed, this side of the Jordan, insofar as they involve a place as well as a time. As a place rather than a time for the community to renew its covenant to hallow the earth, sabbath is wilderness. Actually, the sabbatical place and the sabbatical time can't be separated, as they have been this side of the Jordan, if sabbath is to be the foundation for a way of life.

Hosea prophesies that Israel is to be "led through the wilderness" to her betrothal, "where she shall respond as in the days of her youth, when she came up from the land of Egypt" (Hos 2:14–15). Hosea is a farmer who has no great love of the wildlands, but he knows the full meaning of sabbath. Tabernacles and temples are only makeshift substitutes for wilderness, the sabbatical place in which the covenant community betroths itself.

And in that day, says יהוה, you will call Me "My Husband" and no longer call me "My Master." For I will remove the names of the Master-Owners[4] from her mouth, and they shall be mentioned by name no more. And I will make for you a covenant on that day with the beasts of the field, the birds of the air, and the creeping things of the ground; and I will abolish the bow, the sword, and war from the land; and I will make you lie down in safety. And I will betroth you to Me for ever; I will betroth you to Me in righteousness and justice, in steadfast love, and in mercy. I will betroth you to me in faithfulness; and you shall know יהוה.
. . . And I will say to Not-My-People, "You are my people." And he shall say, "You are my God" (Hos 2:16–20;23).

All the high wisdom that I've gleaned from nearly three decades of errantry is clearly revealed in the opening verses of the Shema.

---

4. *Ba'al*: master-owner, as god, overlord, husband.
The other word here that also means "husband" in this context is *'ishi*, "my man"—"spouse," as one's partner or mate established by steadfast personal intimacy.
To avoid using a transliteration of the consonants with which the Bible's personal "Name of God" is written, יהוה is generally transcribed as "the LORD." This transcription translates *'adonai*, which is another Hebrew word for "my lord and master" that is also sometimes used in biblical Hebrew for "husband." Observant Jews say "Adonai" whenever יהוה occurs—a convention that, at face value, cancels what Hosea says about the covenant of steadfast love. Yet, as a verbal token that stands in for eventual replacement by the Only Name, "Adonai" now serves better than other opaque words, such as "God," for which this opaque usage hasn't been clearly established by convention.
יהוה transliterates into "YHVH" or "JHVH." Innocently mixing the vowel symbols for *'adonai* that the Masoretic text adds to the Hebrew letters transliterated "JHVH," a sixteenth-century Christian arrived at a transliteration hybrid, "Jehovah," which then came into widespread usage. "Yahveh" is the most commonly accepted scholar's estimate of the original pronunciation, which therefore, when spoken, offends observant Jews.

"Hear, Israel: '*Adonai* our God,' '*Adonai*' is One. And you shall love '*Adonai* your God' with all your mind, and with all your strength, and with all your being. . . ."

Historically, the Shema is the form the community betrothal to the One Presence has taken. If the first verse of the Shema were read as a bystander's description of reality's basic unity—"Being is one"—it could serve as the guiding premise of scientific inquiry, that everything exists and is to be understood in terms of its relation to everything else. Yet, <u>the Shema is much more than a bystander's belief. As a pledge of steadfast love to the Creative Presence, it is a dedication of one's life to cocreative unification, through a covenant people.</u>

The Shema's high wisdom is really quite simple and is easily summarized, although it only unfolds through persistent practice, and I'm still just beginning, time and again. This is my side of the love that buoyed me up when I let go, ready to die in that cheap room in Berkeley. From my side, the covenant betrothal to unify the Only Name in daily practice, as steadfast love, starts with trust that I really can take the initiative. I can go out to the Creation's Eternal Presence, just as this love came to me, because it doesn't split into loving and being loved.

I can tell of it only at the risk of using a word that should never be used: This love doesn't split, and I can take the initiative, because it's all one. The love of God *is* God's love.

Beyond that, the highest wisdom is silence.

Look, don't be lazy, but get up out of that bed, and let's go to the country dressed as herders, the way we decided. Maybe, behind some bush, we'll find the Lady Dulcinea disenchanted, if we'll just go look.

—S<small>ANCHO</small> P<small>ANZA'S LAST ADVICE</small>

Appendix A
THE SAGUARD-JUNIPER COVENANT

In acquiring private governance of land, we agree to cherish its earth, waters, plants, and animals in a way that promotes the health, stability, and diversity of the whole community. This entails attentive stillness to meet and know the land as an active presence. It entails study, observation, shared reflection, and cumulative corporate experience to increase and bequeath our understanding of ecosystem health, stability, and diversity. It entails symbiotic naturalization into the land community—a communion of actual nurture and shelter. As elaborated by these entailments, fully accountable governance—stewardship—is the distinctively human way of bonding into one society with all who share in the land's life, which is the foundation for instituting a biocentric ethic among humankind.

—Preamble, *The Saguaro-Juniper Covenant*

FROM OWNERSHIP TO RIGHTS

IN 1988, the Saguaro-Juniper Association formed to acquire 130 acres of deeded land and 6 sections (square miles) of grazing lease

APPENDIX A

near Cascabel, Arizona. In addition to acquiring land under its own governance, the Saguaro-Juniper Association facilitates the acquisition of neighboring land by buyers who will bring it under the Saguaro-Juniper Covenant, which includes the following "bill of rights for the land":

1. The land has a right to be free of human activity that accelerates erosion.
2. Native plants and animals on the land have a right to life with a minimum of human disturbance.
3. The land has the right to evolve its own character from its own elements without scarring from construction or the importation of foreign objects dominating the scene.
4. The land has a preeminent right to the preservation of its unique or rare constituents and features.
5. The land, its waters, rocks, and minerals, its plants and animals, and their fruits and harvest have a right never to be rented, sold, extracted, or exported as mere commodities.

In accordance with these principles, the Saguaro-Juniper shareholders decided on a number of initial restrictions on human activities. New roads, off-road motorized travel, chain saws and other mechanical noisemakers, electric lines of any kind, hunting, shooting, trapping, garden and orchard pesticides, and unleashed dogs or other pets are all prohibited. Predators and wild herbivores are protected, even if they attack livestock or other domesticated animals or eat gardens or orchards, unless there is reason to believe they are rabid. Poisonous reptiles are protected, unless they are in dwellings and cannot safely be moved. Notice and discussion are to precede any construction, any development of a garden site, and any destruction of perennial plants. Tents are preferred; trailers, mobile homes, and manufactured houses or storage sheds are prohibited; any construction will be predominantly with native materials such as rock, adobe, straw bales, rammed earth, and CINVA-RAM blocks. Firewood shall be gathered from wash bottoms, brought up from the river, or brought in from elsewhere.

(Only firewood that can be picked up or broken off and carried without cutting shall be gathered.) All inorganic garbage such as metal cans, glass bottles, and plastics shall be carried off for disposal.

Along with the Saguaro-Juniper Covenant's preamble and principles, these "statutes" constitute a real-estate covenant that runs with the land and is to be attached to the land deeds of the Saguaro-Juniper Corporation and associated covenanting parties. Any of these formulations may be changed by the consent of the covenanting parties and then recorded in amendments to the original real estate covenant. One-time or short-term exceptions to specifics may be granted by the consent of a duly constituted meeting of the covenanting parties. Any exceptions taken to meet emergencies are to be explained to and evaluated by a meeting of the covenanting parties.

The association had the greatest difficulty reaching consensus on the requirement that all dogs be enclosed or on a leash. Everyone readily agreed dogs are a disturbance and often a menace to wildlife, but several of the shareholders also cherish dogs as hiking and riding companions, and dogs are important members of many shareholders' families. Ruling out unleashed dogs put our willingness to adhere to the bill of rights to its first real test, but much more difficult challenges remain. For example, we have yet to deal with the question of unleashed children. When turned loose in wildlands, town-raised children generally behave like a band of marauding chimpanzees. Country-raised children generally learn as hunters to be quietly observant and to avoid making disturbances. Herding also teaches wildland mindfulness—maybe even better than hunting. Whether we can teach shareholders' children to be mindfully observant of the bill of rights will be crucial to the Saguaro-Juniper Covenant's becoming the law of our land.

APPENDIX A

PRIVATE GRAZING ON PUBLIC LANDS

The Saguaro-Juniper Association makes decisions by consensus. The cost of a decision-making membership share is $1,500, payable at about $20 per month, which is based on the investment needed to acquire grazing on public lands that, at the seasonal cycle's low ebb, can provide double the nutrients ordinarily needed by an adult human being—which is slightly more than the grazing needed to support a cow. An additional share of $300 (about $4 per month) entitles members to participate in the herd management and production side of grazing use.

The preservation of wildlands *from* human presence and uses is particularly important in any society for which nonhuman life is just there to be used and enjoyed, but a land ethic is concerned with full human membership in the land community, which includes physical nurture that in this case involves grazing. The Saguaro-Juniper grazing allotment is on one of the arid West's high-capacity rangelands. It usually has good summer and winter rains that support a wide variety of perennial grasses such as blue, hairy, black, sideoats, and sprucetop gramas. The 130 acres of deeded land acquired by the association, which cost $400 per acre, will just support one cow, so a livelihood based on grazing is economically feasible only with access to public land that adjoins the deeded land. Throughout the arid West, livestock grazing depends on extensive use of public lands.

As used here, "public lands" means lands administered by the U.S. Forest Service, the Bureau of Land Management (BLM), and the various Western states.[1] Public lands constitute most of the wildlands in the United States; these lands are mostly in the arid West; and commercial grazing has an extremely destructive impact on these lands. In the West, land redemption will therefore be

---

1. I will just cover basics that are generally applicable to all kinds of public-land grazing permits, which means I'll focus on federal grazing permits and ignore the ways that the state systems vary.

APPENDIX A

more concerned with private grazing on public lands than with establishing real-estate covenants that run with deeded land.

The Saguaro-Juniper Association has bought grazing rights for $1,200 per cow (or five goats)—that is, it has contracted to pay the permit holder $100 per "animal unit month" (AUM) to transfer his permit to the Saguaro-Juniper Association. This comes to about $35,000 for exclusive grazing rights on about 3,800 acres of Arizona State Land. This private market in permits exists alongside the governmental lease of grazing on public lands, the actual lease fees paid to the state or federal government being relatively insignificant: about $1.50 per AUM—that is, $18 annually per cow.

Throughout the West, federal and state grazing permits are privately bought, sold, inherited, used as collateral for loans, and subject to estate taxes. The failure to charge the market value for grazing permits on public lands has converted these permits into private property. In the political arena, discussion of grazing fees and the market value of grazing leases on public lands always degenerates into a semantic shell game, but the moves are easy to follow if you remember this: *The price one must pay to a private party in order to acquire a grazing permit is created by the discrepancy between the government lease fee and the market value of the lease. If there is a private market for grazing leases, lease fees are below market value.*

If the government charged market value for grazing leases on public land, no one would pay the lessee "boot" to transfer the lease. A corollary is that the money paid to private parties for public-land grazing permits represents revenue (the prevailing interest rate on the purchase price) that would go to the public if market value were charged.

Grazing on federal lands that damages watersheds, accelerates erosion, and displaces wildlife is heavily subsidized by the public, even when the loss of market-value fees is discounted. In 1986, the BLM collected $16.1 million in grazing fees and spent $39.1 on range improvements and grazing management. The U.S. Forest Service collected $7.3 million and spent $24.1 million. These figures are typical of the disparity between income and outgo for

APPENDIX A

grazing on public lands. Yet, neither agency is funded for more than token monitoring of the livestock numbers or management practices on grazing permits, nor is it a wise career move in either agency to try to do so. For federal agencies range improvement usually means fencing, chaining, herbiciding, water and corral installations, access roads, and other bulldozing.

No one gets rich from all this waste of resources and degradation of wildlands. A few years back, a cartoon in a livestock trade paper showed a rancher surveying his spread with pride and saying, "I've worked hard for all I owe." For most working ranchers, this is exactly what the privately held permit value comes to. The money that would go to the public for grazing on public lands if the market price were paid goes instead to bankers. Many ranchers have lived their entire lives in economic peonage, giving all proceeds from the sale of livestock to a lending agency and then borrowing back enough to keep going another year. The interest paid on a fully mortgaged grazing permit always equals or exceeds the gap between private and public grazing lease fees, so ranchers who must pay interest on a mortgaged permit and also pay off the mortgage must make the land carry a double burden. (The resemblance to the situation of Third World debtor nations is no coincidence.) The banker's cut is the most common reason that ranchers who know and love the land are trapped into cashing in every blade of grass and selling deeded land to speculators just to make their payments and survive another year.

Depoliticizing the grazing fee system through market mechanisms that recognize, buy out, and retire de facto private property interests could go much of the way toward harmonizing ranch livelihood with the long-range health of the environment on which this livelihood depends. In contrast, using political means to cancel the established private property interest in grazing permits would disorder rather than reorder the system; it would throw everything up for political grabs. For example, since the federal government spends two or three times more on grazing than it receives, AUM buy-outs could save considerable public money over a relatively short period. AUMs the government buys back could return their market value or else be retired.

APPENDIX A

The assumption here is that permittee sales of private-market AUMs back to the public would be voluntary but that future users of government-purchased AUMs would pay a fee that adds the going rate of interest on the public money that has been invested in buying it. When ranchers are in trouble with the bank, the government could buy AUMs or the permit before the bank forces its sale to another private owner. The government could then lease the same AUMs back to the permittee at the market value objectively established by the purchase price, which would ordinarily be the same as the interest the rancher formerly paid the banker. At this point, ranchers would start lobbying for radical reductions in the rated carrying capacities of their grazing permits, since below-market fees have created demands for excessive grazing, but ranchers will want all the grass they can get for each AUM they lease, if they pay the market price.

This is probably too depoliticized to happen any time soon, although it would advance the interests of ranchers, environmentalists, and bankers alike. Professional range managers would be the only adversely affected special-interest group, but even they would benefit professionally (even if not economically) if they could tell the truths about grazing on public lands that are currently heresies that would end their careers.

Meanwhile, a covenant community of 30 or 40 people can easily buy a subsistence interest in grazing on public lands—so easily that even the poor can do it to gain access to subsistence and a home. In terms of direct nurture, five goats and the rangeland to support them can support a human being; in terms of a livelihood in the commercial economy, more than 50 cows (which equal 250 goats in their forage requirements) are needed to support a human being, provided they are heavily subsidized by public funding and below-market lease fees—so the economics of commercial grazing can't compete with the economics of land redemption. For most covenant communities, the real choice is between land redemption and a meetinghouse (or cathedral), if they're too poor to afford both.

Even with massive indirect subsidies, most working ranchers make less on their good years than the property value of their

APPENDIX A

grazing permit would safely return if cashed in and loaned out, and on bad years they lose it. Because the economic conditions that led to the enclosure of the commons in Winstanley's England have become inverted on the West's public lands, the limiting factor for present-day Diggers would be social rather than financial. Thirty or forty people would have to be extremely poor, collectively, to be unable to buy access to subsistence-level grazing on public lands, but they would also have to act as a community. Individuals can buy a subsistence share in a grazing permit only by joining with others who use the permit cooperatively; herding then requires further cooperation, if individual herders are to be free to do anything other than tend to a cow or five goats; and only a community can acquire grazing rights on enough rangeland to follow a rest-rotation pattern of subsistence grazing (an approximation to nomadism, which is essential to noninjurious range use).

The redemption of grazing properties on public lands requires careful herding, monitoring, measuring, and recording of the grazing use in relation to the health and evolution of the land and its life, which in the case of the Saguaro-Juniper grazing permit will be done in comparison with Nature Conservancy land that has been withdrawn from grazing (with which the association shares four miles of fenceline). In addition to provisions in the covenant that already restrict commercial exploitation, prohibit hunting, and protect predators, the association has adopted the following initial framework for grazing use:

1. Any herders' camps shall be moved at least every four months and shall be at least one-quarter mile from permanent surface waters and tanks.
2. No area shall be grazed at the same time of year more than once every three years.
3. Every area shall be entirely free from all livestock use at least once every three years.

Public agencies such as the Arizona Game and Fish Department continue, of course, to administer the public's use of the state land on which the association has exclusive grazing use, but

APPENDIX A

the Saguaro-Juniper Covenant extends the principles and specifics that govern use of the association's deeded land to the grazing permit, as far as members are concerned. Hunting, hiking, and prospecting constitute most of the land use by the public, in addition to grazing. Mining-claim assessment requirements and off-road vehicles compete for second place, as destroyers of public lands that lack commercial timber, but the damage done by prospectors and off-roaders is nowhere near as systemic, extensive, entrenched, and severe as the damage done by grazing. Grazing use is also mandated on most of the lands administered by the Arizona State Land Department, the U.S. Bureau of Land Management, and the U.S. Forest Service; it can't be bought and retired. Grazing use that is in harmony with the untamed biotic community and that displaces injurious commercial grazing is therefore the key to the redemption of these lands.

Appendix B

COVENANT WISDOM

> Far be it from Thee to do such a thing, to slay the righteous with the wicked, so that the righteous fare as the wicked! Far be that from Thee! Shall not the Judge of all the earth do right?
>
> —Abraham (Genesis 18:25)

DOES GOD HEAR THE CRY of the poor? Is the God of the prophets on the side of the oppressed? "I have been young and now am old," the psalmist sings; "yet I have not seen the righteous forsaken or his children begging bread" (Ps 37:25). We can insist on nothing less. Poverty, oppression, sickness, old age, death—all suffering—must be merited punishment, if the all-governing God of the psalmist is just.

PUTTING JOB TO THE TEST

Long ago, in the faraway land of Uz, there was a man of unblemished integrity—just, generous, and merciful. "Job" was his name.

God said, "There is none like Job on earth: of perfect integrity, completely blameless."

Then the Satan said, "He's also the richest, most honored, and least troubled in the land. You see to it that he flourishes in all he does."

"You propose to tempt Me?"

"If no one enters into Your covenant, except to get what all life wants for itself anyway, You're a sovereign without sovereignty, a king without a kingdom. If even a Job won't serve You, gratuitously, then neither a people nor mankind ever will. How could he be said to serve You before all else, unless he suffers for it and has no hope of reward?"

"How could a man enter My covenant, to do right and choose kindness, if he sees that I inflict unmerited suffering, gratuitously?"

"This folktale is about Job's integrity, not Yours. When, for the sake of Your kingdom, he rejects the consolation of religious fantasies, holds to the truth against all the cover-ups devised by Your defenders, and denounces You as he's heard of You, that's the allegiance You need."

"You want to wager My sovereignty and make My kingdom our stakes?"

"You made the bet, when You made man."

"Go ahead, then. Put Job to the test."

Disasters and marauders killed Job's children and stripped away all his wealth. But he held fast to his integrity:

> "Naked I came from my mother's womb; naked shall I return. The LORD gave; and the LORD has taken away; blessed be the name of the LORD."

Then a sickness struck Job. His pains and terrors traced agony's outer brinks, on the boundaries beyond which even torture must be merciful, killing consciousness. The stench of his sores was too repulsive for human society, so he dragged himself out to the dump where lepers wait to die.

Then Job's three friends came to condole with him and to comfort him with religious wisdom. After wailing and weeping and tearing their robes in grief, they sat with him in silence for seven days and seven nights. Hopeful words would have been irritating comforts, his agony was so great.

Then Job spoke. He cursed the day he was born, that it should be struck out of time. Better to have died in the womb or to have been aborted, stillborn, or unclaimed. Nothing life might offer could counterbalance this torture.

Eliphaz the Temanite answered, reminding Job that, when he'd prospered, he had excelled as a counselor of hope against despair. "Think now, what innocent man was ever destroyed; where was the upright cut off? Besides, no one can be righteous before God, so don't despise His chastisements. Repent and be restored."

But Job held fast to his integrity, which outraged his three friends. Against their belief in God's just rule of the world, he insisted that his sufferings were unjustified. To every remonstrance, he claimed innocence of any wrongdoing that could justify the torture.

"Will you speak falsely for God, and speak deceitfully for Him? Will you show partiality toward Him? Will you plead the case for God? Your arguments are proverbs of ashes; your defense, rejoinders of clay.

"I will speak, come on me what may. He will kill me; I have no hope; yet I will defend my ways to His face.

"God has subverted my cause. Behold, I cry 'Violence!' but am not answered. I call out, but there is no justice. I'm innocent, and it's all one. The innocent and the wicked He destroys alike."

Then Job ceased to argue with his friends and made his case to God.

Before, the divine presence had shone on his piety; honors had proclaimed his honor; and well-being had blessed his benevolence. But now, God gave evil for good, cruelty for compassion, torture for mercy, and Job's way had turned to darkness.

To testify to his unblemished observance of the just man's code of conduct, Job put himself under oath, that he should be cursed for any falsehood or infraction. Never had he looked lustfully at a

APPENDIX B

young woman, nor did he let his heart be enticed by any woman other than his wife. He always treated his servants, man and woman, as his equals in humanity. He always shared his food with the poor, the widow, and the orphan, and he clothed any beggar whom he saw in need. He kept his door open to foreigners, wayfarers, and the homeless, so no one in his community would be without food and shelter. He never put his trust in gold; he never coveted wealth; nor did he ever bow to any other idols. He never rejoiced in his enemy's misfortune, nor did he allow his clansmen to plan aggression against foes. Nor had he ever concealed a transgression, feared popular opinion, or kept silent to avoid rejection by the masses.

"Behold, this is my desire: that the Almighty answer me; that my Enemy write out His indictment."

Then God answered Job out of the whirlwind and said, "Who is this that darkens My order by words without knowledge? Who is this that says his right must encompass my Right and his way must be My Way?
"Was it you, then, who laid the Creation's foundations in the primal deep? Did you give the firmament its law, to measure for each day its times, to alternate the seasons, and to assign the stars their watches and the surf its shores? Did you open heaven's gates and inspirit earth with the breath of life?
"You talk at length of just order, but do you know the great goodness of rains that fall in deserts where no man lives? Can you match the wisdom of ostrich stupidity? Do you know the lion's joy in the death screams of a fawn? Can you count out the days till the wild goat kids and then teach her newborn to play on cliffs? Do you know the vulture's taste for a rotting corpse? Can you feed the ravens? Do you free the cimarrons and make them at home in wildlands?
"Look now at the monsters that I've made the lords of swamps and watery deeps. Look at Behemoth and Leviathan. Are you their master? Do you think I glory less in them than in you?"
Then Job answered God, saying, "I have related what I did not understand—things too wonderful for me, which I did not know.

I had heard of You by hearsay, but now I see You. Therefore, I abase myself and repent in dust and ashes."

And then God said to Eliphaz, "My anger is kindled against you and your two friends, because you have not spoken of Me what is right, as My servant Job has. But I will accept a pleading from Job that I should not deal with you according to your folly. You have not spoken of Me what is right, as My servant Job has."

SOME AFTERTHOUGHTS FROM THE JOURNAL OF ELIPHAZ THE TEMANITE

God spoke to me, but I didn't see Him, as Job did. Having heard the voice out of the whirlwind, I now know I was wrong; but I still don't see how God could bless Job's denunciations and then condemn my good-faith praises as though they were idolatrous. My old meanings crumbled but haven't been replaced.

At least I listened. The other two, Bildad and Zophar, now preach about Job's exemplary patience. In telling it, they even add an epilogue in which Job is doubly rewarded for his unwavering belief in God's justice. God doubles Job's properties and replaces his children (with a bonus, that the three replacement daughters are the most beautiful in the land).

Knowing my defense of God was wrong, I now see that the word of God needs an acceptable cover to survive its official handlers, so I won't presume to condemn these sermons that mystify the plain sense of our argument and, therefore, of God's ruling in favor of Job. How else could the word of God survive religious custody, to become scripture that brings future generations into the conversation? Maybe Bildad and Zophar make their epilogue so crass to serve as a cover that will only fool the censor. They do give an accurate report of the argument and ruling; they don't change their account to match their sermons.

I resent God's rejection of my defense. Before, we all thought that the infliction of suffering to punish disobedience, in order to

APPENDIX B

form the enforced order of a human kingdom, must also be the way God shapes the order of His kingdom. In Job's case, God corrected this mistake, then blessed Job for telling the truth about Him. In my case, for my mistaken pleadings that God would never inflict unmerited suffering, His anger flared up and could be placated only by Job's intercession. When I remember that part, I sympathize with Cain. Yet, it doesn't wound my friendship with Job. He isn't the One who shattered my religion. And God did see fit to speak to me, so Job thinks I, too, may some day see Him. That's my remaining hope. Maybe this is how I'm being put to the test: Can my faith survive the loss of my religious beliefs?

Both of us puzzle over the epiphany's blank side. We heard the God of nature, but He revealed nothing about Himself as the God of human history and the covenant—nothing except for the crucial ruling, that Job is truly God's servant, in his sufferings as well as his fulfillment of the covenant. As I heard it, this is the person-to-person confirmation of the covenanted bond: "I will be your God and you shall be my people"—for richer or for poorer, in sickness and in health, for better or for worse, unto death.

Hearing isn't seeing, but Job and I are equally handicapped when we try to tell our children what happened. We can only take the telling as far as words will go, and the truth as words tell it won't guide children into the covenant. Should we tell them that covenant faithfulness is the wrong way to become rich, dominant, and popular? Knowing the truth, what healthy child would choose peacemaking over the way of the wicked?

Maybe that choice can't be taught. Maybe we can just teach the basics on which the choice must be grounded. Maybe it's more like preparing children for a commitment to marriage, when they grow up and meet their mate. In any case, to prepare children to become active members of our covenant community, we must mince no words about the foundation: There is no God but God. Sun, moon, and stars, light and dark, good and evil—everything and all activity is of God. There is no other. There are no independent powers, and God is not at war with Himself or His creation.

APPENDIX B

This is the common ground that Job, Bildad, Zophar, and I shared for our argument, on which we continue to agree.

> I am יהוה, and there is no other.
> I form light and create darkness;
> > I make shalom and create evil;
> I, יהוה, do all these things (Is 45:6–7).

We also agree that God is served with justice and mercy, not sacrifices and magic. Job needed no witch-doctor incantations. God wants no ritual placation. None of us would even consider whether Job suffered because he'd failed to meet some cultic requirement. Only if he had violated the covenant code of just conduct, which is concerned with fulfilling communion in all aspects of our earthly life with one another, could his suffering be justified as a punishment.

> For I desire steadfast love and not sacrifice, the knowledge of God rather than burnt offerings (Hos 6:6).

The other side of this outlook is our agreement about the way of the wicked, who choose death over life by breaking communion. Before, I'd never distinguished between personal well-being and the choice of life over death. I thought that God's justice ties each person's fortunes to communion. Bildad and Zophar still seem to think so. But, in either case, we all agree that the choice of life means entering into communion and the choice of death means breaking communion. The relation isn't external, as cause and effect. Communion *means* choosing life over death, and violation of the life we share *is* the way of the wicked.

> They break all bounds, and murder leads to murder. For that, the earth is withered. Everything that dwells on it languishes. Beasts of the field and birds of the sky—even the fish of the sea perish (Hos 4:2–3).

APPENDIX B

Before, I thought it was only natural that Job excelled in wealth, command, and honors, since he was the model of all righteousness. Now I wonder how, if he was truly righteous, he could have been so rich, powerful, and respected. To be faithful to the covenant of communion, he must stand as a peacemaker on every faultline that fractures humanity's wholeness. How could he share his wealth with the poor and never turn his back on critical needs, yet remain rich? How could he insist that his clansmen treat every alien or foe with the same consideration they show one another, yet retain command? How, if he really set out to practice this chivalry, could his people consider him anything but benighted, to be protected from himself instead of respected and consulted? Maybe Job's case was just a one-time miracle, so God could have the right setting to make His point to everyone who thinks faithfulness must reap personal benefits.

What does Job mean, when he says he saw God? When I ask, he tells me what I already knew, that he can only describe what I saw, too. We saw wheeling stars and crashing surf. We saw desert showers and the untilled land clothed in delicate blooms of such brilliance that they eclipse the finest of Solomon's royal robes. We saw the feeding of lions and ravens, watched wild goats, donkeys, and cattle roam free in the wastelands, and trembled breathless before the monstrous majesties of Behemoth and Leviathan. Both of us saw the great goodness of the untamed Creation, as God's words called forth its wonders. But only Job saw God.

"If I talk of His Presence in the Creation," Job tells me, "it's just another word. If I say, 'The whole earth is filled with His Glory,' those are more words. Let's take still more words, and I'll make them into an illustration.

"Consider a great king, one who excels in every human achievement and knows every human pleasure, yet is overwhelmed with sadness when he thinks that this may be all there is to life. Consider King Solomon as he awaits the arrival of his betrothed, a bride from a foreign land who is said to be the most beautiful woman in the world. The betrothal has been arranged on the strength of this hearsay. But there are also disquieting reports. Some say that she is dark rather than fair, that her black hair is short and curly like the pelt of a desert goat, and that she is a "princess" whose hands are calloused from field work. In the streets, women share the gossip and whisper resentful jokes to one another. In the temple, the priests mutter about alien contaminations of blood and culture.

"She arrives in the king's court, and it's all true.

"I am black and beautiful, daughters of Jerusalem, like the tents of Qedar—like the curtains of Solomon" (Sg 1:5).

"Wait," I interrupt. "Am I turned around? Are you comparing the Divine Glory to this black woman, not to the king?"

"Would you consider marrying a man? If you and I were women (or blacks), I'd tell it some other way.

"Anyway, when the king sees her, he sees Mystery, whose wondrous beauty can't be compared or copied like the charms of his harem girls. Seeing her, he wants her alone, and he resolves that she shall be his queen, sharing fully and exclusively in his realm. Seeing her incomparable beauty, he loves her with all he has.

"Then, on their wedding night, when the king unites his life with hers, he knows Wholeness. All his struggles to grasp more than man's brief breath of personal awareness finds remission in her embrace. 'For love is strong as death' (Sg 8:6). Coupling with her, he loves her with all his life.

"Many years pass, and their love is steadfast; the bond of the marriage covenant holds. One day, the king looks at her and notices that her face is lined with wrinkles and her hair is grey. Looking with steadfast love, he suddenly sees the Glory foreshadowed by her mysterious beauty. The veil of Mystery is thinned, diaphonous. He loves her with all his heart.

"This marriage covenant is quite different from the contract between a landowner and his hireling. This mating serves no *ba'al*, and it isn't a trader's contract. It has nothing to do with rewards for compliance and punishments for noncompliance. Suffering and death remain certainties, and instead of rewards there is just this blessing, that the one whose heart is wholly dedicated, through steadfast love of Her Presence throughout the Creation, shall see God."

THE MAMMALIAN WISDOM OF THE SONG OF SONGS

Philosophy seeks to establish its faith as beliefs. Theology seeks to establish its beliefs as a faith. Errantry seeks to live faithfully; its faith is steadfast love. Philosophers and theologians dedicate themselves to ideals, principles, and creeds, but Quixote dedicates himself to Dulcinea.

For errantry, Wisdom is a woman. The Glory of God, Torah, the Holy Spirit, the Creation's Divine Presence, the Sabbath Bride, Nature, Muse, Mystery, the Light—She has many names. Philosophy knows personal presence as the *persona*—a mask of particularity that the actors take off when the tale is told, so philosophy turns the naming of the Creation's Personal Presence around, as though ideas were being personified to make allegories. Philosophy loves wisdom as an ideal, not a personal presence; errantry loves Wisdom as a person whose presence animates the ideal's mask of characteristics. For errantry, the beloved's names and attributes are tokens and abstractions that must borrow their meaning and truth from direct, personal knowing; its knowing is intimacy. To the seeker who persists in the quest for Wisdom, "She comes to him like a mother and receives him like a young wife" (Sir 15:2).

As intimacy, knowing sometimes finds expression in sexual union. Sexual union is one aspect of communion that, when used as an illustration, stands for all aspects, just as the marriage covenant between man and woman is an aspect rather than an analogy that helps explain the covenantal foundation of steadfast love. The Song of Songs celebrates sexual love and never mentions God, yet Rabbi Akiba was right, in his way, when he said, "The whole world is not worth the day on which the Song of Songs was given to Israel, for all the Scriptures are holy, but the Song of Songs is the Holy of Holies" (Yad 3:5). Sexual love is *the* aspect of one's intercourse with the Creation's kaleidoscopic personal presence that usually awakens human beings to full awareness of another's presence, even when most of the world still seems to be composed of mere objects. Falling in love, one recognizes the beloved as a person with whom one must be united to be whole. This *knowing* that heals separative *knowledge* is always unifying intercourse. (The Hebrew Bible calls sexual union "knowing." To translate this usage into Greek, The Wisdom of Solomon calls it "symbiosis.") The allegorical interpretations of the Song's meaning are theological regressions from the knowing that is communion, back to the realm of separative knowledge.

We are animals whose view of personal intercourse is sex linked. Stand Freud on his head, and his focal point makes sense to virtually anyone: "What does sex stand for?" Having eaten the fruit of the tree of knowledge, we are aware of ourselves as separated, mortal, incomplete beings, and we therefore seek the Other who is our Complement, the Mate with whom we shall become whole once again. Sexual love is an inseparable aspect of communion, which means that "sacred" presence is never pitted against "profane" presence, as though one must choose between loving a fellow creature and loving God exclusively, with all one's resources, life, and heart. To see how sexual love illustrates communion is to see that the personal intercourse of one person with another coheres by virtue of the Presence for Whom there is no other; only in this unity can one person know another, presence-to-presence.

Because we are mammals whose view of communion's steadfast love is sex linked and family formed, covenant betrothal to I-SHALL-BE-PRESENT-AS-I-SHALL-BE-PRESENT is also sex linked. Tradition tells of the Divine Presence as a woman because published mystics and literature's Quixotes have usually been men, but scripture such as the Song of Songs shifts from one side to the other, to incorporate both outlooks. Meditating on the Song's open-

APPENDIX B

ing line, Saint Teresa of Avila writes, "Now, my Lord, I ask you nothing else in this life but 'to kiss me with the kiss of your mouth,' and this in such a way that I should not be able, even though I wished, to withdraw myself from this union and friendship."[1]

The human view of communion is family formed as well as sex linked, and the outlook changes as one grows from infancy through childhood to maturity. Before She receives the seeker "like a young wife" on this side of our exile from Eden, the Presence is first known as Mother, by mammals of both sexes; then, in humanity's exile, as Parent, Teacher, and Pastor, and often as Lord and Master. Outwardly, betrothal to Her Presence throughout the Creation discards the liegeman–overlord relation. Inwardly, the decisive authority of external directors also ends:

> This is the covenant I will make with the house of Israel after those days, says יהוה: I will put My law within them, and I will write it on their hearts; and I will be their God, and they shall be my people. And no longer shall each man teach his neighbor and each his brother, saying, "Know יהוה," for they shall all know me, from the least of them to the greatest, says יהוה. (Jer 31:33–34).

In the Bible, the word for "servant" is the same as the word for "slave and subject"; the concepts are undifferentiated. As the Satan understands it, God bets his sovereignty on Job's integrity, but for God the issue of Job's integrity is whether Job will prove to be someone with whom He can converse, not whether Job will be an obedient slave or child. For genuine conversation, presence to Presence, the master-slave relation must be superseded. Inwardly, Job must maintain his human integrity; outwardly, he must also recognize that the Creation's Presence is genuinely Other—that his Mate can't be reduced to anthropocentric projections. Then,

---

1. P. P. Parente, "The Canticle of Canticles in Mystical Theology," *Catholic Biblical Quarterly* 6 (1944): 142–158, p. 152.

when he clears away all pretense to *knowledge about* God, Job *knows* God as the Unity of his presence-to-Presence intercourse with the Creation.

The outlooks of infancy, childhood, and maturity are followed by the maturity of maturity, the decline to death. Sallying out long after he has passed his prime, Quixote wanders the land as an exile, in search of Dulcinea. Inwardly, his exile is separation from the other who would make him whole. Outwardly, she, too, is in exile—imprisoned and transformed by the spells of conjurers who hide her presence and mask her beauty. This turns out to be the quest imposed by his celibate betrothal to Dulcinea: to free her, not to possess her.

Francis had a choice between family and errantry, and he might have postponed his dedication to Lady Poverty, but empowerment and acquisition must go separate ways in the decline to death. Where the healthy child grasps for more and struggles against every supersession, and the responsible parent must put family first, maturity matures into a letting go and giving away that wants to be superseded and surpassed, to be free from the grasping and getting of growth and reproduction. To be joyful, life at this stage must be predominantly sabbatical. Its empowerment is freedom from the will to power.

In the decline to death, when the postponements imposed by childhood and procreation have run their course, only one way leads to Wisdom. Dulcinea, Lady Poverty, the Holy Presence must be freed from the conjurers' spells. When the Creation ceases to be an object of possession, the whole earth is filled with Her Glory.

Sadness accompanies decline, as grief goes with death. The sabbath delight that over-arches this sadness is like the pleasure an attentive audience takes from a tragedy such as *King Lear*. The playwrite strips away all make-believe about the First Truth; he unmasks our death-row awareness of the doom that is every living creature's destiny; but the audience sees the stage through the eye of eternity, sabbatically. The spectator delights in the great goodness and incomparable beauty of the nobilities that bloom, briefly, only in this tragic tale.

APPENDIX B

> Is this the wisdom of the old?
> —the ripeness only rot can know?
> All touch makes love, when death makes cold;
> bright heavens faded, stars will show.
> Then I have wandered sun-blind through day dreams,
> picked all my finest fruit while it was green,
> instead of stellar course, tracked praise-worn schemes.
>
> As I decay, receding into earth,
> each ache an echo in a carnal tomb,
> this rot that ripens fallows vernal birth,
> until each woman is a girl in bloom,
> and all the passing world I watch grows young
> —and loved,
> > with longings age tills in,
> > > unsung.

THE CONJUGAL RELATION

In the nineteenth century, the report spread that the God praised by the pious and defended by the theologians had died—the just King and protective Parent preached by Job's three friends. Philosophers assumed responsibility for settling probate. Man was presumed to be the sole heir.

The twentieth century confirmed the original report but also discovered that probate had been a fraud. Every undertaking to set the world in order, with man the measure, deepened disaster. We simply haven't measured up, as a replacement for the Deceased.

Job prayed that the God of his three friends be superseded, but by God.

> Earth, do not cover my blood; let there be no resting place for my outcry! . . . Before God my eyes shed tears; let Him arbitrate between a man and God, as between a man and his fellow (Jb 16:18, 20–21).

APPENDIX B

I know that my Vindicator lives; in the end He will testify on earth—this, after my skin will have been peeled off. But I would behold God while still in the flesh, I myself, not another, would behold Him (Jb 19:25–27).

And the tale tells how God does answer Job and does reveal His personal, unifying Presence throughout the Creation, superseding all human imaginings and hearsay, which had been Job's knowledge about God. "Who is this that darkens counsel by words without knowledge?"

Sometimes, words that darken counsel can inform, indirectly, much as the moon shows the sun in a special way during an eclipse. Imagine a philosopher who has seen the unity and goodness of the Creation clearly enough to know that humility and pity are vices, not virtues. Imagine, too, that he has the courage to be the first to announce, publicly, that God is dead.

Maybe this philosopher knows nothing of sabbath delight. Maybe, striving against his own premature decline, he sees decadence as the only alternative to the will to power (which is surely the only alternative, if mortal man really is the dead God's heir). Yet, the philosopher still has eternity planted in his heart and is no more willing than the preacher, Koheleth, to be satisfied with striving and overcoming, just for the sake of striving and overcoming. Running his brief race in boundless time and space, he conceives a finish line composed of infinity itself. In the boundless (he philosophizes) all possibilities must be actualities, somewhere and sometime, and all these actualities must return on themselves, endlessly. My life—this every moment—is eternal in its endless recurrence, both in boundless time and boundless space. Even if the Eternal Presence has ceased to illuminate life, I can (he concludes) know and affirm that every actual presence is eternal in its recurrences.

"This is conjuring," common sense retorts. "Those others who are my stand-ins, in all the innumerable worlds that duplicate this one, aren't me. If I were there, I wouldn't be here." One's awareness of one's own presence takes time seriously; mortal life's time is always unrecoverable. Even if Job's second three daughters had

APPENDIX B

been perfect copies of the first, they wouldn't have been the first, who were irreplaceably lost.

Compare any mortal's relation, first, to the set of innumerable copies projected by the philosopher's speculation about eternal recurrence; and then, to Eternal Presence. It is precisely in this, my irreplaceably singular mortality (which the theory of eternal recurrence obscures), that I enter into a living relation with Eternal Presence. She is the Mate—the Sabbath Bride—who makes me whole and my mortal life a delight, even in tragedy; but the relation is reciprocal. I am Her complement. Without me, the Creation would be irreparably flawed, and the Eternal would also cease to be whole. She needs my mortality.

> Speak, passing day.
> What does the blazing noon sun say?
> I burn; I burn;
> I gayly burn myself away
> to no return,
> in streams of now sped by each ray
> through deepest null.
> Let there be light in farthest night
> to wax time full.
> Eternity needs my delight—
> needs burning, mortal, free delight.

As sanctuary, the covenant entails self-overcoming. "I" becomes "we," and "we" expands to include "them." As betrothal, the covenant begins by reaching all the way, for better or for worse, in trust. Instead of the striving to break through borders and overcome limits, its ground is sabbath. Maintaining my personal integrity, as a cocreator who can't be replaced by any other who ever was or will be, I betroth myself to another, affirming that she, too, is a person who can't be replaced. In observing sabbath, I can also betroth myself to the Creative Presence, through a people that has done so.

Does this Bride join Her groom only in sabbath, when and where a community ceases to strive to bend the world to its will?

APPENDIX B

Some say the old community covenant of steadfast love has been replaced by a new "covenant" of free love among individuals, but this amounts to no covenant at all—certainly not a betrothal. In a society that lives by conquest and possession, individual professions of steadfast love for the Creation's active Presence are make-believe. Free love among individuals can't replace a people's efforts to be faithful to the covenant, as a persisting way of life. A community can begin, fail, return, and begin again, meeting the Sabbath Bride and sustaining the betrothal even in exile. Observed in solitude, sabbath even unites isolated individuals with a covenant people's generations. But this betrothal takes place only when a community observes sabbath in one way or another, celebrating life as an unearned gift, ceasing at least for a time to live by conquest and possession.

I refer to the Sabbath Bride as though I could name Her. I can't, except when I reflect on other people's namings. I certainly can't describe Her as "this" rather than "that," the way Job's friends describe God. If I say she is the Mother who nurtures all that lives, this means that She feeds me some of Her other children now but will soon feed me to the rest of life. What kind of mother is that? The Sabbath Bride who wanders the earth in exile is a good character for folktales—like God, the absolute monarch who holds heavenly court in the Book of Job. Another storyteller might choose some grimmer aspect, from among Her infinite attributes.

All praises and characterizations of "God" are, finally, idolatrous. Saying that God is "this" rather than "that" rejects unity. Even talk about unity leads some to think God is one rather than many, instead of affirming that this is the Only Name—the One for whom there is no other.

"The highest praise is silence."